ON THE WAY TO THE WEB

THE SECRET HISTORY OF THE INTERNET
AND ITS FOUNDERS

————

Michael A. Banks

Apress®

On the Way to the Web: The Secret History of the Internet and Its Founders

ISBN-13 (pbk): 978-1-4302-0869-3

ISBN-13 (electronic): 978-1-4302-0870-9

Printed and bound in the United States of America 9 8 7 6 5 4 3 2 1

Trademarked names may appear in this book. Rather than use a trademark symbol with every occurrence of a trademarked name, we use the names only in an editorial fashion and to the benefit of the trademark owner, with no intention of infringement of the trademark.

Lead Editor: Jeffrey Pepper
Technical Reviewer: John Vacca
Editorial Board: Clay Andres, Steve Anglin, Ewan Buckingham, Tony Campbell, Gary Cornell, Jonathan Gennick, Matthew Moodie, Joseph Ottinger, Jeffrey Pepper, Frank Pohlmann, Ben Renow-Clarke, Dominic Shakeshaft, Matt Wade, Tom Welsh
Project Manager: Richard Dal Porto
Copy Editor: Liz Welch
Associate Production Director: Kari Brooks-Copony
Production Editor: Laura Esterman
Compositor: Dina Quan
Proofreader: Nancy Bell
Indexer: Broccoli Information Management
Cover Designer: Kurt Krames
Manufacturing Director: Tom Debolski

Distributed to the book trade worldwide by Springer-Verlag New York, Inc., 233 Spring Street, 6th Floor, New York, NY 10013. Phone 1-800-SPRINGER, fax 201-348-4505, e-mail orders-ny@springer-sbm.com, or visit http://www.springeronline.com.

For information on translations, please contact Apress directly at 2855 Telegraph Avenue, Suite 600, Berkeley, CA 94705. Phone 510-549-5930, fax 510-549-5939, e-mail info@apress.com, or visit http://www.apress.com.

Apress and friends of ED books may be purchased in bulk for academic, corporate, or promotional use. eBook versions and licenses are also available for most titles. For more information, reference our Special Bulk Sales–eBook Licensing web page at http://www.apress.com/info/bulksales.

For Pat, Larry, Harry, Jerry, James, Ralph, Resnick,
Janet, Ricky, Van, James, Laurie, Chuq, Scott, Akira,
Bill, Peabo, Uwe, Dan, JimSB, Chalker, Eva,
and the rest of the cyberspace night shift

Contents at a Glance

FOREWORD xi

ABOUT THE AUTHOR xix

ABOUT THE TECHNICAL REVIEWER. xxi

PREFACE xxiii

ACKNOWLEDGMENTS xxv

INTRODUCTION xxvii

CHAPTER 1	LOOKING BACK: WHERE DID IT ALL BEGIN? 1
CHAPTER 2	IN THE MONEY 7
CHAPTER 3	MAKING CONTACT WITH COMPUSERVE 15
CHAPTER 4	THE SOURCE. 25
CHAPTER 5	DIS-CONTENT AND CONFLICT 39
CHAPTER 6	EVOLUTION 49
CHAPTER 7	ONLINE EXPERIMENTS. 61
CHAPTER 8	TRIALS AND ERRORS. 67
CHAPTER 9	THE SECOND WAVE 79
CHAPTER 10	AOL GESTATION 95
CHAPTER 11	THE THIRD WAVE 103
CHAPTER 12	IN WITH THE NEW, OUT WITH THE OLD. 115
CHAPTER 13	AOL EVOLVES: EXPANSION, INTEGRATION, AND SUCCESS 127
CHAPTER 14	PRODIGY: THE FLAT-RATE PIONEER WHO JUST DIDN'T GET IT 139
CHAPTER 15	MOVING TO THE NET. 157

AFTERWORD OMISSIONS, ADDITIONS, AND CORRECTIONS 177

APPENDIX A ONLINE TIMELINE 179

APPENDIX B BIBLIOGRAPHY 197

APPENDIX C FOUNDERS 199

INDEX 205

Contents

FOREWORD xi

ABOUT THE AUTHOR xix

ABOUT THE TECHNICAL REVIEWER. xxi

PREFACE xxiii

ACKNOWLEDGMENTS xxv

INTRODUCTION xxvii

CHAPTER 1   LOOKING BACK: WHERE DID IT ALL BEGIN? 1

                 In the Beginning 2

                 Lo! 5

CHAPTER 2   IN THE MONEY 7

                 The First Online Content 8

                 The First Information Superhighway 11

CHAPTER 3   MAKING CONTACT WITH COMPUSERVE 15

CHAPTER 4   THE SOURCE. 25

CHAPTER 5   DIS-CONTENT AND CONFLICT 39

                 Videotex 39

                 Growing Pains at The Source 41

                 Customer Loyalty and Growth 43

                 Usenet Newsgroups 44

                 Microcomputer Bulletin Boards 45

CHAPTER 6 EVOLUTION 49

Games 51

Pirate Software 52

Online Gaming 52

Early File Sharing and User Publishing. 53

Chat 54

Special-Interest Groups. 56

CompuServe Forums. 57

CHAPTER 7 ONLINE EXPERIMENTS. 61

Gateways. 63

New Kids on the Block 65

CHAPTER 8 TRIALS AND ERRORS. 67

Something Old, Nothing New. 68

Newspapers and Newsletters Online 69

Consumer Movement 70

Encyclopedias Online. 72

More Experiments 73

Meanwhile, Back at the ARPA Ranch 76

CHAPTER 9 THE SECOND WAVE 79

DELPHI. 80

More Regional Online Services 82

The First Dot-Com Bust 84

GEnie. 85

AOL DNA, Part 1. 89

AOL DNA, Part 2: Gameline and Control Video
Corporation 89

AOL DNA, Part 3: Playnet 90

CHAPTER 10 AOL GESTATION 95

CHAPTER 11 THE THIRD WAVE 103

American People/Link (Plink). 103

BIX (Byte Information eXchange) 106

USA Today Sports Center 107

The WELL 107

Quantum Link (Q-Link). 108

Trin-what? 113

CHAPTER 12   IN WITH THE NEW, OUT WITH THE OLD. 115

Great Product, Great Customers—Where's the Money? . . . 115

Great Expectations 116

The Entrepreneur Who Wouldn't Go Away, Redux 116

AppleLink–Personal Edition. 117

PC-Link 119

Sour Apples 120

The Competition Wakes 122

Front Ends 122

Another Online Casualty 126

CHAPTER 13   AOL EVOLVES: EXPANSION, INTEGRATION,
AND SUCCESS 127

Independence 127

Promenade. 128

The Great Commingling 129

AOL for PCs: DOS and Windows 131

Planning Ahead. 133

Marketing AOL. 134

CHAPTER 14   PRODIGY: THE FLAT-RATE PIONEER WHO JUST
DIDN'T GET IT 139

In the Beginning 139

Videotex Again? 141

New & Improved 142

Online Advertising? 144

Prodigy Call Home 146

Censored! 147

"Of Course You Realize . . . This Means War!". 149

No, Not Spyware! 150

"Didn't Prodigy Invent the Internet?" 151

Files, Anyone?. 152

Turning On the Meter. 153

Chat, at Last 155

CHAPTER 15 MOVING TO THE NET 157

       International Expansion 158

       Apple Replay 161

       Opening Up the Internet 161

       Online Services and the Internet 165

       One Step Forward, Two Steps Back 169

       Where Are They Now? 170

AFTERWORD OMISSIONS, ADDITIONS, AND CORRECTIONS 177

APPENDIX A ONLINE TIMELINE 179

APPENDIX B BIBLIOGRAPHY 197

APPENDIX C FOUNDERS 199

INDEX 205

Foreword

The Web is everywhere, reaching into the homes of everybody with a computer and a phone line. More and more of us have our computers on all the time, continuously receiving and sending messages and email, frequently looking for information, for pictures, for music.

I do most of my Christmas and birthday shopping online; most of our gifts for weddings and graduations are purchased online and shipped—gift-wrapped—directly to the recipients.

Rumors spread like wildfire on the Web. Sentimental stories (we call them "web weepers") are passed along, jerking tears whether they're true or not. Financial scams, ads for body enhancements, and political fund-raisers pump through the system.

Real news comes from volunteer reporters (bloggers, they're called, whether they're actually writing blogs or not), forcing the traditional news media to deal with stories they would have preferred to ignore. And those political fund-raisers have changed the shape of American elections, allowing some candidates to bypass the traditional fat-cat and PAC fund-raising methods.

All of this is so pervasive that it feels perfectly natural. It's easy to forget how short a time it has been this way.

Twenty-five years ago, in 1983, I moved to Greensboro, North Carolina, to take a job as book editor for *Compute!*, a magazine that covered all the major home computers: Commodore 64 and VIC, Atari 400 and 800, TRS-80, Apple, and a few others that popped up and faded away.

While I worked there—for only nine months—Apple launched their Lisa computer, which in many ways resembled the later Macintosh, and IBM announced the PC.

In other words, the two dominant personal computers did not yet exist.

Meanwhile, the Internet, while it existed, was restricted to academics and Defense Department wonks—civilians like me need not apply.

Yet all the elements of today's computer-centered culture were already in place. So let me tell you about the computers in my life during that crucial period from 1980 to 1983.

~

I wasn't a "computer hobbyist." I wouldn't have spent five seconds or 15 cents on assembling a computer from a kit. All I wanted, back in 1980, was a word processor.

I was a touch typist from eighth grade on. My mother was so fast a typist that if she made a typo at the bottom of a page of a dissertation (with six carbons behind it), it was faster for her to tear up the page and start over than to try to correct the error, even with Liquid Paper. She *blew* through paper at the rate of about 100 words per minute, which meant a page every two and a half minutes. Twelve pages an hour. That was the standard I aspired to meet.

But to reach those speeds, you had to have the right machine. I had learned on a heavy manual typewriter, but at home we had a nice electric. Still, if you typed too fast the keys jammed. So we were thrilled when the IBM Selectric debuted. We owned one as soon as we could afford it. No more jams!

Then it got better: the self-correcting Selectric. The computer actually remembered what it had typed, and if you backspaced it would pop up correction tape and eliminate the mistake—as long as you caught it before you had typed on too far.

Then there was the IBM electronic typewriter, which you could program to remember frequently typed phrases, and did so many tricks you almost wanted to invite it to the prom just to dance with it and look cool.

We knew that these tricks came from having a tiny computer embedded in the typewriter, but we didn't care, any more than we cared that traffic signals were controlled by small computers. As long as they did the job and we could use their particular talents, we were happy.

But then I started hearing how word processors worked. The whole document was kept in memory that lasted even when you turned the machine off. You could go into the document and edit it right in the middle, then print the whole thing out and it would *repaginate itself*.

As a writer—of fiction, and of rewritten articles for the magazine I worked for—the worst problem was that any time you made a significant change, you either had to retype (introducing new typing errors) or cut and paste, adding A, B, and C pages or taping replacement paragraphs over the old version. The result was a messy, nightmarish manuscript that practically begged typesetters to make new mistakes of their own (they seemed to love to find ways to misinterpret our instructions and show us we weren't as smart and precise as we thought).

So the idea of a word processor took hold in my imagination and I knew I had to own one.

A local store (Salt Lake City, at that time) sold "word processors," and I went in and described what I needed.

"What you want," said the salesman, "isn't a dedicated word processor. You want a computer that runs word processing software."

"Why?" I asked.

"Because then it can run other software, too."

"But I only want to run a word processor."

"That's what you think now," he said. "But a dedicated word processor is merely a crippled computer. It does one thing, but it never gets any *better* at it. While with a computer, you can upgrade the word processing program."

"Why would I want to do that? Isn't it good now?"

"Yes. It's excellent. But they'll think of ways to improve it. I promise you. And the computer costs the same. Even less."

I came home with an Altos computer running WordStar on top of the CP/M operating system and it was everything I wanted. It was so blissful to be able to go back and change a character's name, for instance, all the way through the document by using a *single command*. And to insert a scene in the middle of a chapter without having to retype anything that came after.

I also learned about saving files the first time we had a quick power blackout. Lights off, then on again—and 30 pages of a play I was writing were irrevocably gone.

Here's the odd thing, though. When I first started with the computer, nothing on the screen felt real until I had printed it out. I printed things out constantly—on fanfold paper with microperforated edges, using my fancy NEC Spinwriter with proportional spacing.

Within a year, things didn't feel real unless they were on disk. The computer version of the manuscript was more real than the printout, because I realized that as long as I had enough backups, the computer version was permanent and the paper versions were ephemeral, because I could *work* with the file on the computer, but couldn't do anything with the printout.

The computer salesman was right. I also began to buy other programs.

First, it was an upgrade to WordStar. Then a spell-checker—which annoyed me because, of course, all my character names and made-up words were flagged as "errors." Then again, it was fun to see how many new words I made up in each of my books.

Soon, though, I had bought the game Adventure, in which I explored a fantasy environment by typing commands like "left" and "up" and "take sword" and "pay troll."

And only six months after buying my CP/M machine, I upgraded to the multiuser Altos running MP/M. It had a 10-megabyte hard drive so all the novels and stories I was working on could be available to me without inserting a single disk—though of course I backed everything up onto 8-inch floppies.

I bought a second terminal for my wife, who also loved her IBM machines and immediately fell in love with the power of WordStar and the look of documents printed on that Spinwriter.

Here's my shameful secret: I still use the WordStar command set. I've programmed my WordPerfect software to recognize that Ctrl-S means go back a space and Ctrl-G means delete the next character, etc. Why? Because WordStar was created when many terminals lacked dedicated cursor keys and long before there were any mice. So the software used control-key combinations to move the cursor.

And for a touch typist like me, that meant I could do all my moving around the document without ever removing my fingers from the home keys. It sped up my work and still does. When the original Macintosh came out, lacking a control key and therefore forcing users to take their fingers off the home keys and mouse their way through a document, I treated it with the disdain it deserved. It was a toy for people who were going to be passive users of their computer. For serious typists, it was a useless paperweight; it crippled you and slowed you down to a crawl.

Not that I had anything against toys when I *wasn't* working.

~

Right along with my growing love affair with a serious working computer, my Altos with WordStar, I had also fallen for the gaming machines. My favorite videogames in the arcades were Breakout and Asteroids. I was very, very good. But the little Atari 2600 game machine couldn't handle the graphics. To get those great games at home, you had to pop for the Atari 400 computer and insert the cartridges for the games you wanted.

It happened to have a keyboard, but I didn't care. It was Breakout and Asteroids I wanted, and I got them—along with dozens of other games that were sometimes great and sometimes boring. Didn't matter.

And as long as that keyboard was there, why not insert the BASIC cartridge and learn how to program a little? I was like everybody else—once I'd learned a little programming, I couldn't resist going into stores and typing into the demo models:

```
1 PRINT "Buy me and take me home! I'm lonely in this store!"
2 GOTO 1
```

The computer would then sit there and type the stupid message forever—or until a store clerk interrupted it and cleared it out of memory.

I'd only owned the 400 for a couple of months before I absolutely had to have the Atari 800. I'd already learned with my Altos how much better it was to have a disk drive than to save things on a cassette tape, the way you had to do with the Atari 400.

Here were the prices, more or less:

Altos with hard drive: $4,000

Terminal: $3,000

NEC Spinwriter: $3,000

Atari 800: $800

Atari disk drive: $800

That's not including the cost of disks, game controllers, the dedicated monitor I eventually bought for the Atari, and the software.

Nor does it include the cost of the countless hours I spent writing programs and playing games. By now I was going to grad school, working on a doctorate at Notre Dame, and I could hardly keep my hands off the computers. And it was no secret when I was working and when I was playing—working had me in my upstairs office using the Altos, while playing had me in the basement on the Atari.

And I was getting more and more serious about programming on the Atari. I had BASIC for the Altos, too, but my attempts at programming my own text adventure didn't work because I didn't yet understand the conceptual framework of the game. I hadn't got the mental map of it yet.

The Atari, though, had whole programs you could type in from listings in magazines like *Compute!* and see how the bones of the things worked. I began to be a critic of the programs, to see how they could have tightened their code.

And I read the editorial where *Compute!*'s publisher invited people to apply for jobs like "book editor."

I had been a book editor. And since there was a recession right then, the whole novel-writing thing didn't look like it was going to be able to support my family for much longer. I applied, I got the job, and I moved to Greensboro, North Carolina, where I still live today.

Nine months later, I quit the job and went back to freelance writing. In the meantime, though, I had become a reasonably good programmer on the 6502 processor, using the Atari's brilliant design. I had learned machine language and would POKE in superfast subroutines that ran in the graphics interrupts.

I created a set of routines for the Atari that other programmers could use to add music that would run in the interrupts, so it didn't slow down their BASIC programs.

But by the time I was ready to publish it, the market was gone.

IBM killed it.

We welcomed the IBM PC at first. Well, sort of. The graphics were lame beyond belief—only three colors besides black and white, pathetic sound, and the miserable Intel processors that only had 16 registers. The 6502 used the whole zero page as registers! Programming in machine language on the Intel processors was so tedious it wasn't fun anymore.

And IBM's BASIC was also lame. It didn't do any of the cool things you could do with the Commodore 64 or Atari 800—especially the 800, with its Bill Wilkinson–designed "compilerpreter"—a system that compiled your programs as you created them so you never waited for your programs to compile before testing them.

I did, however, like the IBM PC junior— "PCjr." Not with the original chiclet keyboard—that was completely unusable!—but its BASIC was a pretty good one, with a cool system for creating music and drawing lines.

In writing a book for the PCjr, for my former employers at *Compute!*, I created software that I still haven't seen anyone else duplicate. Ostensibly designed to teach programming to PCjr owners, it was really a predecessor to "PC-USA." Only instead of giving you state information, I had researched the electoral vote in every election in US history, and mapped it in.

When you had the program up and running, you could move backward and forward through the years, with the map showing the electoral votes for all the parties, including disputed votes, third parties, and weird candidates. It played like a slide show of electoral history. It was my best real program ever.

And the PCjr died before the book came out.

No point publishing a book for a computer that IBM is no longer supporting. It was never published. Nobody ever saw my program except my wife and kids and me. And the kids were way too young to care.

~

Meanwhile, though, I was still working away on my Altos. I had bought a modem for it, first a 300-baud device and then the expensive upgrade to 1200 bps. That wasn't 1200 characters per second, it was 1200 *bits*, which meant only 150 characters per second. But it was 150 characters per second transmitted over phone lines and appearing instantaneously on someone else's computer.

Only I didn't have many people with modems to send things to.

I joined both DELPHI and CompuServe, but I almost never used CompuServe because I hated having to memorize a string of numbers and DELPHI let me use my own name. Also, CompuServe's menu structure was painful to use, and DELPHI's I learned quickly and easily.

This was now 1984, and I had just finished (right after Christmas of '83) the manuscript of my novel *Ender's Game*. I thought it would be way cool to upload it to DELPHI so other people could download it and read it on their own computers.

The sysop of the science fiction area on DELPHI agreed with me and so I spent hours (and dollars!) one night uploading the whole thing, chapter by chapter.

Each chapter was a separate file, so that if you lost your connection during the download, you'd only have to redo the one chapter instead of the whole manuscript.

Even so, I think it had exactly six downloads. There just weren't that many people online! And certainly not that many who wanted to spend *hours* downloading a book.

It was 452K—452,000 characters. By contrast, MP3s of single songs generally run about three megabytes—3,000,000 characters. You can see that the day for downloading music had not yet come.

And, judging from the six novel downloads, it wasn't time for e-books, either.

But it was free, it was online, and it appeared on DELPHI nearly a year before it was published in hardcover (by TOR, in January 1985). I think it was the first published novel ever to appear online prior to coming out in print. And if any of those six people actually read the whole thing, they were making history with me.

1985—that's not even a quarter of a century ago.

It was a different world. But I loved it then. Your computer still belonged to you, instead of to Microsoft or Apple; you didn't wake up in the morning to find that Microsoft had caused your computer to reboot in the middle of the night as part of a "security update," thereby stopping the process you had wanted it to finish overnight.

Everything was new; you felt like a pioneer. The computer was a fantastic new tool that let you do old jobs a thousand times faster and better—and new games and tasks that simply hadn't existed before.

I was there on Prodigy—a cleverly designed program whose graphical interface was a good idea, but whose human interface was a nightmare of stupidity. They were so determined that nobody could go off-topic in any of the interest areas that in the area called "Orson Scott Card," if someone posted a question like, "Where is OSC doing his next signing?" if I answered by saying, "I'll be signing in NYC on the 18th of June," Prodigy would refuse to post my message because it was "personal." In vain did I explain to them that I *was* Orson Scott Card, and so I was actually answering the question—and providing Prodigy with value for free. It could only help them if they became known as a place where, if you asked a question about an author, the author himself would sign on and answer it!

Instead, I had to write circumlocutory messages that referred to me in the third person; and even then, I actually had a Prodigy employee write to me saying, "We know what you're doing and we're not fooled." They threatened me that if I didn't stop putting up personal messages I would be booted off their system!

No wonder Prodigy failed.

Along came AOL, with a graphical interface my mother could use, and we left Prodigy behind forever.

~

I lived through all the changes. And yet I didn't know what was really going on. I didn't know *why* various programs and machines came and went. Things just happened. Some of them were disastrous—the standardization that

Microsoft brought was good, but the actual product we standardized on was icky. One thing is certain: the better mousetrap does *not* always win. Instead, it's the sneaky, snaky monopolistic business that generally seems to prevail, as long as its product is semi-adequate to the task.

But that's another book and another history. What Michael A. Banks has created here is the story, person by person and step by step, of how we got from those early home computers to the infobahn.

I loved this book. I devoured every word of it. At last things made sense.

Now, there were additional chapters I'd have loved to see. Since I almost went to work for ColecoVision, I wanted a chapter on them; I wanted more about Prodigy just so I could boo and hiss.

Banks couldn't write an infinite book. There had to be a final number of pages. Stuff had to be left out.

But not much! This is a thorough, entertaining, informative, useful history of how our world was transformed during my adult life. Many people in their thirties now have no memory of ever living in a house without a computer of one kind or another. Most people in their teens don't know what it's like to live in a world that isn't online.

And the best thing about this history is that you don't have to know anything at all about how computers work, or what a 6502 processor is, or anything. You just have to know how to read and have a basic idea of what it means to go online.

Orson Scott Card
Author of *Ender's Game*, *Magic Street*,
and the *Tales of Alvin Maker*

About the Author

 **Michael A. Banks** is the author of more than 40 books, among them several titles that deal with Internet topics, including *The eBay Survival Guide*; *Web Psychos, Stalkers, and Pranksters*; *The Modem Reference*; *PC Confidential*; and *Welcome to CompuServe*. He is co-author of *Crosley: The Story of Two Brothers and the Business Empire That Transformed the Nation* (Clerisy, 2006), the biography of twentieth-century industrialist/entrepreneur and communications magnate Powel Crosley, Jr. (This book made *The New York Times* extended bestseller list, *The Wall Street Journal* hardcover business book bestseller list, and the *Business Week* bestseller list. It received a full-page writeup in the February 12, 2007, issue of *Publishers Weekly*.)

He has written hundreds of magazine articles and served as a contributing editor and columnist for *Computer Shopper*, *Windows*, and other magazines.

Banks has been online since 1979, when he caught his first glimpse of CompuServe. During the 1980s, he was involved in a number of Internet firsts, including online book promotion. He has helped maintain BBSs, was a SIG manager on DELPHI for a number of years, and worked in a consulting capacity for CompuServe and The Source. He wrote one of the first guides to online services, *The Modem Reference* (Brady/Simon & Schuster), which introduced hundreds of thousands of users to modems and the online world. Because of his reputation as a modem and telecommunications expert, GEnie and BIX (*Byte* Information Exchange) created special online forums for Banks—early blogs. He has also advised a number of businesses in the area of online marketing.

About the Technical Reviewer

John Vacca is an information technology consultant and internationally known best-selling author based in Pomeroy, Ohio. Since 1982, John has authored 52 books and more than 600 articles in the areas of advanced storage, computer security, and aerospace technology. John was also a configuration management specialist, computer specialist, and the computer security official (CSO) for NASA's space station program (Freedom) and the International Space Station Program, from 1988 until his early retirement from NASA in 1995. In addition, John is also an independent online book reviewer. John was also one of the security consultants for the MGM movie *AntiTrust*, which was released on January 12, 2001.

Preface

The further in time you get from an event, the more garbled the facts are. In books, magazine articles, and newspaper stories, some facts get blurred or omitted. Others are replaced with what an author thinks he remembers. Half-memories that have little to do with reality are often set down as history because they seem right. The truth gets shuffled as deadlines loom.

For these reasons, I went to as many primary sources as I could in researching this book. Paramount among the sources were reports contemporary to the times, and *people who were there*. Occasionally one story or report would conflict with another. In such cases I sought out a third source to verify one or the other.

Hopefully, I have found all the right facts, and organized them clearly without introducing inaccuracies.

Acknowledgments

I was fortunate to be in contact with several primary sources as I wrote this book—people who played important roles in the development of the online world. Leonard Kleinrock and Larry Roberts, two ARPANET founders, provided invaluable help as I struggled to sort out the facts from the unfortunately large number of erroneous assumptions that have been perpetrated regarding the origins and development of the world's first computer network.

Alexander "Sandy" Trevor, one of the original crew at CompuServe's "skunk works" project, MicroNET, graciously permitted me to interview him at his home on New Year's Day. His technical knowledge, insight, and patience with my numerous follow-up questions were and are appreciated.

Bill Louden, a veteran of CompuServe's early days, proprietor of the first dot.com to go bust, founder of GEnie, and the man responsible for getting more people hooked on online games than anyone else, generously shared unique insider information about the economics, personalities, technology, and evolution of online services.

Any factual errors are mine.

The professional staff at Apress were extremely helpful as we went through the process of transforming ideas and a raw manuscript into a bound book. I am especially grateful to Jeffrey Pepper for spotting the idea's potential. He and Richard Dal Porto did an excellent job of managing and moving the process along, and stoically endured the suspense of late chapter arrivals, a thankless part of editing and publishing.

Thanks are due John Vacca for dealing with some puzzling elements, and for catching bloopers and lending insightful opinion and fact.

Even though I disagree with her on the use of a certain interCap, my compliments to Liz Welch as one of the most professional and capable copy editors with whom it has been my pleasure to work. And thanks are due Laura Esterman for her astute transformation of the manuscript into pages.

Special thanks to Debra Morner for proofreading drafts of early chapters. Finally, thanks to Bill Brohaugh for unwittingly giving me the Ven-Tel modem that started me on my way to the Web, all those years ago.

Introduction

Friday was a good day to be indoors and online. It was the middle of a long holiday weekend, with temperatures hovering in the high nineties. Chat rooms buzzed with untold thousands of conversations on everything from television and the stock market to computers and, of course, the weather. Stubborn gamers engaged in mortal multiplayer combat literally clogged some parts of the Internet, while shoppers flooded online malls like lemmings. Online auctions offered the possibility of bargains on hot items like the new Sony Walkman.

It was a good day for online crime, too. More people online meant more victims. Spoofers and phishers collected passwords and other sensitive information like picking up pebbles on a beach. Pseudo-anarchists promoted chaos by uploading free copies of expensive commercial software, and posting public messages with IDs and passwords for a variety of online systems. Hackers lurked everywhere, but few had deadly agendas. Most sought *satori* and empowerment in a realm where they could exist on their own terms.

Elsewhere online, couples "met" for romantic purposes. They flirted, chatted, and emailed, eventually to arrange offline meetings. Some of these encounters ended with marriage. At least one ended in tragedy. Those who were afraid to meet in person holed up in private chat rooms to talk about what it might be like to meet.

This was the online world as the general public perceived it on July 5, 1984. To most it was the internet—the public internet, although the real Internet existed on another plane entirely, walled-off and secure against unauthorized intrusion.

A decade before the Web.

Primitive, fascinating, and seductive, this early public Internet reached deep into the mind, its small-screen glow all but irresistible to those exposed to it. The exposure would be life changing for many.

Thirty-year-old Steve Roberts, for example. On this day, Roberts was in the second year of a high-tech road trip inspired and made possible by the beginnings of the Internet. Riding a recumbent bicycle equipped with solar cell–powered computers and radio gear, the 6'4" technophile would eventually rack up 17,000 miles pedaling into and out of the lives of an ever-changing cast of friends, lovers, and business associates. Along the way he would prove the viability of a high-tech, low-energy consumption, mobile lifestyle. Roberts chronicled his journeys in magazine articles and a book titled *Computing Across America*. CompuServe made his journey possible by providing a link with the world wherever he went, and a forum for reporting on his travels to CompuServe readers. CompuServe email kept him in touch with his sponsors and helped him plan his trips and deal with technical issues.

The online world touched thousands of other lives in less colorful but equally important ways that year. Marriage ceremonies were held online. Computer consultants found themselves in the business of putting businesses online. Writers suddenly had new books to write (writing guides to online services would become a minor industry in itself).

That was just the beginning. The online services that brought the Internet into homes themselves created jobs—in engineering, programming, marketing, and customer service. Manufacturers ramped up to supply modems and communications software to millions of new computer owners. New magazines explained how to get online and what to do once you got there.

Entrepreneurs partnered with services such as CompuServe, The Source, and DELPHI by creating products to bring more people online and keep them there longer. For this, some received a share of the revenue generated. Others, functioning as "helpers," were content just to have free time online.

Some of these early online entrepreneurs were stunningly successful. Beginning in 1983 Paul and Sarah Edwards founded a work-from-home industry based on telling others how to work from home. The foundation of their empire was a CompuServe Forum. The Forum, profitable in itself, spawned books, magazine articles, and columns, as well as syndicated radio and TV programs. Self-referential, but it worked.

Other special-interest groups—particularly those devoted to a specific brand of computer—enjoyed similar successes. Content providers such as *The Wall Street Journal*, *The New York Times*, and other print media found it profitable to be online. Online game designers, though few, might earn as much as $30,000 per month in royalties from one game.

Obviously, the online world was booming in those pre-AOL days. And that's a strange fact to ponder if, like many people, you thought the Internet came along sometime after 1990, with the Web hot on its heels.

In truth, the Internet goes back a lot further than that. Just how far back depends on what you're talking about. If you mark the beginning of the Internet by the very first communications between two computers, you'll have to go back to the 1950s, or maybe the 1940s. Multiple computers communicating and sharing resources from several locations? That would be ARPANET, the government-sponsored research program that most histories peg as the beginning of the Internet (and which just happened to begin the year CompuServe and its network were founded: 1969).

ARPANET *is* a likely candidate, responsible as it was for developing the technology that makes the Internet possible. And so many major events cluster around it. But we can break it down further than that, if you like. Maybe the Internet began with the first ARPA long-distance computer communications experiment, which created the first wide area network (WAN). Or was it the first message sent from one computer sitting next to another? Could it have begun with the very concept of networked computers?

It's your choice. There are other possibilities set forth in the pages that follow. But hold your judgment until you've read the whole story of what happened on the way to the Web, once we got started. Here you will find tales of not only technology, but also of the people behind the technology and institutions that led to the Web.

You'll meet the visionaries and engineers (and at least one psychologist) who set up the first experiments in networking and established the earliest online outposts. Among them are some clever people who turned the limitations of computers into assets, along with the first online information hucksters—people who, as you'll see, could make money from (almost) nothing.

And that group connects us to the people who created the first Information Superhighway in the early 1970s. In between are those responsible for commercializing ARPANET technology (without which it would never have achieved its fullest potential).

Equally as important as those who made the Internet are those who made it public. They're in this book, along with the entrepreneurs who made the public Internet possible, and made their fortunes on the way to the Web. Not to mention the companies—US Robotics, AOL, The Source, DELPHI, PLink, Telenet, Playnet, and dozens more that put us on the road to today's Internet.

And of course there are the people responsible for the shape of the Internet—its customs, rules, traditions, appearance, and more. You may be one of them. Read on and learn how they affected the paths we followed on the way to the Web, and how they continue to shape the Web today.

Looking Back: Where *Did* It All Begin?

That was the first breath of life the Internet ever took.
—Leonard Kleinrock, ARPANET founder

A history of the Internet ought to begin at the beginning. But determining when and how the Internet began is difficult, not unlike defining the moment at which life begins, or determining who was responsible for the atomic bomb.

One is tempted to say that the Internet began with the first connection of two computers; no one knows for certain when and where that occurred. We do know that in the 1950s the U.S. Air Force developed the SAGE (Semi-Automatic Ground Environment) radar system, which relied on computers communicating with one another from several different sites, using some of the earliest modems.[1] In the commercial realm, we find the SABRE airline reservation system going on line with two IBM 7090 mainframe computers in 1960. But who knows which researchers in other industrialized nations were working on similar projects at the same time?

Besides, while those computers were communicating, they weren't networked, with each system's resources available to every other system on the network. That had to wait for the first true computer network, the Advanced Research Projects Agency Network, or ARPANET.

But where and how did ARPANET begin? What was its genesis?

---

[1] The first modem designed to transmit digital data was the Bell 103, which operated at 110 and 300 bits per second. Note that the proper term to designate a modem's speed is bits per second (bps). "Baud," which is often mistakenly used in place of bps, is the number of times a modem changes its signal state each second. When operating at 300bps, the Bell 103 also used 300 baud (one change in state for each bit transmitted). In contrast, a 1200bps modem operates at 2400 baud, but manages to send 4 bits with each change of signal state, thanks to a different modulation technique. People confused the terms and baud has been erroneously used to represent modem speeds ever since.

In the Beginning . . .

The generally accepted story is that someone at the Pentagon decided it would be a good idea to build a computer network that could survive a nuclear strike. The Advanced Research Projects Agency (ARPA) built a network called ARPANET; it initially connected university computers. The Department of Defense (DoD) later changed the name to DARPANET (for Defense Advanced Research Agency Network) and more computers were added.

Access to the network was limited to academics and other researchers. Those favored few not only accessed data, but also sent email, posted on bulletin boards, and played games. Eventually, the public got wind of all this and clamored for access until the government decided to share.

Part of that is true, but much of it isn't. As often happens with history, the story has been altered by many retellings. But it is such an article of faith with most people that it might just as well be codified into scripture, perhaps something like this:

> *In the beginning there was no Connection. Then—Lo!—ARPANET was brought forth upon the land. Scholars learned to Connect among themselves, whereupon the Department of Defense took note and said, "Let there be DARPANET!"*
>
> *And the DoD saw that this was good, and declared, "Henceforth, let only scholars and soldiers be Connected!" And it was so, for the DoD was mighty, and all feared Its wrath. TCP and IP were created, and the word was "Internet," and it was good.*
>
> *But the people, led by the merchants of the land, were sorely vexed and prayed leave to Connect . . .*

The *real* story of ARPANET—and the online world in general—goes back to at least 1957. It was that year that the Soviet Union successfully launched the first artificial satellite, Sputnik, and thereby proved that the United States was in second place when it came to technology.

It is difficult to imagine how this affected America and Americans, unless you were there. Suffice it to say that the general attitude was that something had to be done about this, and soon. Government-backed research in rocketry, electronics, and atomic power mushroomed. Science became the number-one priority in schools. Recognizing the need for an all-out effort to close the technology gap, President Dwight D. Eisenhower called on some of the most brilliant minds of the American scientific community to meet the challenge. As a result, on February 7, 1958, ARPA was created by DoD Directive 5105.41 and Public Law 85-325. An arm of the DoD, ARPA's mandate was to promote and underwrite scientific research in all disciplines, and to foster technological advancement on all fronts that might be connected with defense.

ARPA funding went out to research programs at universities across the country. The number of researchers increased and the demand for computer services soon outstripped the supply. At the same time, computing was among the less-crowded fields of research, perhaps because it had not achieved the popularity of disciplines such as information theory and architecture.

For this, among other reasons, MIT grad student Leonard Kleinrock was attracted to computing. Kleinrock had come to MIT in 1957 to earn a master's degree in electrical engineering. Having earned the degree and accumulated practical experience at MIT's Lincoln Laboratory (where SAGE was developed), he had no notion to seek a doctorate until a professor urged him to do so.

For his PhD work, Kleinrock chose the relatively unexplored realm of computer communications. Having worked with computers, he foresaw that computer communications would be vital to future research. He also recognized the inadequacy of the telephone system for linking computers.

With these ideas in mind, Kleinrock developed mathematical theories for packet networks (though the term was unknown at the time). In 1962 he published a paper presenting the idea of organizing and transmitting data in fixed-length blocks for accuracy, control, and reliability. His PhD research, published as a book in 1964, addressed routing, distributed control, message packetization, and other elements that serve as the foundation for today's Internet technology.[2] (The book is *Communications Nets*, whose 2007 edition is available from Dover Publications.)

Also at MIT during this period (though the two were unaware of each other's work) was psychologist J.C.R. Licklider, a pioneer in psychoacoustics. While working with the department of electrical engineering on improving the military's use of computing technology, Licklider introduced a concept he called the "Galactic Network." He envisioned the Galactic Network as a worldwide network of computers through which people would interact and share information. A researcher at any location could access "a universe of data" and run programs at all the other sites. (Several science fiction writers, among them A.E. van Vogt and Isaac Asimov, had by this time introduced similar concepts in their work, though they weren't likely to realize them.) This would be the ultimate solution to the shortage of computers in academia.

Licklider also inferred new forms of social interaction through computers. He foresaw a kind of symbiosis between humans and computers, with computers facilitating social interaction at a level impossible without them. It's probably safe to say that we have achieved the Galactic Network concept, but we are still working on the human-computer symbiosis.

---

[2] *Interestingly, parallel work on packet-switching technology was under way by Paul Baran at the RAND Corporation and Great Britain's National Physical Laboratory (NPL). Donald Davies of NPL coined the term "packet."*

The Nuclear Strike Myth

It is widely believed that the initial purpose of the Internet was to create a communications network that would survive a preemptive nuclear strike. This is appropriately dramatic, but is not strictly true.

The nuclear strike story resulted from people confusing ARPANET development with a separate project, conducted by the RAND Corporation, aimed at developing a voice telephone communications network that used message-packetizing technology. The intent of that project was to create a network that could function if some of its links were taken out, as by a nuclear attack.

Soon after circulating his Galactic Network proposal in a series of memos, Licklider took the job of head of ARPA's Information Processing Techniques Office (IPTO). While there, he succeeded in convincing two men who would succeed him in this position of the importance of the computer network concept, Ivan Sutherland and Kleinrock's fellow MIT researcher Larry Roberts. Kleinrock, in turn, sold Roberts (his officemate) on the idea of computer communications via packets, planting a seed for future development.

In 1964 Kleinrock accepted a faculty position at UCLA, but he would work with Larry Roberts again, thanks to Licklider's evangelism for the Galactic Network. Ivan Sutherland, who took over at IPTO immediately after Licklider, saw the computer network concept as a solution to the problem of satisfying researchers' need for computing power.

Back at MIT, Sutherland followed up on the computer network idea in 1965 by giving Larry Roberts and Thomas Marill (another of Licklider's protégés) at System Development Corporation (SDC) an ARPA contract to get two computers to communicate. SDC had previously developed the time-sharing system for ARPA's AN/FSQ32 (or Q-32) computer, and so was a logical choice for the experiment. The computers in the experiment were the Q-32 in SDC's Santa Barbara, California, lab and a TX-2 at MIT's Lincoln Lab.

The cross-continental computer hookup, at 1200bps, was the first wide area network (WAN) and served as a proof-of-concept. In addition, the experiment validated Kleinrock's idea that conventional telephone circuits were inadequate for computer communications. Packet switching would indeed be necessary, as Klcinrock had predicted in his thesis work.

A year later, Sutherland (now in charge at IPTO) recruited Robert Taylor of NASA to be associate director of IPTO. Like his predecessor, Taylor recognized the need for an ARPA computer network to facilitate research and general information sharing, and set about making it happen. Taylor hired Larry Roberts as chief scientist for IPTO in 1965. Roberts, already educated on the importance of computer networking and packet-switching methodology, was the ideal person for the job and perhaps the only individual who could handle it.

In 1966, Roberts, together with Marill, wrote the first proposal for a network of timesharing computers. In April 1967, Roberts organized a design meeting among ARPA principal investigators. The basic network design was worked out and in October Roberts presented it in a paper at an Association for Computing Machinery symposium.

It was at this meeting that Roberts for the first time became aware of parallel, independent work being conducted by Paul Baran at the RAND Corporation and by Donald Davies at Britain's National Physical Laboratory. In June 1968 Larry Roberts wrote a plan for an ARPA network, in which, according to Kleinrock, "he proposed that ARPA build a working network which would permit researchers to log on to one another's computers and gain access to the many resources of each such computer." Taylor approved the proposal and by mid-year Roberts had written a proposal for network hardware and sent it out to 140 potential contractors. Bolt, Beranek, and Newman Corporation (BBN) won the contract.

By this time, Kleinrock was in charge of the Network Measurement Center at the University of California in Los Angeles, with a Scientific Development Systems (SDS) Sigma-7 computer among his assets. Because of Kleinrock's early work with packet-switching and the facilities available there, UCLA's Network Measurement Center was selected to be the first "node" of the new network.

Kleinrock led a research team of computer science grad students. There was also a hardware engineer named Mike Wingfield. Kleinrock assigned the job of establishing and refining network communications protocols to a team led by Steve Crocker and including Vinton Cerf. Their work would prove to be vital to making a network that was robust and scalable.

At BBN, Frank Heart was the team leader and Robert Kahn the system designer in developing the hardware (that is, the interface between the mainframe computer and the rest of the network). What BBN had signed on to do was build something called an Internet Message Processor (IMP). The IMP was actually a Honeywell DDP-516 minicomputer. It would receive data packets sent by other computers on the network, reassemble the packets into their original form, and pass the data on to the host computer. (Each host computer, or node, would have an IMP working between it and the network.)

Lo!

BBN delivered the IMP in August 1969, just eight months after winning the contract. Kleinrock and his team, along with BBN engineers, cabled the IMP to UCLA's SDS Sigma-7 mainframe computer and went to work. On September 2, data bits started moving back and forth between the two machines. According to Kleinrock, "That was the first breath of life the Internet ever took."

The First Internet Message

The first message sent over a computer network was supposed to be "login," but it was truncated to "lo" by a system crash. In one sense this was appropriate, "Lo!" being short for "Lo and behold!"

It took an hour to bring the system back up before "login" could be transmitted from UCLA to Stanford.

Within a few weeks, UCLA's IMP was communicating with another IMP and mainframe at Stanford University. On October 29, Kleinrock sent the first-ever computer message from UCLA to Stanford. By the end of 1969, computers at two more universities—UC at Santa Barbara and the University of Utah—were connected to the network.

ARPANET was up and running, although it went pretty much unnoticed. As Kleinrock is fond of pointing out, "In 1969 the first man landed on the Moon, the Woodstock Festival took place, the Mets won the World Series, Charles Manson went on a killing spree, and the Internet was born—and nobody noticed!"

A UCLA press release announced the network in advance, on July 3, 1969. Headed "UCLA to Be First Station in Nationwide Computer Network," it hinted that computer networks just might grow into something really big. Kleinrock was quoted as saying, "Computer networks are still in their infancy. But as they grow up and become more sophisticated, we will probably see the spread of 'computer utilities,' which, like present electric and telephone utilities, will service individual homes and offices across the country." Kleinrock's statement was more prophetic than anyone knew.

In the Money

*. . . we were going to be able to share all the knowledge of the world
between all the computers.*
—Larry Roberts, ARPANET and Telenet founder

Computers were not originally a mass-market product. They were more like
airplanes, in that their cost and complexity ensured that the market wouldn't
be huge. With computers, as with aircraft, the first profitable enterprise was
producing machines for sale or lease. But other opportunities would be developed by those who could figure out the right angles.

As it happened, it was possible to turn the very factors that limited the
market for computers—cost and complexity—into opportunities.[1] Most businesses could not afford to own or lease a computer, so IBM and other manufacturers began offering technical computing services to business and industry.
They sold access to computers and to their employees' expertise. These services, which cost hundreds of dollars per hour, required clients to hand off their
data processing jobs to the computer companies, which usually delivered
results in the form of large printouts several days later.

Early computer service bureau customers had to adapt their schedules to
the machine's work schedule because computing jobs were processed one at a
time (called "batch computing"). In 1957, a researcher named John McCarthy,
inventor of the LISP programming language, built the first time-sharing
system.

The basis for time-sharing was the fact that a computer spent much of its
time waiting for user input or responses from printers or other hardware.
McCarthy devised a way for a computer to work on other jobs during these

---

[1] *Interestingly, the same thing happened with radio, but in a different way. In 1921, Powel Crosley Jr.,
on observing that early radio receivers were overpriced and overly complex, determined that he would
manufacture simple, low-cost radio sets that anyone could afford, and thereby touched off the broadcast industry.*

waiting periods, thus eliminating the waste of significant amounts of computing power and time. Computer operations were so fast, even then, that any delays caused by time-sharing were not perceptible to humans.

Commercial time-sharing computers made their debut in the early 1960s, and soon became the standard model for computer service bureaus.

Mainframe computer owners were soon copying the manufacturers, selling computer time to organizations that could not afford to own their own systems. Selling time helped amortize the investment, and business was so good that it often paid for the computer. By the mid-1960s, time-sharing had grown into a billion-dollar business—big enough that companies were developed to buy mainframe computers for the sole purpose of selling computer time and services.

Some time-sharing clients needed more than occasional access to computers, though still not enough to justify buying one. Time-sharing services accommodated the heavier users by setting up remote connections to their computers. Teletypes, or more modern terminals with a video display (then called CRTs, or Cathode Ray Tubes), connected with modems (again, available since the 1950s) and telephone lines, allowed customers to operate the remote computer from their site.

Of course, time-sharing clients paid to lease or buy the terminal equipment. And this wasn't the only "extra" income for time-sharing companies. If a client did not have its own system operators and programmers, the time-sharing operation provided them, at a charge. There were also charges for storing data, and for special "conditioned" leased telephone lines to keep a direct link between the terminal and the computer open.

Software development was yet another source of income. Time-sharing companies charged to develop the software, and to maintain and update it. And the more astute time-sharing services recognized that money could be made from their customers' own programs. If a simulation program developed by a client was particularly effective, the time-sharing company might offer it to other clients to use, with a royalty or license fee paid to the client/developer.

The First Online Content

During the 1960s, a new role developed for companies that owned computers. No matter what their primary business, they could put their computer expertise to work for other computer owners. Some organizations that owned computers (as opposed to depending on time-sharing operations for computing tasks) found managing computer systems outside their areas of expertise and interest. Rather than hire trained engineers and programmers, they hired companies like the Lockheed Corporation, Bunker Ramo Corporation, General Electric, and System Development Corporation (the same SDC that participated in the first ARPA computer communications experiment) to manage their computer operations.

Several of these relationships involved the development of databases and remote computer access. In 1966, for example, Lockheed, the aerospace company, received a contract to help compile and manage NASA's Scientific and Technical Aerospace Reports (STAR) database. STAR was a project that NASA had started in 1962, to create hard-copy abstracts and indexes of technical journals that were of interest to the agency.

Lockheed had for several years been developing a data-retrieval system it called Dialog, which gave it the expertise needed for the project and the tools to manage it.[2]

Bunker Ramo was given the contract to provide remote access to the database. Both of these companies would find the experience gained valuable in creating publicly accessible online databases over the next few years.

Bunker Ramo also put together NASA's RECON (short for REmote CONsole information retrieval system), another bibliographic database. RECON is notable for being the first multisite bibliographic retrieval system. It was also the first online search system with the capability of ordering source documents, a standard feature on Dialog and other commercial information retrieval systems today.

Bunker Ramo withdrew from the contract after a two-month trial period, and Lockheed took over. In both contracts, Lockheed retained ownership of the software, a wise move, considering future developments. In effect, the software development was underwritten by NASA.

Concurrent with these developments, SDC was developing information retrieval systems for the U.S. Air Force and the U.S. Office of Education (USOE, predecessor to the U.S. Department of Education). The USOE project was called ERIC (for Education Resources Information Center).[3] Lockheed was given the contract to provide leased-line terminal access to ERIC.

Other database management contracts with various government agencies followed, among them the Nuclear Science Abstracts (NSA) Database and the National Library of Medicine's (NLM) MEDLARS (Medical Literature Analysis and Retrieval System) index of over 2,000 medical journals. (Although MEDLARS was developed by General Electric for NLM, SDC had a contract to back up the database.)

By the end of the 1960s, Lockheed and other organizations had accumulated extensive expertise in developing, managing, searching, and providing remote access to large computer databases. Here again, software development, the building of databases, and the experience gained were underwritten by various U.S. government agencies.

---

[2] *Dialog remains in business, on the Web at* http://www.dialog.com.

[3] *ERIC was and remains a program of access to bibliographic records of journal articles and other educational resource material. Today it is available on the Web at* http://www.eric.ed.gov.

None of these databases were open to the public at large. Each government agency limited access to its employees or a group of fee-paying institutional users—mostly other government entities, libraries, and universities.

In the eyes of the computer contractors, commercializing the databases—offering public access for a fee—was the natural next step. It went almost without saying that elements of business and industry, as well as the libraries and institutions that weren't a part of the original user base for remote database access, would be more than willing to pay to use the vast data repositories that had been developed. Even some individuals would find the information products attractive. It is likely that each contractor had thoughts of offering the databases to the public from the beginning.

The expected conflicts with data owners over making the databases available to the public arose, but in the end both Lockheed and SDC succeeded in going commercial. Royalties were paid to the agencies that owned the databases' content. But the new information retrieval services costs of systems hardware, software, data management techniques, and database content were essentially paid for by government agencies.

Lockheed put Dialog online as a commercial service in 1971. It offered three databases: the NASA RECON database, ERIC, and Nuclear Science Abstracts.

Close on the heels of Dialog, SDC put MEDLARS online as MEDLINE, then went live with a new program called ORBIT (necessary because SDC did not retain ownership to the software it developed as a contractor). ORBIT (Online Bibliographic Retrieval of Information Time-Shared) offered not only the NLM database but also its backup of ERIC, Pandex (a general science abstracts database), and Chemical Abstracts Condensates.[4]

Bunker Ramo took a different approach to commercializing institutional computer development; it went straight to the private sector. Already well versed in automating financial systems, Bunker Ramo began developing the NASDAQ system in 1969 and had it online in 1971. That same year, a partnership between Bunker Ramo and Dow Jones called the Dow Jones–Bunker Ramo News Retrieval Service went online. (This became the Dow Jones News/Retrieval Service, or DJNS, in 1979.) The service provided recent news and other information published by Dow Jones News Service, *The Wall Street Journal*, and *Barron's*.

A few years later Bunker Ramo was responsible for installing the world's largest online bank teller terminal system, interconnecting over 1,000 branches of the Bank of America. The company's ventures into public online information services diminished after that, and it eventually became part of ADP (Automatic Data Processing, Inc.).

Dialog and SDC ORBIT continued adding new databases and customers. As they grew, competitors such as Bibliographic Retrieval Services (BRS) went

---

[4] *Orbit is now Questel, at* http://www.questel.orbit.com.

online, at times offering some of the same databases. Other commercial information providers, Data Central's LEXIS among them, provided proprietary databases that no one else could offer.

The online information retrieval business was off to a flying start, sowing the seeds of the Internet.

The First Information Superhighway

When SDC, Dialog, and others began putting content online, there were no commercial packet-switching networks like we have today. The connect charges for dialup or leased-line phone access were a source of concern, as users' telephone bills often exceeded charges for computer access.

It was enough of an issue that in 1970 NLM experimented with Teletype access for MEDLINE via AT&T's TWX (TeletypeWriter eXchange) network. A descendent of the nineteenth-century telegraph system, TWX cost less than telephone access, but was slow and cumbersome, operating with speeds as low as six characters per second. (Modem/telephone line connections were 50 times faster.)

Teletype proved to be grossly inadequate, but a better solution was coming from the time-sharing industry. By this time, time-sharing operations had developed various methods to ensure reliable telephone data hookups for their clients. Tymshare, founded in 1966, had in 1968 developed a "circuit-switched" network to carry traffic for its time-sharing clients. This differed from packet switching in that data was sent in a continuous stream, like water through a pipe. The network wasn't the best, but the large-scale use of leased lines meant an economy of scale that greatly reduced data transmission costs.

In 1972 (1973 by some accounts), Tymshare initiated plans to make its network (now called Tymnet) publicly available. This was made possible by a new Federal Communications Commission (FCC) directive that allowed the company to link computers in the manner of an Internet service provider (ISP), as opposed to becoming a regulated data carrier. Tymnet's first customer was MEDLINE/SDC. The charge for Tymnet access was a mere $6 per hour, as compared with $27 per hour for direct-dial phone service. The service offered local telephone numbers in 40 cities. Dialog signed on soon after.

Larry Roberts was still running the IPTO at ARPANET at this time. But it was no longer ARPANET; its name had been changed to DARPANET, the "D" denoting "Defense." Roberts decided that the time had come for packet-switching technology to be developed commercially. He approached AT&T about running DARPANET and taking over development of the technology, but the communications giant felt that a packet-switching network was, as Roberts put it, "incompatible with their future."

Having missed this golden opportunity, AT&T tried several times over the next couple of decades to create their own data network, but failed, according to Roberts, because the company would not put managers who had the appropriate technical knowledge in charge. (AT&T would eventually buy an existing network and develop it.)

In trying to get DARPANET's technology commercialized, Roberts' mission was to get the technology to the public as soon as possible—his goal from the beginning of the ARPANET project. He knew the demand for computer communications and networking would increase, and that packet switching was the best possible way to meet the demand.

Roberts' vision was a network far larger than most people could imagine—but nowhere near what the Internet became. Some 35 years later, Roberts said of taking the network public: "I thought it would become a worldwide activity that would be very important because my thinking was that we were going to be able to share all the knowledge of the world between all the computers. I didn't envision that everybody would have their own computer, that there would be millions of computers. We thought there would be thousands."

After AT&T turned down the offer to commercialize DARPANET, an FCC official suggested that Roberts set up a packet-switching network as a regulated communications carrier. Among other benefits, this would help control leased-line costs and protect the company against loss claims in case of service outages. Creating such a service had only recently become possible, thanks to the telephone system going competitive and the establishment of companies like MCI.

Roberts took the idea to BBN, which was still DARPANET's contractor. BBN concurred with Roberts, and made the decision to invest in the commercial packet-switching network. Roberts was asked to be president, but could not go to work right away because he had to choose his successor at IPTO. BBN moved ahead with organizing the company, called Telenet, and hired people to work on filing the tariff with the FCC.

By the end of 1974 Telenet was a going concern, under Roberts' leadership. It was up and running as the world's first commercial packet-switched network (PSN) in 1975. (As noted, Tymnet used circuit switching, and other packet-based systems inspired by DARPANET were experimental.)

Telenet not only provided PSN services, but also manufactured switches and other equipment. Before long, a large number of organizations were setting up their own networks using Telenet technology and equipment, among them Southern Bell. Telenet was easily able to interconnect with these networks, which only increased the company's rapid rate of growth. Its customer base went far beyond time-sharing companies, and included corporations like General Motors, government agencies, and just about any other organization that needed computer communications links. International links with British Telecom (BT) and other communications companies were not far away.

Telenet's nationwide system of switches, routers, and leased lines provided a low-cost, high-speed data communications service that was more reliable than simple leased lines and direct dial—and certainly more reliable than Tymnet. Equally important, Telenet created a way to connect computers to the network without a specialized hardware interface like ARPA's IMP.

Taken together, Telenet and Tymnet constituted the world's first "Information Superhighway," particularly in the sense that they were open to the public. The local-number access these networks provided eliminated what might have been a significant psychological barrier to many online database customers: the per-minute charges of conventional long-distance telephone calls. For the same reason, Telenet and Tymnet would be vital to the consumer online services yet to come.

DARPANET had not remained static through all this. In 1972 Ray Tomlinson at BBN developed a program to send small mail messages to users on Digital Equipment Corporation (DEC) PDP-10 computers, and another program that enabled the recipients to read the "electronic mail." With a small hack, he was able to send mail to users on another machine, and decided to try sending mail across the network. He worked out a means of using the file transfer protocol then being developed for DARPANET.

The mail had to be directed not only to the desired recipient, but also a specific computer on the network. This required formatting the address in two separate parts: the user's name and the name of the machine the user was on. A character would be required to separate the user name from the machine name. Tomlinson chose the @ character. It was not likely to appear in a user's name, and it had the advantage of saying "at."

DARPANET users were still left with two separate systems for sending and reading mail. There was no way to reply to a message; to respond to the sender, one had to use the sending program to create a new message. Email wasn't sorted, and was stored in one big file. Some users had to print out all of their email to get at a message.

In 1973 Roberts solved these problems with the first email-handling system. He wrote code that gave users a menu of messages, and allowed them to reply to, delete, or file messages. With 75 percent of DARPANET traffic consisting of email, it was a welcome program.

It was natural that the email concept would carry over to commercial networks, just as other DARPANET elements. Telenet developed Telemail. Some of the information retrieval services made internal email available. Time-sharing services, among them Dialcom and CompuServe, also offered email services to clients. By the late 1970s private email systems connected corporate and government offices across the United States and in many other countries.

As these developments unfolded, DARPANET's developers, among them Vint Cerf and Bob Kahn, began thinking about interconnecting DARPANET with radio and satellite packet networks. TCP (Transmission Control Protocol) and IP (Internet Protocol) were born. Commonly known as TCP/IP, these protocols would replace ARPA's original Network Control Protocol (NCP). (See Chapters 1 and 8 for details.)

At this point the online world consisted of four major elements: time-sharing services, ARPANET, the information highway of public computer networks, and private and commercial online databases.

Each element was a cornerstone in the foundation of consumer online services. Time-sharing services established remote access to computers as a marketable commodity. Along with Telenet, ARPANET validated PSN technology, commercially as well as technically. Tymnet and other time-sharing networks further validated the viability of computer communications. And online databases set the precedent for marketing online content.

Making Contact with CompuServe

They called it schlock time-sharing . . .
—Jeff Wilkins, CompuServe founder

For its first decade, the online world was elitist in the extreme. Getting in required . . . well, connections. Affiliation with a university or government agency that had computer or terminal equipment could get you online. So could an employer who was willing to underwrite access and qualified as a government contractor, though that usually meant adhering to a rigorous set of rules. And even though other networking projects were under way, they weren't intended for the public, either.

Things had to change if the online world were to be accessible to everyone. The instrument of change would be the microcomputer.

~

A recent engineering graduate of the University of Arizona, Jeff Wilkins returned home to Columbus, Ohio, in 1969, to work for his father-in-law, Harry Gard Sr., who ran a successful insurance company called Golden United Life Insurance. It was a subsidiary of another Gard company, Golden United Investments (that company's name would be changed to Ilex in 1973).

Like many large enterprises in the 1960s, Golden United used computers to track finances, make business projections, and for general number crunching. But the insurance company did not own computers, nor did most businesses that used computer services. A computer cost hundreds of thousands of dollars, and few organizations had enough data processing needs to justify buying one. Most bought time on computers owned by companies that specialized in computer time-sharing.

Jeff Wilkins had accumulated some experience with a mainframe computer at the University of Arizona's Analog Hybrid Computer Lab (AHCL) and was very familiar with time-sharing. In fact, he and two fellow students, Alexander "Sandy" Trevor and John Goltz, discussed starting a time-sharing service, to be based on a DEC PDP-15 computer, the same model owned by AHCL. Wilkins decided that his father-in-law's business could benefit greatly by buying its own computer and getting into the time-sharing business. It would eliminate an expense and add a potential profit center.

When the trio graduated, the U.S. Army called Sandy Trevor, but Goltz (now Dr. John Goltz) followed Wilkins to Columbus. They talked Golden United's board of directors into letting them set up the time-sharing service, which they named CompuServ Networks, Inc. And Goltz, who would serve as CompuServ's first president, talked the company into buying a more powerful (and expensive) KI-10 system.[1]

Wilkins and Goltz assembled a superb technical team. For the front office, business computing experts were recruited from organizations such as IBM and Xerox—experts whose button-down shirts and attitudes matched those of CompuServ's target market.

Time-sharing depended on data networks. Most time-sharing outfits used packet-switching networks (PSNs) like Telenet or Tymnet to connect their computers to clients' terminals. Information services like DJNS and Dialog also used PSNs to connect with customers.

But CompuServ built its own data network, based on leased lines provided by AT&T. The company's engineers developed proprietary network hardware and software that enabled the CompuServ network to outperform PSNs and AT&T's own networks, using standard telephone lines as opposed to the much more expensive "conditioned" lines normally used for data communications. (CompuServ's network employed DEC minicomputers to service as switches in routing data.) This rankled AT&T managers who, as future events would demonstrate, did not like the idea of CompuServ besting their technology.

In addition to saving money by leasing regular telephone lines, CompuServ was able to negotiate a favorable bulk rate because it used so many thousands of hours per month. CompuServe paid only a tiny fraction of AT&T's standard long-distance rates. AT&T wouldn't have sold time so cheaply if FCC regulations didn't require it, which was another thorn in the telephone monopoly's side.

CompuServ was as innovative in creating products as it was in setting up its hardware and network. The traditional time-sharing company's role had been to give clients basic access to computers, leaving it up to them to provide their own software. Wilkins changed that business model by introducing packaged business applications. These programs were installed on CompuServ's computers and maintained by the company. Clients paid extra to use them. One of the first, logically, was a data information system for life insurance companies. The company also developed financial and experimental modeling programs,

---

[1] *Although Jeffrey Wilkins is widely regarded as the first president of CompuServe, Dr. Glotz was the initial president.*

and occasionally partnered to make a particularly outstanding client-developed application available to other customers.

Wilkins was equally innovative outside of business. When he built a house in the mid-1970s, he installed a DEC minicomputer and programmed it to automate environmental controls and security—very leading edge at the time.

Trevor returned from working with an IBM 360-40 in Saigon in 1971 and joined the rapidly growing operation. In 1975 it was spun off into a separate public company (NASDAQ: CMPU SRV). By 1977 it had more than 600 customers, served by two dozen sales offices in major cities. In May of that year, the board changed the name to CompuServe Incorporated, based on a study that showed wider acceptance of that version of the name by potential clients.

By now the company had two computing centers, one in Upper Arlington, Ohio, and another in nearby Dublin, filled with DEC KAs and 2050s, respectively. Teams of engineers were constantly improving both the hardware and software aspects of the computers.

In addition to providing computer access and software, CompuServe experimented with information products. Among the first of these was a database that provided new and replacement costs for an extensive list of consumer merchandise. This was originally developed for insurance companies, who used it for a reference in calculating loss. The database would be the foundation for a membership-based shopping network called Comp-U-Card. (The company was not operated by CompuServe and despite the name, customers didn't shop by computer. Comp-U-Card service representatives used the database as they helped members place orders by telephone. However, members would eventually be able to access the service by both computer and cable TV.)

Obviously, CompuServe was highly successful. The only real flaw in the works had to do with the fact that the centerpiece of CompuServe's services, its computers, sat idle about half the time.

As was true of time-sharing operations in general, all the action was during business hours. Though the huge computers ran 24 hours a day, virtually no one logged on at night or on weekends. As Wilkins told *The Wall Street Journal* in a 1979 interview, "It's a network that's there and not in use during off-peak hours." This didn't represent a loss, but Wilkins viewed the situation as a terrible waste of resources. So CompuServe's staff gave considerable thought to how the computers might be put to work.

The solution came from an unexpected quarter: the growing ranks of microcomputer owners.

Microcomputers, as personal computers were then known, had been around since 1974, when the first computer kit, the Altair, was introduced.[2]

---

[2] *The earliest microcomputer may be the Datapoint 220, a programmable terminal manufactured by Computer Terminal Corporation (CTC) in 1970. However, Intel released two different chips that in themselves were microcomputers, the MCS-4 and the MCS-8 CPU. Another candidate is the Kenback-1 (1971), which, while it used transistor-transistor logic (TTL) logic rather than a microprocessor, functioned like a microcomputer.*

The Altair and other early systems like the IMSAI weren't for the general public; they were essentially boxes with lights and switches, and microprocessors and other circuitry inside. These required extensive electronics knowledge to build and maintain. The only buyers were engineers or dedicated hobbyists—early personal computer geeks. Many hobbyists were stumped by the intricate assemblies and endless solder joints required, and paid a premium price to have their kits assembled.

Nor were these early micros very powerful. Today's pocket calculators have more capability and are simpler to use. Microcomputer owners programmed and recovered data from their systems through a series of switches and indicator lights. Most computer hobbyists enjoyed this: it made computers mysterious and flattered the users' intellects. More sophisticated and well-heeled computerists expanded their systems with expensive Teletypes for input and printed output. Paper tapes stored data and programs.

Though the first-generation machines were anything but user-friendly, just about any technically minded person with a lot of patience could teach themselves to use one. Newer machines were easier to assemble and use, and preassembled systems hit the market. This broadened the customer base considerably, helped along by marketing that presented the small computers as serious learning and business tools.

Keyboards and monitors replaced switches and lights. Increased memory, along with data and program storage on cassette tapes and disks, resulted in simplified operation and more power. The comparatively low cost of these sophisticated microcomputers helped them achieved the status of consumer products less than three years after the first crude kits came on the scene. By 1978 companies like Apple and Radio Shack were selling computers by the thousands.

Wilkins had taken notice of microcomputers when the Altair made its debut, and from time to time he had followed the industry. Wilkins wasn't a microcomputer hobbyist, but he recognized microcomputer owners as a potential market for CompuServe. So he hired his brother-in-law, a recent college graduate, to buy computer magazines and track what he called "the newshole," as the mainstream press was still largely unaware of the nascent computer revolution.

~

About the time the microcomputer began to ease its way into the American consciousness, the prices of mini- and mainframe computers were beginning to drop. DEC and other companies were offering mainframe systems that cost $150,000 or less. At this price point, many companies that were being billed $4,000 to $8,000 per month for time-sharing services would find it expedient to buy their own systems.

This represented a threat to the $1.7 billion time-sharing business. Time-sharing companies like ADP, Boeing Computer Services, CompuServe, and Tymshare began devising strategies to keep customers from buying their own systems.

The major tactic was the relatively new concept of distributed processing. A time-sharing operation would install a minicomputer at a client's business, giving the client on-site processing power as well as a link to the time-sharing company's big mainframes. Much of the processing load would be handled by the on-site computer before the information was sent on to the central computer, reducing the billing for the use of the host system.

Still, perhaps it was time for time-sharing companies to look for a new source of customers.

~

Wilkins learned that there was more interest in microcomputers than he had thought. People were spending serious money on microcomputers; a typical system with keyboard, monitor, and a cassette tape recorder for storage cost between $600 and $1,200. But price didn't discourage computerphiles. Word was spreading and people were literally fascinated by the idea of owning a computer. Demand often exceeded supply, as evidenced by the experience of Radio Shack. The company introduced its TRS-80 Model I on August 3, 1977, thinking it might sell 1,000 a year at most. Ten thousand were sold in the first month, and 55,000 the first year.

Most of those early buyers bought their microcomputers sight unseen. Aware that no more than 5,000 of any microcomputer had ever been sold, an overly cautious Radio Shack management had ordered only 3,000 TRS-80s built.[3] Since there were some 3,500 Radio Shack stores, the decision was made to sell the computers direct from the catalog, rather than put demo units in some stores and not in others.

This was asking customers to accept quite a lot on faith. Americans were accustomed to instant gratification, especially when it came to big-ticket items. But the faithful were not to be dissuaded. Enthusiasm generated by magazines and word-of-mouth brought them to Radio Shack stores in droves.

The company did not provide demos even when production began to catch up with demand. Store managers were sure they could sell a lot more computers if they had demo units. But the warehouse would ship a computer only if it was sold. Hence, if store managers wanted a demo, they had to buy it—for $599.

---

[3] *Another reason only 3,000 were built was that Tandy President John Roach figured that if the computers bombed, they could be used in the stores, in which case building them wouldn't be a complete loss.*

Bill Louden was a Radio Shack store manager in Columbus in 1977, having recently returned from several years working in Japan. He was an instant convert to the TRS-80 and was sure he could sell large numbers of the little machine, if only he had one to show. Since the company refused to provide demo units, Louden bought his own, over his wife's protests. It was serial number 10.

Louden's instincts served him well; by early 1978 he had sold nearly 200 TRS-80s, with a 10 percent commission on each sale. His was the only demo unit in the Midwest, which made him the region's "expert." Anyone who wanted to see the computer had to travel to Columbus—like the attorney who flew in from Chicago to buy one. Other buyers included engineers from Bell Labs in Columbus, and an engineer named Russ Ranshaw from CompuServe. The latter would prove to be a fortuitous connection for Louden, and not just because Ranshaw brought others in to buy Radio Shack computers.

To promote sales and information exchange among TRS-80 owners, Louden started the Central Ohio TRS-80 Users Group, better known as COTUG, in June 1978. Membership swelled to over 500 by year's end.

Springing up all over North America, clubs were an important element in the development of the personal computer. As with radio enthusiasts at the beginning of the twentieth century, clubs not only advanced the technology, but also created more enthusiasts and helped sell computers, peripherals, and programs.

~

Though the microcomputer market was big, it was difficult to define. Buyers were predominantly male, but otherwise represented nearly all demographic groups. And the reasons people bought computers were almost as varied as the buyers themselves. Home computer users played games, balanced their checkbooks, inventoried collections, tracked expenses, and gave up typewriters in favor of computers and printers. People who had never kept files of recipes started keeping them on personal computers, and many a parent put forth the vague argument that "the kids can use it for their homework" to justify a computer purchase.

Businesses small and large learned to harness the power of primitive database and spreadsheet programs. Hackers broke "unbreakable" programs and shared copies with their friends just because they could. Engineers created gadgets to add to their systems. Anyone who could afford it expanded their system with a printer, and just about everyone tried their hand at programming.

But no matter what programs or peripherals they added, personal computer owners wanted more. They were constantly on the lookout for something new and novel, not unlike people who browse the Web today.

So they bought more software and added printers. They spent money on books to learn how to make their toys do new tricks. When they reached their systems' limits, they added memory or upgraded to a new system, then began looking for something more.

It didn't take long for computer-makers and telecommunications equipment manufacturers to see the market potential for modems. But in a way it was a market with no rationale, for there was little for the home computer user to dial up in 1978, aside from other modem-equipped computer owners, with whom they traded programs and data. Professional information-retrieval services like Dialog held almost no interest for computer hobbyists, though some of the earliest information professionals (searchers) were building lucrative small businesses for themselves doing research and training.

Still, people were buying modems, certain that there was *something* they could connect to. It only remained to be discovered . . .

It was an entrepreneur's dream: all these modem buyers were a growing market in search of a product. And Wilkins had the product, in the form of idle mainframe computers and a data-carrying network with local phone numbers in every city. It was an almost perfect business proposition. With the computers and network already in place, there was no capital investment to be made, and almost no overhead. The startup costs would be laughably small—advertising, mainly. If the venture failed, the loss would be minimal.

Wilkins knew he had a winning idea. All that remained was to convince personal computer users to connect with CompuServe's computers. He knew how to reach them—through magazines and marketing partnerships with computer and modem manufacturers. But what kinds of services could CompuServe offer?

CompuServe executives were of little help in answering that question; in fact, they seemed suspicious of the idea of a consumer service. "The corporate organization was staffed by a lot of ex-IBM Service Bureau and GE people—people who were very familiar with how companies bought computer services," according to Wilkins. "But there were no hobbyists, no one who had any idea of what might interest consumers with microcomputers."

Still confident in his idea, Wilkins put together an in-house task force, a sort of skunk works, to consider how the services CompuServe offered its corporate customers might be presented to the consumer market.

Working through the summer of 1978, the group came up with three application categories. The first was raw access to the DEC computers. Home computerists would appreciate the mainframes' speed and power, and of course the novelty of using the big machines would be a draw.

The second application was storage, a problematic area for microcomputer owners. At the time, nobody made hard drives for microcomputers, and few users owned floppy disk drives because they cost $500 and up. Most stored their data and programs on slow, unreliable cassette tape systems. CompuServe's DEC mainframes used several 20MB hard drives. Compared to cassette tapes, using the system via modem would seem faster than using the disk drives in their own computers.

The final application from the CompuServe skunk works was person-to-person communication—both private and public. CompuServe already had an email system. Called "Infoplex," it was originally developed for American Express and other corporate customers. And a public "bulletin board" system, where users could read and leave public messages in subject "threads," could be easily set up in a few days' time.

Always a marketer, Wilkins also had a notion that personal computer users might be interested in buying software for download. There were already so many different kinds of computers that no computer store could stock programs for all of them. CompuServe's virtual "shelves" would always contain enough units to meet the demand. Downloadable software would eliminate the logistics problem and offer the kind of instant gratification that some people couldn't resist. And from the software producer's viewpoint, selling programs online meant reaching markets not otherwise available, and eliminating expensive packaging. It would prove to be a profitable enterprise.

And so it went as Wilkins and his group laid out the basics of an online world for consumers that was loosely modeled on European "Videotex" services (see Chapter 5). Convinced that the personal computer would become a common household appliance, he intended to develop a service that would appeal to everyone—not just hobbyists. Wilkins named the service "MicroNET." The idea of the name, he said, was "to get microcomputer owners' attention and suggest the power of the computer network."

With the basic concepts in place, Wilkins turned to his potential customers for help in expanding it. He invited the members of a local computer user group called the Midwest Computer Club to meet with CompuServe staffers at the company's Arlington Center offices and talk about what MicroNET might offer them. The owners were a mixed group of people with Apple, TRS-80, homebuilt, and other kinds of microcomputers.

There was a lot of discussion about what Wilkins called "hardware/network play versus services play." Hardware play simply meant raw access to the DEC mainframe computers, using the same programs and features provided corporate clients. The concept of services was more consumer-oriented, and included Infoplex and bulletin boards as well as access to some of CompuServe's databases, all applications that the nontechie microcomputer owner would find of interest.

Midwest Computer Club members took to modems like ducks to water. Some of them had written programs to handle communications and file transfer between their systems, and these were easily adapted for use in communicating with the DEC mainframes. And when Wilkins sent CompuServe engineer, and TRS-80 computer owner, Russ Ranshaw to invite COTUG members to log on and try out MicroNET, it turned out that they had been doing the same.

Louden remembers the online offering as "a hacker's dream." It was also a good way to sell modems, which at the time gave users a choice of two speeds: 110 or 300 bits per second.

And a hacker's dream it was. Most of CompuServe's programs were written in FORTRAN or an extended BASIC similar to that used by Radio Shack computers, and the computer club members could download and convert quite a few to run on their own computers, including games. (Popular games included Star Trek, SpaceWar, and Adventure. There were no graphics, only text and numeric readouts. All the action took place in the player's mind.) Users could also upload and run programs they had written, and they could create, edit, and store text files on the DEC system. Having MicroNET access was the next best thing to owning a mainframe computer!

Word spread and by August 1978 MicroNET was a haven for scores of hobbyists. While they didn't pay for their time online, they did serve as an online focus group. There are reports of as many as 1,200 hobbyists using the service on this test basis. Giving them free network access "was worth it," Wilkins said, "to let the users get a taste of what might be possible, and give the company an idea of their needs."

The group tested the limits and security of the system in every way imaginable, a valuable contribution. They also tested a modified DEC feature they called the "SEND" program, which allowed users to send one-line messages to one another in real time—not really chatting, but exciting just the same.

So it was that MicroNET's initial membership was made up mostly of hackers and techno-geeks. But Wilkins retained his vision of an online service that would appeal to the mainstream—the kind of people who wanted to *use* computers rather than program them.

Of course, supplying this free service ran against the grain of CompuServe's corporate culture. The company was, after all, based on running the meter. Free service added to a perception on the part of CompuServe management that MicroNET was not a business, but a dalliance for the CEO and a few kooks. "Why waste our time on this, when we're servicing Goldman-Sachs and Morgan Stanley?" they asked themselves, though not too loudly. The sales force began to refer to MicroNET as "schlock time-sharing." The service was, according to Trevor, "developed almost clandestinely."

But the money would come. As 1978 drew to a close, Wilkins, serving as CEO of MicroNET, moved Trevor to the position of vice president of computer technology. Other engineering and support staff were brought over from CompuServe, among them Harry Gard Jr., Russ Ranshaw, Rich Baker, and several more, creating a core group of 15.

A pricing structure was set early in 1979, and the hundreds of hobbyists who had been enjoying MicroNET for free either logged off for good or became paying customers. Most stayed on. After a $9 startup charge, non-prime-time usage (6:00 PM to 8:00 AM, all day holidays and weeks) was $5.00 per hour at 110 or 300 bps during non-prime-time hours, and $12.00 per hour for daytime usage (300-bps access soon became a premium service, but only until 1200-bps modems arrived on the scene).

The world's first commercial online service for consumers was unofficially up and running. According to *Business Week*, which offered a brief paragraph about the new service in its September 10, 1979, issue, most of the 1,200-odd paying users owned TRS-80 microcomputers. In November, *The Wall Street Journal* reported that CompuServe had begun selling downloadable software to microcomputer owners. "It's a very small revenue producer, less than one percent of our business," Wilkins told the *Journal*, but added, "It could have a positive impact on our earnings next year." During the second quarter of 1979, CompuServe had overall revenues of $4.2 million.

Louden, personal computing promoter *extraordinaire* and already deeply involved with CompuServe's MicroNET (soon to be renamed "CompuServe Information Service"), would join the company to help create a more sophisticated consumer version of MicroNET that offered far more than hacker toys. He would also develop the online world's most fascinating—and profitable—product areas—gaming. Users would spend hundreds of dollars per month on it. At the same time, once MicroNET members were given the tools, they pitched in and started building new products and adding files to share. It was the very beginning of the user-generated content revolution that would sweep the Web in the coming century.

The Source

This is the beginning of the Information Age!
—author and futurist Isaac Asimov

As Jeff Wilkins was assembling his skunk works at CompuServe in Columbus, a Virginia entrepreneur named William F. von Meister was pondering his next business move. The 36-year-old had recently been ousted from his position as CEO of a high-tech startup called TDX—a company he had founded two years earlier.

This was not a new experience for Bill von Meister, who seemed surprisingly inept for an entrepreneur. His business practices were questionable—and sometimes questioned in court. He started nine companies in ten years; the longest he stayed with any was two years, and he was forced out of most of them. His reputation was such that people called him "von Shyster" behind his back.

Outside the office he was described by more than one acquaintance as "a wild man and a magnificent rogue." He lived high and fast, chasing women and pursuing hobbies that included fine wines, fast cars, guns, and boats, with a few sets of tennis thrown in now and then.

But he had some good ideas, one of which became Western Union's "Mailgram" service. And he excelled in finding backers for those ideas. He was so good at selling ideas that, in his obituary in *Washington Technology* in 1995, a former backer was quoted as saying that von Meister "could raise money from the dead."

So, despite his business incompetence, von Meister made money—enough to support eight children, a rambling mansion in suburban Virginia, and his hobbies.

Coming as he did from a wealthy family tinged with royalty, he may have felt entitled to living well. He was certainly accustomed to it. His father, Friedrich Wilhelm "Willy" von Meister, was a godson of Kaiser Wilhelm II, and his mother was an Austrian countess. A naturalized U.S. citizen, Willy von Meister was a prosperous businessman. He headed up the U.S. operations of *Deutsche Zeppelin-Reederei* (DZR, German Zeppelin Shipping), the company that operated the *Hindenburg* until the airship's 1937 disaster, an event that gave him an unwanted 15 minutes of fame as the spokesman for DZR.

The *Hindenburg* disaster seems to have left the senior von Meister unscathed. By 1938 (the year William Fredrick von Meister was born) he was heading up a division of General Aniline & Film Corporation, a major U.S. chemical manufacturer. But investigations early in World War II led to von Meister's indictment on charges of trust violations, and he was ousted from the company.

The investigation also involved von Meister's ties to Germany. However, he emerged from the scandal with his reputation and fortune intact, probably aided by the fact that he and his wife were members of Washington's social elite. Following this brief interruption, von Meister continued his career in other realms of industry.

Growing up in Far Hills, New Jersey, Billy von Meister and his brother and sister enjoyed a privileged childhood. A household staff attended the family at an estate—a 15-room, six-bath home on 28 acres called "Blue Chimneys." The children of course attended boarding schools.

An amateur radio operator at the age of 11 (amateur license number K2ZRK), young Billy was something of a whiz kid. He was constantly tinkering with gadgets for use around the house. One such was an "early warning" radio signaler that transmitted an alert when his father's car was nearing home on his way from work, so the family's maid would have his tea prepared.

The young man attended a Swiss finishing school after high school, then enrolled in Georgetown University's School of Foreign Service (a likely choice for the scion of European gentry). He soon grew bored with the program, however. Financed by his father, he turned to racing and trading in exotic sports cars, from time to time returning to Georgetown for a few courses. Five years of alternating school and racing produced no profit, but it did produce an ultimatum from his father: finish college and start a career. So at the age of 25 von Meister returned to school full time, this time at American University where he earned an MBA in 18 months, wrapping it up in 1973.

His education completed, Bill von Meister didn't go job hunting. His father's example had left the young man determined to start as the boss—or to at least work under his own direction. Accordingly and in keeping with a personal interest, he started a liquor-distribution outfit he dubbed "Spirits of America."

The business seemed promising, what with the rate of liquor consumption in the D.C. area. But once the business was off and running, it didn't last long. Von Meister found day-to-day operations boring, and Spirits of America suffered from his lack of attention. As has been true for many another entrepreneur, the challenges and thrills of getting a business off the ground meant more than running a successful business. In addition, his own rate of liquor consumption was high.

This was a preview of Bill von Meister's future. He would never be happy just running a successful (or unsuccessful) enterprise; he always had to be starting something new. As one of his future backers, Jack Taub, later said, "von Meister is a terrific entrepreneur, but he doesn't know when to stop entrepreneuring."

Von Meister's tenure in the liquor business ran less than a year. His next venture was to market himself simply as a "business consultant." He had cards printed up and started handing them out to everyone he met. Some combination of family contacts, persistence, and luck won him a consulting job with Litton Bionetics, a diversified Virginia company. There he helped computerize the records of test animals used in a cancer-research program.

Going in, von Meister knew little more than the basics of what computers could do, but he learned quickly, motivated in part by the growing mystique of "thinking machines." Working with the existing staff, he developed a successful records program, then lost interest in the job. And then it was time to move on to something else.

In 1974 he moved on to another consulting position, this time at Western Union. There he put the knowledge he'd gained at Bionetics to work creating a computerized billing system.

A few months into the job at Western Union, von Meister learned that the company was scrapping a large quantity of tube-based electronics equipment that had a huge potential salvage value. When no one bid on the equipment, von Meister put in an offer of $750. He won and arranged to have the material hauled away and sold by a junk dealer. The junk dealer salvaged and sold gold contacts and other valuable material from the haul, and split the profit with von Meister. Bill von Meister netted $250,000 on the deal without having to move or sell anything. This fed his already exaggerated opinion of himself and probably added to the sense of entitlement that prompted him to take such liberties with his future employers' resources.

But this was only the beginning of what he would take away from his association with Western Union. While there, von Meister expanded his knowledge of computer applications with the help of Western Union employees, in particular an engineer named Bernard Ryder. And working with Telex systems inspired von Meister to conceive a system for speeding up business mail, whereby a letter could be transmitted by Telex to the city nearest its destination, there to be printed out and mailed for next-day delivery. (Western Union at the time had a similar fax-based service, but it was less efficient.) This was in 1974, when email was unheard of and fax was not yet ubiquitous.

Von Meister laid out a business plan that added call centers to which customers could phone and dictate letters for cross-country transmission and mailing. But Western Union wasn't interested in anything beyond their existing data-transmitting systems. So von Meister continued working on the idea until he found a backer, at which point he left Western Union.

With the backer—Xonics, Inc.—he put the concept in operation as "Telepost." The name was already in use by the Canadian Post Office for a combined telegraph-letter service, but von Meister was able to trademark it in the United States.

Telepost was successful enough to attract Western Union's interest, and the telecommunications giant eventually bought out the company. But Xonics forced von Meister out of the operation before that, in a dispute over von Meister's spending and lack of attention to the business. Telepost went on to become Western Union's Mailgram service, and von Meister reportedly received $1.2 million as his share of the buyout, after a legal confrontation.

The reason von Meister hadn't been giving Telepost much attention was because he was working on yet another new business, this one in concert with Bernard Ryder, his engineer friend from Western Union. Ryder had devised a formula for analyzing and controlling the routing of bulk telephone communications so that the optimum, least-expensive paths were always used. The two developed a computerized system to implement the idea, and after applying for a patent, von Meister formed a company called TDX Systems, Inc., to capitalize on it. (The initials TDX stood for nothing; it was a letter combination that von Meister thought sounded impressive.) They named the product "Telemax."

TDX soon reached the point where further growth mandated an infusion of capital. Von Meister went looking for backing and found it in the form of a British company, Cable & Wireless. The company's history stretched back to 1872 when it was founded as the Eastern Telegraph Company, which had for decades served as a sort of internal Internet for the British Empire. (Eastern remains a telecommunications service provider today and in one sense the online service called The Source—and hence its descendent, AOL[1]—could be said to be descended from the Eastern Telegraph Company.)

It was easy for von Meister to convince the company that TDX Systems was a good opportunity. Cable & Wireless wanted a way into the lucrative North American business telephone market, and TDX was just the ticket. Cable & Wireless signed with TDX in 1975.

TDX marketed Telemax to corporate customers with nationwide operations and high long-distance bills, like Manufacturers Hanover and the Marriott hotel and restaurant chain.

Telemax was a corporate accountant's dream. It kept a complete record of each call: who made the call, from which extension, and when; the duration; the cost; how much money was saved; and the department to which the call should be billed. If a Telemax user got a busy signal, the system would monitor the number dialed and notify the person making the call when the desired line was free. Such features are common today, but in 1977 they were all but unheard of. MCI and AT&T offered "least-cost" routing systems, but they were far less sophisticated and neither offered the savings of Telemax.

Combining existing technology in new ways was fast becoming von Meister's métier. Discussing Telemax during a 1977 newspaper interview, he

---

[1] See *Chapters 9 through 12*.

boasted of his technique. "This is," he told the reporter, Michael Schrage, "the first time somebody took the microcomputer, coupled it with a large mini-computer, and used it to do telephone switching. All the parts were available, but nobody had ever put them together this way before to get this effect."

Such was von Meister's knack for visualizing the potential of new combinations of technology. When he looked at a piece of equipment—a router, for example—he didn't see the equipment. Instead he perceived its function in relation to the functions of related equipment. A logic that instantly recognized this sort of relationship: "Unit A and Unit B together enable Unit C to perform this action." This is not necessarily a rare ability, but von Meister was fortunate in that he was in a position to bend the ears of those with the money to turn his concepts into reality—a position that was likely based on family contacts.

What happened after von Meister got Telemax up and running was predictable: he lost interest in it as new ideas caught his attention. In fact, even as he was drawing $70,000 per year to run TDX, von Meister was developing three new businesses on the side. One was a TDX-based venture, but the other two were strictly private enterprises.

The TDX-based operation was something similar to Mailgram, called "Datapost." (He may have borrowed the term Datapost from the British Post Office, which used the name for an express delivery service. Von Meister registered it as a trademark in the United States.) Marketed as a means of expediting collection letters for businesses, Datapost used fax rather than Telex to transmit letters to the U.S. Post Office's Express Mail Center in Chicago, where they were processed for next-day U.S. Mail delivery in any of 55 cities. (If von Meister had a no-compete clause in the buyout agreement with Western Union, this must have stretched it to the limit.)

On the private side, von Meister and a partner, Mark Sandground, were planning to open a restaurant to be named the McLean Lunch and Radiator Shop. The establishment would feature a table-side telephone system that diners could use to make free telephone calls to anywhere in the country—one call per customer.

In an arrangement that added insult to the injury of von Meister developing the business on his employer's time, the calls would be handled by TDX's own computerized routing system. Presumably, TDX would derive some token benefit from not-so-free advertising to the restaurant's customers.

Von Meister's other private venture was a variation on his theme of combining computers and communications. Working with engineers Michael Hills and Clay Durret, von Meister devised an information network based on "piggybacking" digital data on an FM radio broadcast, using a sideband. Such use had been legalized early in 1978 by the FCC, and used the same portion of the FM broadcasts as the Muzak music service.

The system, which von Meister named "Infocast," could transmit data up to the limit of an FM broadcast (about 75 miles). A "black box" receiver would decode data broadcasts and display the information on a computer terminal screen.

Von Meister envisioned a system that would send news, weather, ski reports, stock market prices, and sports results from a central location, to be relayed to FM stations around the country by computer-controlled PSNs and phone lines. Homes would tap into the data broadcast with receivers rented from the company. Von Meister also planned to allow those same users to send data, and even exchange messages.

In concept it was the public Internet . . . wireless and well before its time.

Initially Infocast would be deployed on a much smaller scale. Von Meister came up with a plan to sell the system to large organizations that needed to move data quickly to far-flung locations, following a business plan similar to that of a competing company, Fax Net, which carried data for large grocery chains.

Commercial Infocast clients were offered private two-way channels through which they could transmit sales and production reports, training material, company directives, product data, or anything else 24 hours a day. Infocast would lease computer terminals and receivers to clients, and charge for data traffic.

Once Infocast was established, it would provide the technological basis and part of the funding for a wireless consumer network. Von Meister told *Business Week* that a network of 50 FM stations across the country, connected by PSNs and controlled by computer systems, could reach more than 90 percent of businesses in the United States. A message from a user on such a system could be routed to an individual recipient, or copied to hundreds.

There was some discussion with the FCC as to whether Infocast should be assigned common carrier status (and thus fall under strict regulation), but von Meister patented the idea and formed a company called Digital Broadcast Corporation (DBC) to produce and market Infocast, all with Cable & Wireless money. He lined up sources for terminals and receivers, then set up offices and a technical staff in a building on Old Springhouse Road in McLean, Virginia. A small sales force went to work marketing Infocast to corporations and institutions, and in November 1977, WGMS-FM of Washington, D.C., began on-air tests with Infocast hardware. Before long, FM stations in New York, Dallas, and Atlanta were also carrying Infocast data.

With the system operating and paying customers online, von Meister further disengaged himself from TDX activities and set about trying to expand Infocast beyond the commercial sector.

Von Meister did not try to hide his connection with DBC from Cable & Wireless. He spoke freely about the operation to newspapers and traveled to make presentations to prospective customers—at TDX's expense.

Predictably, his haphazard spending and ignoring TDX in favor of his own projects soon got von Meister into trouble. TDX showed a $4.5 million loss for 1977, and von Meister was shown the door by Cable & Wireless early in 1978. He picked up $700,000 on his way out. TDX would not turn a profit until 1981.

Von Meister was no longer drawing a salary from TDX, and although Digital Broadcast Corporation remained viable, it would soon be in need of cash. Still in startup phase, it wasn't generating enough money to pay its CEO, and von Meister's personal finances edged toward negative cash flow.

With the huge house and family to support—not to mention his hobbies—von Meister was edging toward disaster. Plans for the restaurant were jettisoned as he got busy looking for a backer for DBC.

Working his contacts, he found a backer in just a few weeks. The April 19, 1978, edition of *The Wall Street Journal* announced that Consolidated Industries of America, a packaging manufacturer, planned to buy half the company's stock for $5 million, with the promise of an additional $25 million in long-term financing. Consolidated's major shareholder was an entrepreneur named Jack Taub, about whom we'll hear more later in this chapter. (Some stories maintain that Taub had met with von Meister in the fall of 1977, and from there worked out the backing deal for DBC while von Meister was still working for Cable & Wireless.)

Von Meister was once again the head of a growing concern. His $275,000 home and Porsche Turbo were safe, as was his flamboyant lifestyle. And high-volume customers were signing up for Infocast—like Lucky Stores, a grocery chain with 1,500 locations nationwide. Using Infocast to send price changes and other data from its California headquarters to stores in Maryland and Virginia cost Lucky only 10 percent of what it had been spending on conventional communications.

Moving beyond the commercial sector, Infocast cut a deal with the Illinois Farm Bureau to buy 100 terminals for tests in the homes of farmers. A similar deal with a University of Kentucky farm information project fell through, however. DBC next convinced the national nonprofit corporation Online Computer Library Center (OCLC) to conduct a three-month test of Infocast's suitability as a means of home delivery of library services. (This was a USDA program known as Project Green Thumb.) After testing the system at multiple sites from February through April, 1979, OCLC was optimistic, but found that Infocast technology had "not been fully developed or proven." There were also some reservations about cost.

It soon became apparent that Infocast was not feasible for the kind of national consumer network von Meister had envisioned building. Supplying 1,500 receivers and terminals to a corporate customer at a cost of a few million dollars was practical. Outfitting millions of households with terminals and developing the infrastructure for a two-way system was not. Consumers would have to be educated about the system before it even could be marketed. There was no way to raise the hundreds of millions required.

Had today's cellular telephone network existed then, von Meister might have found a ready market, one he wouldn't have had to equip with receiving devices. As it was, his proposed information network had nowhere to go and no one to broadcast to.

As he had already discovered, new ideas worked easiest when piggybacked on existing technology. So, von Meister started "entrepreneuring" again, casting about for another technology into which he could plug his idea.

He had seen reports on a cable television–based information network with which Warner Cable was experimenting in Columbus, Ohio. Using something called "Videotex," Warner's QUBE system transmitted data along with conventional programming via coaxial cable. The data channels carried textual information like weather and stock market reports.

These same channels could handle two-way traffic as well. Viewers might, for instance, vote on weighty matters ("Do we want twice-weekly trash collection?" or "Is the guy singing on this talent show any good?"), respond to polls, shop, and even bid in "online" auctions. They could also exchange messages through basic electronic mail.

There were problems and limitations, of course. Compared with today's Web, Videotex was awkward. The home cable controller didn't have a full keyboard, and by today's standards the onscreen text and graphics were blocky. But they were advanced for the time. QUBE could also transmit photographs, using a protocol that resulted in high-resolution color display.

Those problems could be overcome, but von Meister could see that Videotex wasn't going to be the basis for a nationwide data network, either. Only about 20 percent of homes in America had cable, and the majority of cable networks were one-way systems; they could only send information to subscribers. Creating a nationwide two-way cable network would require a whole new cable system, a project so enormous that not even a government would consider it.

But a two-way communications network was already in place, and it was connected to just about every home on the continent: the telephone system. All that was needed to turn it into a data and graphics information network were terminals. And the terminals were already making their ways into hundreds of thousands of homes, in the form of microcomputers.

Combining the concept with his recent experience with computers and telephone systems, von Meister decided he could create a nationwide information service that linked home computers to a central computer—and one another—through telephone lines. It would have none of the disadvantages of cable, and all its advantages (bandwidth excepted). The network would provide electronic mail, which von Meister felt was vital because of its intensely interactive character, along with airline and TV schedules, news, weather, and anything else von Meister might conjure up.

Unlike MicroNET, von Meister's information network would not be about using computers. Instead, it would focus on user communication and information access.

However (and also unlike MicroNET), von Meister had no mainframe computers to host the service. Nor did he have software, a data network, or even data to transmit. All he had was the idea.

But the idea was enough for von Meister. He focused on developing the product, confident of finding financing when the time came. He spent most of 1978 occupied with organizing the business under the aegis of Telecomputing Corporation of America (or TCA, following von Meister's penchant for three-letter names), which was created in July as a subsidiary of DBC. Funding it in part with his own money, but largely with support from DBC, von Meister established offices in a building in McLean, near his Vienna home.

The name of the information service would be CompuCom, suggestive of computer communications. The company behind it was organized as TCA.

Von Meister assembled CompuCom literally one piece at a time, putting together off-the-shelf technology just as he did with Telemax. Email would be the service's hub, so he went looking for that first. He found it at Dialcom, a Maryland company headed by an acquaintance named Bob Ryan. Dialcom had recently developed an email program for the U.S. House of Representatives. Von Meister licensed the program, at the same time striking a deal to use Dialcom's Prime mainframe computers to host his CompuCom service. As was the case with CompuServe, Dialcom's computers were idle in the evenings. In exchange, Dialcom received a 10 percent stake in the new company, plus a royalty deal.

Along with Dialcom's resources came Bob Ryan to serve as TCA's president. Von Meister's reputation preceded him, and Dialcom and Ryan were probably aware that someone had to keep an eye on the entrepreneur. Besides, Ryan found the idea of a consumer computer network interesting. Plus there was the appeal of getting in on the ground floor of a new technology.

CompuCom would also have a public bulletin board (a concept that was rapidly gaining currency in the academic computer field). For this component von Meister turned to a Massachusetts company called Participation Systems. The company produced a feature-rich computer bulletin board system called PARTIcipate (more often, simply PARTI) that had been used on mainframe computers since the early 1970s. This was a good choice; PARTI would develop an intensely loyal following—so loyal that it would outlast The Source.

The next item on the list was a data network to connect computer users with CompuCom. Building a network like CompuServe's was out of the question; it wasn't exactly something that could done overnight, and it would cost too much. Sticking with his off-the-shelf strategy, von Meister went shopping for a packet-switching network.

There were several commercial PSNs in the United States at the time, each of which charged as much as $15 per hour during peak periods. This was completely out of line with the few dollars per hour von Meister felt the home market was willing to pay. In those days people would pay three or four dollars to spend less than two hours at a concert, ballgame, or movie. It was logical to assume they would pay that much for an hour online, for an experience that would give them more lasting value than a film or sporting event.

But for TCA to offer the service at a rate that would attract customers while ensuring profits, von Meister determined that data network access would have to be a fraction of a dollar per hour.

That would mean getting a PSN to reduce its price by 95 percent. But von Meister had one thing in his favor: like time-sharing services, PSNs saw little usage during evenings and weekends. Naturally, when von Meister approached the largest of the PSNs, GTE Telenet (later SprintNet), with the prospect of generating income during its off hours, the company was interested.

Von Meister negotiated a rate of 25 cents per hour, per user, to connect people from anywhere in the United States with CompuCom's computers in Virginia.

It was a win-win deal. For Telenet there was no up-front cost, and the overhead was virtually nil. Being restricted to evenings and weekends did not present a problem for CompuCom because it would be marketed for use between 6:00 PM and 9:00 AM, and on weekends and holidays, the hours the network had the lowest traffic and lowest rates. (Users who wanted to log on during business hours could pay the going rate.) Getting government approval for the rate meant filing for a special tariff with the FCC, but von Meister foresaw no obstacle there.

Von Meister had the tariff approved and a pricing structure in place by September. After a $100 signup fee (CompuServe members paid only $29.95 at first, and later just $9), members would pay a flat hourly rate of $2.75 to use CompuCom, which included the 25 cents per hour for Telenet. Charges would be accrued at 4.6 cents per minute and paid by credit card. Each user would pay a $10 minimum monthly charge.

This was a bargain compared with the $100 hourly charge of *The New York Times* Information Bank, not to mention five-dollars-per-minute services like Dialog.

Out of the gross would come 15 percent in royalties for Dialcom and other service and information providers, which would leave CompuCom a net of about $2 per hour per user.

Industry estimates at the time varied widely, but it was generally believed that there were at least 200,000 computers in U.S. homes in 1978, and maybe as many as 500,000. Von Meister was confident that CompuCom could sign up 5 percent, or 10,000 computer users the first year. This would bring in $1 million up front, and generate a minimum of $1.2 million the first year. Of course, von Meister planned on signing up far more than 10,000 customers, and he predicted that an overwhelming majority of customers would spend more than $10 per month.

CompuCom was to be an information service, but it would not create information. Just as he had with software and hardware, von Meister went shopping for information providers.

He brought *The New York Times* on board as the first information provider, with its product information database. Prentice Hall signed on with consumer tax information, and Dow Jones agreed to provide delayed quotes of selected stocks and commodities, business news, corporation information, and text transcripts of public television's "Wall Street Week." (There would be no photos; in 1978, personal computer graphics and sound were primitive. Video was out of the question.) *The Wall Street Journal* and other Dow Jones publications were not included, as they were marketed with DJNS.

Many of the offerings were predicated on the expectation that most CompuCom members would be upscale, due to the high price tags on personal computers. This in turn implied people who would have investments to track, and businesspeople to access the business services.

CompuCom would also offer wine lists, horoscopes, selected local entertainment guides, and an online shopping service with the somewhat familiar-sounding name "Comp-U-Star." There was even a Mailgram-like service called "Data Post."

For entertainment, CompuCom users could play online games already implemented for mainframe computers, like Star Trek and Hammurabi. Meanwhile, von Meister had Dartmouth College's Kiewit Computer Center busy developing additional games for the online service.

In June 1979, TCA announced a cooperative agreement with United Press International (UPI) to bring news right off to the wire to computer users in a service called "NewsShare." This greatly enhanced the service's credibility and image. Von Meister was already talking about The Source's email service as a serious business product, too, apparently trying to impress both the home and business markets.

Von Meister began referring to CompuCom as an "information utility." "We want information to come out of CompuCom like water comes out of a faucet," he told *The Washington Post*. It would be a while before that flow increased beyond a trickle, though.

To help those who didn't own a computer get online, von Meister offered modem-equipped terminals for $595. Plans had been made for a factory in Charlotte, North Carolina, to produce more terminals especially for CompuCom, the money for which would come in part from a $2.9 million government-guaranteed small-business loan arranged by DBC backer Jack Taub, ostensibly for Infocast terminals. Part of the idea was to create employment opportunities, something with which Taub already had experience, having set up a New York factory with government aid to create jobs. The loan, from a North Carolina bank, would later become the object of a Commerce Department investigation.

With the hardware, software, and content in place, the big question was the interface—what subscribers would see when they logged on to CompuCom. Over at MicroNET, users simply typed commands to find and run programs and to access data, just like they did with their own microcomputers. They would soon have a menu, however.

The command line–driven environment was foreign to von Meister's idea of an information service for the public at large, so naturally he wanted a menu, something like a TV channel listing. If CompuCom was to grow into the kind of service that he envisioned, it would have to be simple to use—like cable TV. The object would be to use the service, not learn how it operated.

But, as a nod to the likelihood that many early users would be computer-philes, CompuCom users would be given a choice of accessing the menu or going into command mode at logon. This would permit advanced users to go directly to a service without winding their way through a series of menu choices.

Von Meister hired a computer consultant and former DARPANET engineer named Mark Seriff to help lay out the service and its menus. This was a complex job, but Seriff was more than equal to the task and before long he was hired as the company's chief technical officer. The executive lineup was rounded out by the addition of Marshall Graham as sales and marketing manager. Graham's background included stints at IBM, Xerox, and the Credit Card Service Corporation (CCSC).

At this point it was time to bring in someone with operating capital.

With Marshall Graham and von Meister talking up the service, newspaper stories and magazine articles about CompuCom began appearing by the end of the summer of 1978. Thanks to the publicity, von Meister didn't have to look far for backing. In fact, DBC backer Jack Taub found him, or so the story goes.

Taub was a rags-to-riches story. Born in Brooklyn, his education ended with the eighth grade. But along with his brother, Bert, Jack turned a childhood passion for stamp collecting into a booming enterprise. Together they started a magazine called *Stampazine*, on which they built a philatelic investment and auction business.

Jack Taub eventually became chairman of the board of the Scott Publishing Company, which was responsible for the definitive annual *Scott Stamp Catalog* and *Scott's Monthly*. From that base he created a number of stamp-collecting accessories and sold the U.S. Post Office on carrying them. The business made millions for both Taub and the Post Office. It also made Taub the target of Jack Anderson's investigative reporting; it seemed that Taub directed some of the new postal business to a company in which a deputy Postmaster General had previously been an officer. There was also a Justice Department investigation into whether Postmaster Benjamin Bailar had been given reduced prices on rare stamps by Taub's company. The Postmaster later resigned his government post, though an investigation cleared Taub of wrongdoing.

Taub first learned of von Meister's computer service when he read about it in *Business Week*. Taken with the idea of a nationwide information network, Taub arranged to meet with von Meister while on a business trip to Washington, D.C. Taub was particularly interested in the educational potential of CompuCom, always mindful his own lack of same. (As a philanthropist, Taub would later fund several educational initiatives.) He was probably sold on the venture before the meeting; if he wasn't, the persuasive von Meister soon made a believer of him.

As noted, Taub was a principal in Consolidated Industries of America, DBC's backer. This no doubt fueled his interest in CompuCom, though one must wonder why he was seemingly unaware of the relationship between von Meister's DBC and CompuCom. In any event, after signing on to back von Meister's TCA, he became a director of both DBC and CompuCom, with control of 42.5 percent of the company.

Now everything was in place. An article in the December 16, 1978, issue of *The Washington Post* detailed CompuCom's offerings and noted that DBC had "an undisclosed number of Prime and Honeywell computers with thousands of time-share ports" to meet the anticipated demand for the service. The computers and data ports of course belonged to Dialcom and Telenet.

The startup date for local (Washington) access was set as "sometime in April." Taub envisioned reaching the break-even point in six months.

The *Post* went on to note that the service would be provided to the Washington, D.C., area, and that 10,000 local customers were anticipated by year's end, which would mean one million dollars in signup fees. The *Post* story was a bit confusing, implying that CompuCom would be a strictly local service. This is understandable; after all, the reporter was dealing with an entirely new concept. In any event, CompuCom was nationwide; deals were already in place for access via the Tymnet packet-switching network as well as Telenet.

A more formal announcement of CompuCom appeared in the trade journal *Computerworld* a month later. The story opened with, "Probably the first low-cost time-sharing network for home use will be offered soon by Digital Broadcasting Corp. (DBC)." The publication was apparently unaware of the parallel developments in Columbus, Ohio.

CompuCom finally went live in late spring 1979—but not as CompuCom. The name was changed to "The Source." The change could have been made for any of several reasons—the most likely being that a Texas company called CompuCom Systems that dealt in computer systems was already using the name. It might also have been that Taub felt that CompuCom sounded too technical and limited, while The Source could be . . . well, the source of *anything*.

The whole ball of wax remained under the umbrella of DBC. As described earlier, DBC was built with resources from Cable & Wireless, which had been founded as the Eastern Telegraph Company. Hence, The Source was linked with one of the nineteenth century's greatest communication empires, though not by design.

Censored!

UPI news came to The Source right off the wire, at the same time as it was transmitted to hundreds of newspapers and other outlets across the country. This meant that the service's members could read news, weather, sports, stock prices, and syndicated columns before they appeared in the papers.

It was standard practice to send out some columns and features one or two days ahead of publication. Investigative reporter Jack Anderson, whose popular column was distributed by UPI, was incensed when he learned some Source members could read his columns online as much as two days before they were published in newspapers. His displeasure may have been intensified by the fact that he had blown the whistle on the business relationship between Jack Taub and the deputy Postmaster General two years earlier.

Anderson's protests quickly resulted in the columns being delayed until after they were published in hard copy, perhaps the first instance of online information flow being censored, or at least disrupted.

Early subscribers were signed up manually, offline. Prospective members either telephoned or mailed a coupon to The Source's McLean office. In response they received a membership agreement, which had to be signed and returned with a hundred-dollar signup fee before a Source ID and password were issued. These were sent by return mail, after which the new Source user could finally sign on.

The practice was ironic for an online, computer-based business. Many members complained about the company taking weeks to get their membership materials (which included a posh ring-bound member manual) to them.

The Source's official rollout took place on July 9, 1979, at New York's Plaza Hotel, where a press conference formally announced The Source as "the information utility the world's been waiting for!"

Celebrated science fiction author and futurist Dr. Isaac Asimov, already a spokesman for Radio Shack computers (he was portrayed in magazine advertisements using the high-end TRS-80 Model II), was on hand to say a few words. After an appropriate introduction, Asimov declared, "This is the beginning of the Information Age!"

The Good Doctor (as he was known to his fans) was right about that. It was also one of the first stops—though no one knew it at the time—on the way to the World Wide Web.

On Saturday, July 14, The Source hosted an "open house" at its headquarters on Anderson Road in McLean. Newspaper ads invited Washingtonians to come in for giant-screen demos of all The Source's services. The ads and demonstrations pushed all the buttons. Education, business, gaming, communications, personal investing—no matter what your interest, The Source had something for you.

Asimov wasn't on hand for this one, but it was clear that The Source intended to be part of the future. A slogan declared, "By the 21st Century, The Source will be as vital as electricity, the telephone, and running water."

Dis-content and Conflict

Von Meister spent money as though he were building General Motors.

—Jack Taub, investor who took over The Source in 1980

As 1979 dawned, the mainstream and trade press had yet to take The Source and MicroNET (recently renamed the CompuServe Information Service, or CIS) seriously. Each was regarded as a limited system serving a niche market. The press would almost completely ignore equally important developments in computer communications that year.

But publications such as *The Economist* and *Business Week* were quite taken by a new French Videotex service called Minitel, initiated in 1975 as *Telematique*. Perhaps it was the exotic flavor that came with something from far away, but the media seemed to expect a Videotex system to pop up and take off in the United States any day now. Computers, after all, were for geeks.

Videotex

The term Videotex was coined to describe any two-way communications system that allowed users to receive and display text and crude graphics on television or computer terminal screens. Communicating via telephone lines, Videotex allowed users to send as well as receive data.

The Minitel Videotex system was offered as a substitute for printed telephone directories. It provided faster access and could be updated instantly. The French government supplied terminals with small screens and keyboards to the public at no charge in the beginning. Increased telephone usage and advertising (plus the money saved by not printing telephone books) paid for the service and helped the country rebuild its aging telephone system. Minitel grew rapidly with the addition of services such as news and sports, along with shopping, email, and message boards. Advertising and independent commercial information providers were also a part of the service.[1] There was talk of marketing the system in the United States, particularly because it was so simple to install—just plug it in and go.

The United Kingdom was not far behind France in developing its own Videotex system, called Prestel (derived from *press* and *tele*phone).[2] Like Minitel, Prestel linked users through the national telephone system, and simple information retrieval was expanded with a variety of two-way services. The government did not, however, supply terminals; Prestel was designed to work with television sets equipped with a special terminal/decoder.[3] As with Minitel, users were charged for connect time, and there were surcharges for some data.

A simpler, one-way approach called *teletext* saw parallel development during the 1970s. Instead of sending information over telephone lines, teletext broadcast data via an unused portion of television broadcasts (the vertical blanking interval between the transmission of image frames). Bill von Meister's Infocast and other systems like it were distant cousins of teletext.

Although the systems based on teletext—Ceefax (originally Teledata) and Oracle in England—were one-way, they had the advantage of not being affected by the number of people using them. Teletext systems cost the user less as well.

Prestel, Minitel, Ceefax, and Oracle grew in popularity. There was even talk in England of installing coin-operated terminals in bookshops. Other countries began investigating similar systems. In Brazil, Germany, Canada, Japan, and elsewhere, governments spearheaded development, as had been the case in France and England.

Not so in the United States. This was largely because American telephone and broadcast systems were commercial enterprises. Even though they were regulated by the government, focus on competition tended to retard innovation and discourage cooperation on things like technical standards. The government's regulations kept various kinds of communications services from cooperating anyway, and the flagging QUBE interactive TV experiment and the failure of AT&T to deliver oft-promised videophones (the famous PicturePhone) made it easy not to expect anything startling from the established commercial powers, in any event.

Still, there were some early American experiments involving teletext. Two years after the FCC gave the go-ahead in 1975, the CBS television network ran tests of both Ceefax/Oracle- and Minitel-type systems, as did individual television stations. The best AT&T could come up with was an "intelligent

---

[1] *Perhaps not surprisingly, the most prolific were providers of pornographers, who advertised in Paris with billboards and posters.*

[2] *Prestel was preceded in the United Kingdom by a system called* Viewdata, *a simple two-way system that used a dedicated terminal and allowed users to request specific data from a database by telephone, and retrieve the data in video form via a separate channel.*

[3] *As the service grew, television sets with built-in decoders became available.*

phone system" to replace phone directories. There was some talk of intelligent TV sets that would supplement news and information on TV, and maybe provide database and educational services.

Little came of these experiments and ideas, beyond establishing that text could be broadcast. Cable television–based hybrid systems fared equally bad.

It would be left to entrepreneurs like Jeff Wilkins and Bill von Meister to see a potential market for consumer information services—and go after that market.

Growing Pains at The Source

According to the company's advertising in fall 1979, The Source was rolling hot. Large print ads with Peter Max–style graphics touted airline schedules; restaurant guides for major cities; a Mailgram-like service called Datapost; a library of 2,000 programs; and other appealing offerings. (The glitzy art was necessary; text on a green computer screen would not convey the proper excitement.)

In reality, the airline schedules would not take off for a year, and restaurant guides were limited to D.C. and New York. Datapost was still months in the future. Only a tiny portion of the planned program library was in evidence. Worse, Digital Broadcasting Corp. (DBC) and The Source were bogged down by more than $5 million in debt and neither could meet their payrolls.

It was not a new situation for von Meister. Around the end of the summer, Taub came to the conclusion that von Meister was mishandling company money. "Von Meister," Taub said at the time, "spent money as though he were building General Motors!"

Because Taub and his brother owned 42.5 percent of the stock in DBC and The Source, in October Taub was able to give von Meister the boot. He paid von Meister an insulting penny a share for the 314,000 shares of company stock, with a promise to increase that payment to a dollar a share in three years, *if* The Source started showing a profit. Presumably, von Meister accepted the $3,140 check, but he didn't consider this the end of the matter. Meanwhile, Taub sued von Meister, stating that the latter had misrepresented the financial situation of his companies when Taub came in as a backer.

At the same time, the bank that had loaned DBC $2.9 million for Infocast's North Carolina terminal factory was calling on the federal government to make good on the loan, which it had guaranteed. Some 300 other creditors were demanding payment, and Taub claimed that The Source had only $1,000 in the bank.

Once he got von Meister out the door, Taub set up a new company, Source Telecomputing Corporation (STC), in an attempt to insulate it from the creditors who were pestering DBC and TCA. Next, Taub fired 45 of the company's 70 employees in a cost-saving move.

Former employees agitated against the company for months, demanding undelivered paychecks and claiming they had been fired without cause. In what may have been the first online privacy scandal ever, several claimed that Source executives could access private member files online. The company denied that this was possible, and the question was left unresolved, though one employee noted that, "Sometimes we do get information on our screen that we're not supposed to have." To which he added, "Electrons can cause problems like that."

Von Meister took a consulting job with Telenet—now GTE Telenet—and announced that before he left The Source he had been in discussions with GTE about the communications company buying DBC (including The Source).[4] This appears to have been a fabrication by von Meister.

On top of everything else, The Source was experiencing severe growing pains. While some members complained about the promised services that hadn't materialized, many more complained about problems with the service itself. There were problems with logging on during peak evening hours.

Plus, only 80 to 100 customers could use the service simultaneously, and many had to wait up to 10 seconds for a response to a command. This not only inconvenienced members, but also limited billable minutes. Taub responded to the complaints by promising to increase capacity—enough to serve 2,000 users at once and cut the response time to five seconds or less—and opened negotiations with Tymnet to carry member traffic. But those improvements would be as much as a year away. Taub also conceded that The Source had in the beginning advertised far more services than it could provide.

Members continued logging on—some because The Source was all they knew, and they didn't want to forfeit online access because things weren't perfect. Others tried CompuServe and said goodbye to The Source. But at least as many rejected CompuServe and returned to The Source because it had been their first online experience—which meant that they judged the other service on standards they had established on The Source.

By Source standards, CompuServe was an alien world. Even CompuServe's superior offerings couldn't lure those to whom The Source was "home." For example, The Source's primitive sequential bulletin boards lacked such sophistications as topic threads, but this seemed normal to those whose first online experience was with The Source. The additional features and unfamiliar set of commands and menus offered on CompuServe were confusing and made some users uncomfortable.

---

[4] According to Larry Roberts, GTE bought Telenet to enable Telenet to get contracts with companies like General Motors, which did not like to do business with operations that weren't backed by a large corporation.

Customer Loyalty and Growth

Beyond all these things there was the community. People got to know one another through those cranky bulletin boards, and used email to stay in touch with relatives and friends across the country whom they'd convinced to sign up for The Source. (There were no email connections with other services.)

Plus, The Source had features CompuServe lacked, just as CompuServe had features The Source lacked. In addition to unique elements like Jack Anderson's columns and the limited restaurant guide, there were the users who published data or literary work in their private file areas, material available only if you were a member of The Source. Some were paid royalties for the amount of time users spent viewing or downloading such files.

Certain games developed loyal followings. And there was *Sourceworld* magazine, which reinforced the feeling of connection, as did the handsome slipcased manual all Source members received. Taken together, these things, along with the familiar menu and command structures and other features, constituted a real community, one you gave up if you left The Source. As a Source member put it, "CompuServe is technically superior to The Source, but it doesn't have any of the excitement or the evolution of The Source."

This sense of community went a long way toward keeping members onboard. Besides, members wanted what The Source promised strongly enough to put up with the service as it was, for a time. It was early days, and most Source members regarded the service as still in the development stage.

Just how many members The Source had during the waning months of 1979 is open to debate. When von Meister left, someone at The Source was telling newspapers that there would be more than 1,000 members when 1980 rolled around. This implied that the service's membership was in the hundreds.

But a couple of months later, in January 1980, *The Wall Street Journal* reported that the online service had "well over 3,000 paying customers, or double the total of only two months ago," and was signing up new members at the rate of 500 per week. There was also a claim of $100,000 monthly revenue. There seems to have been some hyperbole or wishful thinking in there somewhere—a bit of a front to assure potential new members that The Source was a viable and growing entity, perhaps?

Whatever the figures, Taub was positive about The Source's future growth. "By midyear," he vowed at the time, "we'll be in the home like Tupperware!"

Over at CompuServe, membership was edging toward 3,000. Customers still paid $9 to sign up, and $5 an hour to use it in 35 major cities and $7 an hour in another 225 cities. There were none of the problems that plagued The Source's management, because CompuServe was an established, well-funded entity going in. Problems that CompuServe experienced behind the scenes stayed there, and product development, customer service, and marketing moved smoothly ahead—hence, CompuServe's faster growth.

Modem users who started out with CompuServe were as loyal to CIS as Source members were to their home service. CompuServe management also recognized the importance of personalizing the service with a magazine and began publishing *Online Today* in 1981. As one company document put it, "intrusive member communications in a familiar magazine format would offset the still unfamiliar online environment." (The term "intrusive" was used to indicate the marketing approach.)

In the case of each service, the phenomenon of discovery was an important factor. Members felt they had discovered something unique, embraced it, and became experts on it. To Source members, The Source was what computer networking was all about. To CompuServe members, CompuServe was *it*. No competitors had come forth to challenge the services. If they had, they would have found it tough going.

While not exactly competition, new experiments in computer communications were under way. Both involved public discourse and were essentially free of charge to their users.

Usenet Newsgroups

In 1979, just as CompuServe and The Source were beginning to get off the ground, an entirely separate computer communications system popped up. Called Usenet, it was (and is) a decentralized discussion system that functions like a bulletin board—but a bulletin board to which millions of people have access because all content is distributed to multiple computer systems worldwide (thus, it can be called a distributed system). Each system is a host to the board, and each automatically sends out and receives updates several times daily.

More familiar to most people as "newsgroups," Usenet features "threaded" discussion systems, meaning that all replies to a message are connected to that message and can be read in sequence, and replied to separately or together. The management system for this threaded message system—newsreader software—also manages sorting major topics and their subtopics.

Usenet began as a two-node bulletin board system connecting Duke University with the nearby University of North Carolina. Usenet gained distribution early on via FidoNet and other microcomputer BBS systems. Other institutions were added and eventually distribution expanded via TCP/IP and DARPANET to the Internet. By 1984, there were over 900 Usenet hosts. Today Usenet is a massive system that carries over 3 terabytes (TB) of traffic per day.

In the beginning, Usenet was largely a forum for discussing computing issues. Gradually it became necessary to designate specific topic areas so that discussions of classic cars, for example, would not obscure threads about the Internet. Usenet ended up being a set of 9 newsgroups, each with as many subtopics as needed. The nine newsgroups are

- *comp*: Discussions on computing and computer-related topics
- *humanities*: Literature, philosophy, fine arts, and related

- *misc*: Miscellaneous topics

- *news*: Discussions about Usenet

- *rec*: Recreation and entertainment

- *sci*: Discussions related to science (both "soft" and "hard")

- *soc*: Sociological, society, and related

- *talk*: Discussion on controversial topics

- *alt* (for alternate): Everything else

Over the years Usenet has developed a specific culture and set of customs to which most participants adhere rigorously. It has also been an important forum for new ideas involving the Internet, among other topics, and was in fact where the World Wide Web was first announced.

An interesting aspect of Usenet is that its posts are archived, a project begun by Deja News in 1995 and taken over by Google as Google Groups in 2000. Archives of some topics go back to 1981.

Microcomputer Bulletin Boards

Usenet was not a system that you could dial up and log on to, like CompuServe and The Source. It was like DARPANET in that it had its own system of hosts, and you couldn't get in unless you had access to one of the hosts.

But there were bulletin boards that anyone with a microcomputer (or a mainframe or minicomputer, for that matter) could access. Most were not connected to any kind of network, but individually they connected personal computer users with other computer users and provided a sort of non-real-time network. (Later many would join in store-and-forward networks, and even host Usenet newsgroups.)

This kind of bulletin board, more commonly known as a BBS or just "board," was a modem-equipped personal computer with special software that allowed it to accept calls from and communicate with other computers and manage such tasks as validating callers (via user ID and password), transferring files, handling email, and managing message boards. A few BBSs were based on minicomputers or even mainframes, but the vast majority were hosted on microcomputers.[5] Nearly all were free.

---

[5] There's a bit of a terminology problem in talking about BBSs. At one time, "bulletin board" was used by many with reference to CompuServe or anything else that would answer a modem call. It can get confusing. Today, the term bulletin board is also used to refer to online messaging systems. To keep things straight, web sites or online service areas where people leave messages are referred to as "messaging systems" or message boards.

Today they're fairly rare, but at one time BBSs were a vital part of the online world, with uncounted numbers of users worldwide. It's likely that a BBS was the first online experience for tens of thousands (if not hundreds of thousands) of personal computer owners. Collectively, their users outnumbered those on The Source, CompuServe, and other online services for several years.

Free BBSs were the ideal training ground and test bed for novice modem users. (Believe it or not, it was easier for many people to dial up a BBS than to try to connect with a friend's computer by modem and telephone.) As such, they were an important element in the evolution of the online world. They gave many who were uncomfortable with the idea of paying for time online a reason to buy modems. Thanks to free BBS access, modems and telecommunications software became easier to use, and costs dropped as demand increased. The net result was to speed migration to online services and, eventually, the Internet.

In the beginning, BBSs were little more than cranky systems run by an underground elite of hackers and experimenters (and maybe a few gnomes here and there). But within five years they evolved into an important and accepted element of personal and business computing online. This was thanks in large part to the fact that early BBSs rarely charged for access. Most were operated as a public service and to satisfy the curiosity, personal and professional interests, and egos of their operators (aka "sysops," short for "system operators").

Boards ranged from simple public message boards to sophisticated systems that offered software downloads, multitopic bulletin boards, email, and even games.

BBSs running certain software packages (like FIDO and GTE PowerComm) formed the basis for national networks that relayed messages from one "node" (a group of boards in a given region) to another via a chain of computers that made calls over the shortest possible distance at times when rates were lowest. It's likely most used a system not unlike that developed by Bernard Ryder and Bill von Meister for TDX Systems.

Messages were relayed from one computer to another—automatically—until they reached their destination. Users may have had to pay a small charge for message-relay service, but it was a thrill to be able to communicate with someone on the other side of the world by computer whether or not it was free.[6]

These relay systems were called "net mail," "echomail," "relay mail," or any of several other names. They were fairly fast and efficient, although it typically took two days to get a reply to a message sent to Europe.

More prevalent (and usually free) relay systems handled topical message boards and newsletters, duplicating them on BBSs around the country. There were also BBS equivalents of listservs. The precedence of these networks

---

[6] *Quite naturally, American BBS callers were curious about BBSs in other parts of the world, and a few dialed up boards in Europe and elsewhere, capturing their online sessions in ASCII text files and sharing them as uploads to American BBSs.*

made it easy for the BBS world to adopt Usenet, and thus increase the connections of the fledgling Internet.

The first bulletin board was set up by Ward Christensen and Randy Seuss in 1978. Christensen (who later developed the pioneering Xmodem file transfer protocol) and Seuss set up the board to allow their computers to communicate, partly as an experiment. They called it CBBS, for "Computerized Bulletin Board System." Christensen made the bulletin board publicly available in 1979. It didn't take long for the idea to spread through the personal computing community.

In the beginning, most boards were devoted to sharing programs and information for specific types of computer. If you had a TRS-80, for example, you dialed up a TRS-80 board, hosted on a TRS-80 computer. There you could get help with your computer problems and read the latest on new peripherals and software. But soon enough, special-interest boards started popping up. There were boards for radio-controlled aircraft enthusiasts and for people looking for dates. Boards were devoted to travel, to cities, and to sex, hacking, and just about anything for which you can find a web site today.

By the mid-1980s, computer hardware and software manufacturers began setting up customer support BBSs, which served the same purposes as customer support web sites do today. Message boards, downloads, and information files were readily available for the cost of a long-distance telephone call. By the late 1980s, outfits that were anything but computer-centric, including magazines like *Popular Mechanics* and *Thrasher* skateboarding magazine, were setting up BBSs to complement or substitute for their presence on online services like CompuServe or AOL.

In addition to being free, a major difference between BBSs and online services was that you had to dial the boards directly. This often made for faster communication than a PSN, but you also had to pay any long-distance charges involved. Eventually, BBSing got so popular that not only were there publications devoted to BBSs (like *Boardwatch*), but Telenet, in its new persona of SprintNet, offered callers access to their network for a flat monthly fee. Using the service, one could call boards in certain areas through a local (to the caller) telephone number.

The world of BBSs grew rapidly throughout the 1980s, inspiring magazines and at least one annual convention for sysops and BBS aficionados.

After 1985, commercial bulletin boards developed as an alternative to online services. Users were lured by lower prices or special interests. An IBM/PC BBS like ExecPC might draw users by offering an immense collection of software and data files, as well as access to other PC hobbyists, for a flat monthly fee. (Users still paid their own long-distance bills.) Real-time chatting became popular. And a few X-rated boards flourished during this period, along with boards hosted by companies or dedicated to a specific theme like gaming. Eventually, some of the largest and most successful boards set up PSN access for their users, and ended up being almost miniature versions of CompuServe and The Source. Some could handle as many as 256 users at a time.

Packet Switching for PC Users

In 1985, Telenet/SprintNet offered a product called "PC Pursuit." With PC Pursuit, any modem-equipped computer user could dial up a local Telenet number and use the system to dial into a bulletin board's number anywhere in the United States without incurring long-distance changes.

The cost was $30 per month for 30 hours of usage. Additional hours were billed at $7 to $14.

The company did a fair amount of business this way, but angered many users by not allowing access to the service at 2400bps and up.

As you'll learn in Chapter 4, some boards also emulated the commercial online services in offering access to various aspects of the Internet, like Usenet. But try as they might, BBSs could not quite match the lure of the major online services, with their tens and then hundreds of thousands of users, superior offerings and, eventually, flat-rate pricing. By the time the Web came along, the online world would be morphing into a mainstream institution. Computer bulletin board systems would go into a steep decline. Getting online with ISPs would become too cheap and easy for BBSs to match, except for those that became ISPs themselves.

By 1980 the online world was growing faster than it ever had. DARPANET was approaching 200 hosts and had crossed the Atlantic and Pacific. As of 1975 it had been turned over to the Defense Communications Agency (DCA). Usenet was growing and developing a distinct culture. BBSs provided an important meeting place for personal computer enthusiasts to trade knowledge, software, and ideas. They were also serving as test beds for networking techniques and communications hardware. CompuServe and The Source began to find their identities, and all of this was fueling the market for computers, modems, and communications software.

Evolution

We saw ourselves in the center of the universe, enabling a way to allow
everybody to communicate . . .

—Sandy Trevor, CompuServe Chef Technical Officer

The Information Superhighway—composed of both packet-switched and
circuit-switched networks—was growing. Telenet and Tymnet expanded
through new nodes and international links. Regional data networks like
ALASKA/NET and ConnNet were also in the mix. In Canada, Bell Canada
and Northern Telecom operated Datapac. These data networks carried traffic
for time-sharing services, banking and other transaction networks, airline
reservation systems, and the growing number of information retrieval or database services. They also provided links for corporate WANs and remote access
of mainframes by employees and customers. And they carried traffic for the
consumer online services. At the same time, ARPANET continued to add
hosts (nodes) at a steady rate; by 1980 the number was over 100.

Public, experimental, and private computer networks were, of course,
being developed in other nations. Still, there were probably fewer than
100,000 people online worldwide at the end of 1979.

What was it like? What did people see when they logged on? The simple
answer is "text." The menu and default text display on most systems was set for
"the lowest common denominator" in terms of computer displays. That meant
32 or 40 columns by 16 lines of text, though some systems could take into
account wider or narrower displays.

If you had logged on to CompuServe's MicroNET in 1979, you would have
seen some announcements, and then something like this:

```
User ID: 70000,2721

Password: SECRET
```

```
Job 45 on MicroNET at 10:21
24-Oct-79 on T08CLJ

Welcome to MicroNET,
 For more information enter: NEWS

 OK
```

There was no menu at this point. The **OK** was the system prompt, but would be changed to **!**. To access different parts of the service, such as email or bulletin boards, or to run programs, you had to type a command at this prompt.

A computer that operated like this was called a *command-driven* system, as opposed to *menu-driven*, and it required that commands be entered in a precise syntax. For example, if you wanted to view a list of MicroNET access phone numbers (which of course were CompuServe access numbers), you would have to enter **TYP SYS:PHONE**.

Fortunately, each new user was given the *MicroNET User's Guide*, which included a detailed list of commands. And there was online help.

Offerings included email, bulletin boards, online storage, a feedback and customer service system, and a few games like Adventure, Hangman, and Blackjack. The entire service was hosted on one computer, and membership hovered around 1,200.

The system would not remain command-driven for long. The CompuServe menu was released in August 1980. CompuServe CTO Sandy Trevor attended the 1980 Videotex conference in Wembley, England, where he was able to see Videotex systems like Prestel and Minitel in action. He returned to set the top-level specifications for the CIS menu-driven, paged online service, improving on the types of menus he had seen. (The name MicroNET was changed to CompuServe Information Service on June 9, 1980. After that, the service was commonly referred to as "CompuServe" or "CIS.")

The new menu system resembled this example of the main or "TOP" menu:

```
CompuServe                    TOP

   1 Newspapers
   2 Finance
   3 Entertainment
   4 Communications
   5 CompuServe User Information
   6 Special Services
   7 Home Information
   8 MicroNET Personal Computing
```

```
Enter your selection number,
or H for more information.
!
```

Most menus led to a series of submenus, with which the user could navigate to the desired area, pyramid-fashion.

In addition to the menu, a set of mnemonic "GO commands" allowed users to take shortcuts. For example, if a member wanted to check stock prices, she could type **GO STOCKS**. Similarly, **GO COMPUTING** took the user to a menu of computer services, from which she could select an item, or proceed with another GO command. (These would be reduced to single-word commands, like **MAIL**.)

The Source offered a similarly straightforward menu:

```
MENU OF SERVICES
1 News and Reference Resources
2 Business/Financial Markets (NEWS)
3 Catalog Shopping
4 Home and Leisure
5 Education and Career
6 Mail and Communications
7 Creating and Computing
8 SourcePlus

Enter item number, (H)elp or <Q>uit:
```

Like CompuServe, The Source offered a command mode. Most commands were single words. It also had an online help system, and there were online demos for some features.

Both services sought to present an easy-to-use front end, especially as there were so many people who were uncomfortable operating a computer. As with just about anything to do with personal computers, the idea was to put as little as possible between the user and the content or program she was after—hence, The Source's emphasis in its advertising on being able to navigate the system using "plain English."

At this point, both companies offered a similar range of services, including email; bulletin boards; news; and stock, commodity, and bond prices, all in text format. Other text-based products included programs that produced horoscopes and biorhythms.

Games

There were also games similar to games that computerists could buy for their own systems at a computer store. In some instances, they were the same games that stores offered, *sans* packaging and manuals. (See the discussion of SOFTEX, in a moment.)

The main differences between the online and offline products were diversity and the relatively low cost of buying online. You would find more games online than in any computer store. There were freeware games that you didn't have to pay for as well as shareware ("try before you buy") programs that you were supposed to pay for.

Even if you paid to download a commercial software product, it still cost less than you would pay in a store. The overhead of packaging, shipping, and inventory didn't exist.

Pirate Software

You had to know the right people, or just where to look, but thousands of illicit copies of programs could be found online. In cooperation with software publishers, the online services waged a largely successful battle against software pirating, a battle that continues today.

Pirate BBSs were another matter. There were enough that local law enforcement and the FBI couldn't be persuaded to crack down on most offenders. When a pirate board was taken down, it was usually one that charged membership fees. Quite a few such boards escaped getting busted by changing locations and phone numbers periodically.

Online Gaming

As noted, buying a commercial game online usually cost less than buying it in a brick-and-mortar store—if you could find it online. Some games—notably those that included some sort of artifact to help in copy protection—weren't available online.

Playing games online was another matter. As many CompuServe and The Source members quickly found out, one could rack up three or four hundred dollars on the ol' credit card in just a couple of weeks. Adventure, MegaWars, and role-playing games really burned up time. And those were all text; the highly addictive simulations and multiuser graphic games were still several computer generations away. But a multiuser text-based game was enough to hook thousands—the key being multiuser.

As might be expected, online gaming grew into serious business. We'll take a closer look at this subject in later chapters, but suffice to say that Bill Louden, who had been CompuServ's product manager for Games as well as other services, and who went on to found GEnie, was instrumental in developing much of the online gaming establishment.

Early File Sharing and User Publishing

There were also file exchange areas, where members could upload and download information and program files (most of the latter being shareware or freeware).

On CompuServe the file area was called ACCESS and was open to all. It offered a little extra in the form of optional password protection that allowed an uploader to password-protect a file. The uploader would give the password only to those she wished to have access to the file, and no one else could download it.

Unique to CompuServe was SOFTEX (from *soft*ware *ex*change). This was Jeff Wilkins' idea for selling software online. It was successful, and would remain with CompuServe in one form or another for the rest of its existence. (The author—along with many others—used SOFTEX to sell programs direct to users in the late 1980s and into the early 1990s.) Initially it was the only service where you could download programs for every kind of home computer—IBM, Atari, Apple, Commodore, Tandy, and so forth.

The Source did not initially sell software, but offered a file-exchange setup called "Sharefile." Members could transfer files there from their personal file area. The only way another user could download the file was by knowing the filename, a rather straightforward method of security.

If that was too complicated, The Source also offered a feature that allowed members to open portions of their personal file areas to others. One enterprising Source member decided to use this feature to publish a newsletter in his personal file space, the idea being just to share his thoughts and writing talents. Email comments on the newsletter told him that it was popular but he had no idea just how popular it was until he used a Source feature that showed him which members had accessed his newsletter and for how long.

It turned out that Source members were cumulatively spending a significant number of hours in his personal file area reading the newsletter. He was generating thousands of dollars in revenue. Shouldn't he get a share? He asked Source management and they set him up as a content provider with a 17.5 percent royalty every month.

This is not to say that others weren't publishing their prose and making it available in online databases, but few were getting paid for it until The Source began publicizing that it would pay royalties to people who published work in their private file areas.

There was no precise counterpart to this on CompuServe, but members would soon have the opportunity to become paid content providers in a big way.

But a new offering would soon eclipse all of these. It was a little something called the "CB Simulator."

Chat

Like many other mainframes, CompuServe's computers had a program called "Send" or "Talk," by which one user could send a one-line text message to anyone logged on to the system. It's a primitive form of what we call "instant messaging" today, and dates back to the early 1960s.

These early one-line systems were simple setups, no neat progression of text in a window like we have today. The sent line simply appeared on the recipient's screen. To reply she had to initiate another one-line message. These lines and responses either disappeared or scrolled off the screen as soon as a new line was sent.

CompuServe's regular users did not have access to this feature. But in early 1980 they would get something even better—something that would take personal communications to a level that J.C.R. Licklider may not have imagined.

It started late in 1979, when CompuServe added a new feature consisting of writable memory segments that could be shared among multiple users on the system. This gave Sandy Trevor an idea for a product where several users could type to one another, and everyone would see what was written. It was like CB radio, though users would type and read rather than talk and listen.

Trevor called the new system the "CB Simulator." The name was perfect; it explained the concept in an instant. And, as it turned out, CompuServe users took to it like the American public had taken to CB radio.

Trevor at first worked with CompuServe developers on the idea. But their approach was to treat it like a business product, trying to design the system to ensure that no messages were lost, and in general make it more complicated than it had to be. Trevor's view was that the product was more like a game. And since CB radio users were accustomed to less than perfect communication, the CB Simulator didn't have to be perfect.

As Trevor explained later, "I couldn't convince them to just do a quick-and-dirty approach. They had all these designs for features like queuing. So I decided to write it myself over the weekend, at home." He set up the system with 40 "channels," just like CB radio.

CompuServe's CB Simulator went online on February 21, 1980. Lives were changed immediately. People stayed online longer and later, fascinated with the ability to interact with several people at once. The online world and its denizens took on a new aura of reality, and the online experience grew far more entertaining and unpredictable.

Some people couldn't get enough of it, often overindulging to the point where they couldn't pay their online service bill. A member of a chat group would mysteriously disappear, only to return a few weeks later, remarking, "I had to pay down my credit card; I had a $700 chat bill last month!" (This happened regularly on all the online services that had real-time chat systems, not just CompuServe.)

Online Chat and the Real World

Online chat has changed millions of lives, offline. No one knows how many intense two-person chat sessions turned into marriages or other domestic partnerships. Some turned into heartbreak and ripoffs, too.

Businesses have been launched after entrepreneurs met in chat rooms, as have many other sorts of partnerships and organizations. Chat rooms have been the basis for gaming and just about every other kind of social interaction. Any number of suicides have been prevented in chat rooms (see the Web for stories), and lots of people who had nothing in their lives found themselves revitalized by the people connections made in chat rooms.

Education has been conducted in online chats, but more often online chatting has provided raw material for dozens of dissertations and theses—a field that will continue to be mined for decades to come.

CompuServe CEO Jeff Wilkins didn't understand the appeal, and at first didn't want to put the CB Simulator on CompuServe's menu. Instead, people learned to type **GO CB** from CompuServe announcements or other users. But when CB got to be CompuServe's largest-billing product, it went on the menu.

Refinements were added, like "squelch" (tune out a specific user), and the ability to record and monitor one conversation while participating in another. CB users could also create "handles" or nicknames, following the CB metaphor. A system of protocols gradually evolved so that everyone wouldn't be typing at once (simple things, like typing **GA** at the end of a line to let people know you're done "speaking"). Still, multiple conversations often overlapped one another, and quite a bit was lost.

The Source had what it called a "chat" feature, which allowed two members to send one-liners back and forth, but it did not add a real-time conference system until after 1983. A persistent rumor has it that when Bill von Meister was kicked out of the company he took or destroyed some vital programming code that prevented updating much of The Source.

When is Conferencing Not Chatting?

One of the problems with computing has always been the terminology. Consider the term "bulletin board." As discussed in Chapter 5, "bulletin board" or "board" might not only be used to refer to a microcomputer that accepts phone calls, but also an entire online service, or just a place to post messages—or message base—hosted by the online service. The word "forum" has also been used to denote a message base.

When The Source first began operation, there was no real-time chatting system, but there was a bulletin board system called PARTIcipate, or PARTI for short. As marketed by the company that created it (who had developed it for use on mainframe computer systems) the PARTI software was called a "Conferencing System." The developers of PARTI obviously gave no thought to the directions that computer communications might take in the future. They felt that "conference" was the perfect name for a place where people come together to exchange thoughts. In fact, "conference" was already used on many mainframe systems to refer to any public message base.

As online services and BBSs developed, the word was co-opted to mean real-time chatting. It certainly made for a lot of confusion when members of The Source (and some mainframe users) started using other online services. They would ask for a place to post messages and end up in a chat room!

Not incidentally, the PARTI system was so popular with its users that several heroic efforts were made to keep it alive after the demise of The Source. You'll read about those in a later chapter.

Special-Interest Groups

In addition to channels being designated for specific topics, there were also clubs that met on certain channels at the same time every week or so. Some of them called themselves "special-interest groups," or SIGs (perhaps borrowing the term from Mensa, the high-IQ society).

SIGs included TRS-80 owners, Apple users, and many noncomputer interests, like aviation. Early on, members of several SIGs (including John Strom of the Control Program for Microcomputers, or CP/M, SIG) got the idea of putting the various tools and human resources surrounding them to work. They trolled for new members and posted to one another on the National Bulletin Board. And they uploaded files to ACCESS, sharing in CB meetings or via email lists of available files. This was all unofficial; it was a matter of picking up tools and seeing what could be made with them. It was a unique opportunity to combine resources in a way they'd never been used together.

Phishing

We hear a lot about "phishing" today, and experience it as we receive idiotic spam telling us that our password or financial information has been compromised, and therefore we must click on a link and enter our ID and password.

To many this is a recent phenomenon, but it was almost as big a problem in 1980 as it is today, although the term "phishing" wasn't coined until 2003. CompuServe users routinely cruised CB chats claiming to be CompuServe employees (often creating a handle that looked official) and requesting passwords. Once they got the passwords, they usually ran wild, burning up time on CompuServe until the victim got his bill—at which point he complained and was issued a new password.

Most of the victims were new users who didn't know how to get the real ID behind the criminal's CB handle, so the phisher usually got away with it.

CompuServe Forums

The way some SIG members were combining online products gave Compu-Serve engineer Russ Ranshaw an idea. Why not create special areas of CompuServe devoted to specific interests? Each of these areas, or SIGs, would be a sort of "mini-CompuServe" with a sheaf of existing CompuServe services on one menu: bulletin boards, file libraries, and CB. Small extra features, such as member directories, were later added.

SIGs were a brilliant marketing concept, a way to package disparate services on one menu, under a uniting theme or "brand." Instead of moving around the system to use the CB Simulator, bulletin boards, and the ACCESS file system, a user could go to the Journalism Forum or the IBM Forum and enjoy convenient access to all three products—plus interest-specific announcements, information on other members, and so on.

In a way, it was like Procter & Gamble's brand marketing. Just as Dreft and Tide were the same products packaged for different market segments, so did the IBM Forum and the Atari Forum reach out to their own markets.

For a few months the groups went by the names SIGs. But that seemed ungainly. Someone came up with the name "Forum," which implied an organized meeting place, an association of equals with a purpose.

Unlike online service products, the Forums required management. Someone had to be responsible for making sure commercial software wasn't uploaded to Forum file libraries. Someone had to watch for inflammatory postings, libel, and other problems in Forum bulletin boards. A Forum manager was usually referred to as the "sysop," short for system operator, as with BBSs.

A sysop's job also included bringing in new users and encouraging people to spend more time in her Forum. Sysops maintained the libraries and posted announcements about new files and events. They organized CB conferences and online interviews with celebrities and experts.

Running a Forum was a time-consuming proposition. But there was compensation. Forum managers were not billed for their time, and they were paid a percentage of the total billing for time users spent in their Forum. This gave them an obvious incentive to be efficient, and to be creative in getting users to spend time in their Forums. They also had the capability of granting free time (often known as "free flags") to CompuServe members who helped run the Forums.

Forums soon grew to be CompuServe's highest-billing product, followed by CB.

The Source did not add SIGs until 1985. Instead of SIGs, it followed a strategy of finding businesses to sponsor SIG-like areas with bulletin boards and files. There were few companies willing to pay to place product information and interact with customers in such an unproven venue, and the idea was eventually abandoned.

Interestingly, CompuServe developed a reputation (especially among Source users) of being devoted to technically oriented computer owners. Source members were warned (by other Source members) that they would find nothing but computer geeks on CompuServe, and that if they weren't themselves technically oriented they would be shunned. In fact, CompuServe hosted many noncomputer Forums—for model aviation enthusiasts, science fiction fans, writers, private pilots, coin collectors, and amateur genealogists, to name a few. (The real shunning happened when AOL and Prodigy came along.)

⁓

By the middle of 1980, CompuServe had 3,000 customers, each paying $5 per hour. The Source also claimed 3,000 subscribers . . . and sometimes 4,000. The service continued to charge a $100 signup fee, and kept the hourly rate at $2.75.

CompuServe was signing up hundreds of members through a highly successful $29.95 "Snapak" promotion with Radio Shack stores. The Snapaks were sealed, numbered membership packets that contained CompuServe documentation and signup information, along with a user ID and temporary password for the service. The buyer received most of the $29.95 back in free online time.

Marketing efforts included ads in computer magazines, and then deals with modem manufacturers to bundle signup materials with free time in with their products. It was an ideal promotion: put CompuServe in front of 'em as soon as they get their hands on a modem! And any book about modems, specific online services, or telecommunications in general included offers from one or more online services in its back pages. But the company still kept the advertising budget on the low side.

The Source spent even less on advertising, most likely due to financial unsteadiness.

But new marketing strategies waited in the wings—along with new ownership for each of the online services.

Online Experiments

> *It is unlikely that cable TV, telephone lines, and microwave links will*
> *serve to deliver information from remote databases to the consumer.*
> —Bill von Meister, founder of The Source

The Source and CompuServe were watching each other carefully. CompuServe watched as The Source tried and failed to sell small networks to businesses (its Professional Exchange program). Scratch one idea. The Source didn't take the hint from CB Simulator and Forums, which set it back competitively. Then both companies tried to broaden the market base by selling the one thing most potential customers didn't have: a computer.

Actually, they would offer individual terminals, dedicated computers that did one job—communicate online. The Source planned to market The Source terminal, which was a French-made Minitel terminal that GTE had gotten a deal on and apparently wanted to unload. (GTE had plans—probably originating with Bill von Meister—to market a service like Britain's Prestel in the United States. Prestel's terminals were made by Minitel in France. GTE shut down the project for no stated reason, but it was observed that the highly vaunted Prestel system in New England had only 4,000 subscribers, while CompuServe had more than twice as many subscribers.)

The idea was to offer a package—a membership to The Source and the terminal for somewhere between $500 and $700. (Perhaps a portion of the price was earmarked as The Source's signup fee.)

It really wasn't worth the price, even with built-in software and some dedicated functions. For the same money, you could buy a used computer (or in some cases a new one) to use with The Source and get all sorts of other functionality as well. Not surprisingly, few were sold.

CompuServe was working a deal with Tandy. It had given Tandy a two-year exclusive agreement selling the CompuServe Snapaks. And now Tandy was bringing out a product that would make it easier to get online: a dedicated system manufactured by Radio Shack called TRS-80 Videotex. It was based on the Tandy Color Computer (or Coco), and sold for $399. The terminal used a television set for a monitor, and booted up in terminal mode—no software to load. For another $29.95, you got a CompuServe Snapak with a free hour on CIS. They threw in a sigup offer with a free hour of Dow Jones News/Retrieval Service, too.

The origins of the Videotex terminal (and the Color Computer) were in a joint Radio Shack/Motorola program to develop an easy-to-use dedicated terminal and modem setup that farmers could use to get information on weather, crop prices, and related matters to help manage farm operations. This was tied in with the U.S. Department of Agriculture's Project Green Thumb, aimed at using new media to deliver useful information to farmers, ranchers, and other agricultural operations. A few were sold by Tandy as "AgVision" terminals, but the Videotex version was more popular, if different only in some elements of its appearance.

Interestingly, von Meister had run a pilot program with the U.S. Department of Agriculture's Project Green Thumb, implemented at the University of Kentucky, to supply terminals driven by his Infocast FM broadcasting system in 1978, but the deal fell apart—at which point Tandy apparently got involved. (See Chapter 4 for more information.)

Radio Shack got its Videotex terminals into stores late in 1980. The Source was shooting for fall 1981.

～

As The Source and CompuServe were busy adding members and refining their offerings, other organizations were looking on with interest. In newspaper interviews, Jack Taub had made it plain that he was looking for investors to help The Source recover from what he called von Meister's earlier mismanagement. The Reader's Digest Association stepped in during September with an offer of $3 million to buy 51 percent of The Source. Taub went for it. Reader's Digest immediately set about cleaning things up, replacing a lot of people. They brought in an RD executive named Graeme Keeping as CEO, and hired 50 new employees to bring the company back to where it was before von Meister left. Marshall Graham stayed on as president.

Bill von Meister was already suing Taub over who owned DBC, and for setting up The Source as a separate company from DBC, when he heard about the Reader's Digest deal. He went roaring back to court and obtained an order prohibiting Taub from selling additional shares. Taub was also barred from using any of the $3 million he'd received from Reader's Digest.

The messy situation was settled in December when Taub agreed to pay von Meister the actual value of the stock for which he'd given von Meister a cent a share. And he had to give Reader's Digest another 29 percent ownership. In exchange, Reader's Digest paid off over $2 million of DBC's and The Source's debts—after which it owned 80 percent of The Source. Taub may not have been completely happy with the settlement, but he'd get his back in a couple of years when von Meister set up a business to download music (decades before Napster).

Reader's Digest announced plans to place some of its book and magazine content online. Keeping was quoted as saying, "Any publisher today, if he doesn't get into electronic publishing, is either going to be forced into it by economic circumstances or will have great difficulty staying in the paper-and-ink business."

Keeping's statement was a bit ahead of its time. (It had to wait for the Web.) And as for *Reader's Digest* putting content online . . . it sounded good, but somehow nobody got around to posting condensed books and magazine features.

In all, it was a lot of trouble for something that was supposed to be entertaining, educational, and part of the future. The arguing, firing, and hiring—not to mention all the changes in management—stunted The Source's growth tremendously.

CompuServe was acquired, too, but things went a lot smoother. H&R Block made an offer and issued a statement that said its "previously announced merger with CompuServe, Inc. had become effective" on May 13, 1980. Most of the management remained in place.

Both companies benefited from infusions of cash. Among other things, The Source bought two new computers, and CompuServe got more computers and improved its network.

Gateways

Everything was growing. The Source was claiming 10,000 members; CompuServe had 12,000. The number of ARPANET hosts exceeded 200. The University of Illinois cancelled buying a new mainframe, in part because access to ARPANET gave it all the capabilities it needed. And uncounted thousands of BBSs were running in basements and spare bedrooms across the country.

Computer information retrieval was almost mainstream in the business world. After Dow Jones/Bunker Ramo had blazed the trail, *The New York Times* followed closely with its New York Times Information Service, which provided bibliographic citations for books and magazines, and occasional abstracts and actual content from the *Times* and other sources. (When the service was announced in 1969, it planned to offer photos and other graphic material for retrieval. That was an overly optimistic plan. The service did not go live until 1973. As it was, the content was little more than abstracts or headlines, like "Reagan-Carter Race Not Expected to Be Close.")

Prices for the database/information retrieval services were still steep by consumer standards. Access to ERIC through BRS, Dialog, or ORBIT could cost as much as $30 per hour, under certain conditions. The New York Times

Information Service was priced at $100 per hour. Some of the more abstruse databases hosted by Dialog cost $500 per hour.

The high pricing had a precedent in the general time-sharing business. Businesses were accustomed to paying $30 and up per hour of access, a toll on every kilo character transmitted.

With this kind of pricing, it is no wonder that personal computer owners didn't jump on the modem bandwagon until the low-priced consumer online services came along. (Well, low-priced except for The Source's $100 initiation fee, which was probably responsible for more people choosing CompuServe over The Source than anything else—even The Source's lack of chat rooms. It was probably von Meister's idea, thinking that to anyone who laid out $600 or $800 for a computer system, another hundred wouldn't mean much. He was wrong.)

In any event, the cost of business-oriented services didn't drive away business customers. Dow Jones News/Retrieval had a healthy customer base of 11,000 subscribers. Most DJNS users were brokerage firms, who paid $50 per month plus $40 per hour of usage. This made The Source's $100 signup fee seem less significant, though not by much.

Soon enough, CompuServe and The Source offered many of the same news, stock quotes, and even brokerage services as DJNS, but DJNS was more attractive to managers. They assumed (correctly) that switching to the lower-cost consumer services with all their varied offerings would be turning employees loose on virtual playgrounds where they would waste time, costing them productivity as well as online charges (rather like the Web today).

There wasn't a lot to play with on DJNS, with few offerings beyond stock quotes, airline guides, selected news items from *The Wall Street Journal* and *Barron's*. Shopping and movie reviews provided some diversion, but that was it. Email would not be offered until 1983, when MCI Mail started up and became the email service provider for DJNS.

Those businesses that needed email service, as well as information access, could always go to Dialcom or, later, Telemail, or MCI Mail. But CompuServe and The Source had become adept at running private email systems for corporate clients and government agencies. These could be customized to create private networks with selected information services in addition to email. The rest of the online service was invisible to the private networkers, and vice versa.

The large database services like Bibliographic Retrieval Service (BRS) and Dialog continued to grow, and some were experimenting with "gateways" to other services. BRS had set up a gateway for its users to access DJNS. A BRS user who accessed DJNS through BRS paid a surcharge, which appeared on the BRS user's bill.

Serious email providers like Dialcom added gateways to Official Airline Guide (OAG) and health and agriculture news. And similar gateways to popular services like Dialog and the OAG, Eaasy Sabre, Knowledge Index, and other database services would soon begin to show up on CompuServe and The Source. (And, once MCI Mail set up to provide DJNS with email service, MCI Mail offered a gateway to DJNS for its users.)

New Kids on the Block

New entities were showing up. Comp-U-Store made its services available to computer users, and some 30,000 computer owners took advantage of it. (The majority of its business was still through 800-number calls to operators.)

Several cable- and telephone-based Videotex services were tried out. These seemed to represent existing media trying to get a hold on the new media. In Coral Gables, Florida, Knight-Ridder (the newspaper publisher) and AT&T set up an experiment to provide interactive newspaper content to 200 homes. Access required a special terminal, and information was delivered by telephone and displayed on the home's television set. The services included online shopping for home delivery and advertising.

The Dallas Morning News experimented with a local Videotex system, working with Belo Information Systems. This system offered email, as well as news from the AP, UPI, Reuters, and *The New York Times*. Local information on the system included airline schedules, business and financial reports, entertainment guides, and local news, sports, and other features. The system lasted for about a year, and generated a little over 200 subscribers.

The famous QUBE two-way interactive cable TV experiment was still running in and around Columbus, Ohio, but it was beginning to lose money. And PBS station WETA in Washington, D.C., was experimenting with teletext.

The biggest event of the year in telecomputing was something that almost had to happen: newspapers going online. The Source already had UPI news, and AP was a provider at CompuServe. The obvious next step was to put the entire content of newspapers online.

The program was announced in June 1980, at a conference of the American Newspaper Publishers Association (ANPA). Katharine Graham, president of ANPA and CEO of *The Washington Post*, commented that the newspaper industry was on the brink of being able to deliver fixed-sized national advertising by satellite.

That idea got lost among all the other ideas being thrown around, but 13 big-city newspapers went online during the year-old program. Full text of news and features went up every day, but there were no graphics. The first paper up was *The Columbus* (Ohio) *Dispatch*, which went online in June. The other papers were *The Washington Post*, *The New York Times*, *The Minneapolis Star Tribune*, *The Chicago Sun-Times*, *The San Francisco Chronicle*, *The San Francisco Examiner*, *The Los Angeles Times*, *The Virginian-Pilot/Ledger Star*, *The Middlesex News* of Framingham, Massachusetts, *The St. Louis Post-Dispatch*, and *The Atlanta Journal* and *The Atlanta Constitution*. The experiment was set to run for a year, with CompuServe members able to access papers in the cities where they lived.

Views as to the benefits of putting newspapers online were split. Jim Batten, vice president of Knight-Ridder Newspapers at the time, presaged the sentiments of newspapers in the twenty-first century with his statement, made July 7, 1980: "Our concern was that if people might get their information in this way, they might no longer need newspapers."

John C. Quinn, vice president for news at the Gannett Company, saw online services as "A new development on the communications scene. My own view is that it will evolve into an additional service for the public, not unlike what happened with television after World War II. Remember how TV was going to kill radio and newspapers?"

And a generation before that, newspaper owners were sure that radio would steal all their advertisers. That didn't happen: television didn't kill radio or newspapers—but it changed them. And as we know from our vantage point, three decades later the Web does threaten to kill off newspapers.

In the middle of all this, as both commercial online services were growing and old media was tentatively embracing new media, von Meister came out as a contrarian to the whole idea of online services for home use. Perhaps as a parting shot to Jack Taub and STC, von Meister used his position with GTE Telenet to throw cold water on the idea of personal computer communications. He told *Computerworld* magazine and other publications, "It is unlikely that cable TV, telephone lines, and microwave links will serve to deliver information from remote databases to the consumer. Cost will be a major obstacle to getting home information technology established. Telephone is the most likely avenue for home information systems, although present telephone resources would be swamped with the traffic volumes."

Surprising talk for the man who had created one of the early wireless data networks, and one of the first home computer networks.

But von Meister himself wasn't out of the game—far from it. He was still seeking a way to pull money from the air. And this time he was confident of success. As soon as he could line up investors, he would start the world's first music download service.

Von Meister's "Home Music Store" would bring music direct to consumers—their choice of songs over eight channels. There would be five channels for listening, one for previews, and (this would really get him in hot water) two for recording downloaded music.

Worse, his nemesis, Jack Taub, was developing an idea for something very similar that would use one of von Meister's own ideas against him.

Trials and Errors

I do not think that teletext and Videotex will ever obtain the kind of advertising revenues we see from the traditional media forms.
—Michael Drexler, Doyle Dane Bernbach, 1982

Bill von Meister's GTE Telenet gig lasted just long enough for him to be certain GTE wasn't going with his idea for a Minitel-based online service.[1] Then he lined up some investors (including the singing Osmond family) to back a project he'd had in mind for some time: he would sell music to cable TV subscribers via satellite download.

Announced in the middle of 1981, the Digital Music Company, operating as Home Music Store, would provide music on demand 24 hours a day. Digitally recorded from studio masters, the music would be computer-encrypted and beamed to the Westar IV satellite. Westar IV would, in turn, transmit the coded music signal to cable TV stations that had signed on to carry the service.

From there, the encrypted signals would travel by cable to subscribers' homes to be decoded by a "black box." All of the technology—the digital encoding, computers, satellite transmission, cables, decoding, and billing—would be computer-controlled and invisible to the end user. A customer could listen to three preprogrammed channels of music, plus a preview channel and two channels from which she could make tape recordings of favorites.

This service would cost subscribers $6.95 to $9.95 per month, with an additional charge for taping (the equivalent of 20 to 60 percent off an album's list price).

Once again, von Meister was assembling a product using off-the-shelf technology, put together in ways no one had thought of before: bootstrapping

---

[1] As noted earlier, GTE had bought thousands of Minitel terminals, and would cut a deal to sell them to The Source when it canceled its online service idea.

it. Von Meister thought it was a great idea. So did his backers. Music delivered to your home with a sound quality better than records or tapes? Titles on demand at a big discount? Who wouldn't like it?

When an announcement of the service appeared in *Billboard*, record retailers were livid. If people were buying music in their homes, they wouldn't be going to record shops. Store owners threatened to refuse to offer records from any label who worked with the Home Music Store. Copyright holders and organizations that represented them, like the American Society of Composers, Authors, and Publishers (ASCAP), had a few things to say as well.

As most people could have predicted, the idea didn't fly because the record companies refused to take the risk of dealing with von Meister. Von Meister protested that people who would download music from his service weren't the type who went to record stores, anyway. And besides, he told the record companies, the profits would be bigger because there was no need to manufacture, package, and ship records. Those, along with a few other lame arguments, got him nowhere. Although he claimed to have "informal agreements" with Warner Brothers and some other, unnamed record companies, he never got anything on paper, so the Home Music Store didn't get off the ground.

At Warner Brothers, one executive who liked the Home Music Store idea suggested he try the idea with computer games. Warner owned Atari, who made the hottest game console on the market, the Atari 2600. Millions of gamers owned 2600s, and each and every one was a potential market. If von Meister could make his music idea work with video games, the executive said, it could be big . . .

Something Old, Nothing New

Meanwhile, Jack Taub was setting up to profit by one of von Meister's earlier ideas, now lying idle. When the lawsuits and dust settled in December 1981, *Reader's Digest* fired Taub from The Source, but the court gave him DBC, the von Meister company he had backed before The Source. DBC was the parent company of Infocast, which used FM sideband signals to transmit digital data to special receivers that translated it into a format a computer terminal could use. (See Chapter 4.)

Taub reorganized the company as National Information Utilities (NIU). He managed to get the idea in front of National Public Radio's vice president, Thomas Warnock, and convinced him that NPR should join him in a venture not unlike von Meister's 1978 version of a wireless Internet. NPR would become a major stakeholder with an investment of a half-million dollars.

Why would NPR get involved in a commercial enterprise? Because it was hurting from Reagan budget cuts. The idea was that NPR would transmit digital data to affiliate stations around the country. Those stations would broadcast the data on an FM sideband, to be picked up by home users with

NIU terminals and personal computers. Subscriptions and maybe a few advertisers would generate cash flow.

What sort of data would this new iteration of Infocast broadcast? Computer games and other programs. With this system, once the infrastructure was in place, there was virtually no overhead; all you had to stock was one copy of every program (like Jeff Wilkins' SOFTEX on CompuServe).

There might also be a provision to enable NPR listeners to record their favorite shows while they were away from their radios—for a fee.

NPR and NIU would operate the system under the aegis of INC Telecommunications. The program generated a lot of buzz and pulled in a few more investors, among them Kemmons Wilson, the founder of Holiday Inns. Apple cofounder Steve Wozniak agreed to help set up the software broadcast component, and perhaps select programs to offer.

But the idea went nowhere. A little over a year after the service was announced, NPR bowed out, accepting the return of $500,000 of its investment in INC and a promise of 5 percent of future profits. The whole thing quietly faded away after that.

Newspapers and Newsletters Online

The yearlong CompuServe/American Newspaper Publishers Association (ANPA) newspaper experiment ended disappointingly in June 1982. After the initial novelty wore off, only about 10 percent of CompuServe's members used the newspaper service consistently.

As part of the test, a selected group of computer owners, who were not CompuServe members, were allowed to use the service for free. They complained about the lack of pictures, the service tying up their telephone lines, and difficulty in finding what they wanted. (Still, a third of this group became paying CompuServe members after the trial.)

The test brought out quite a bit of data about online demographics and reading habits. Most users were males in their thirties, with decent incomes. They logged on for email, news, shopping, gaming, banking, and so on. But newspaper publishers weren't as interested in these things as they were in assurances that online services were no threat to newspapers and their advertising base. They got that assurance from AP spokesman Larry Blasko, who told them, "There is no danger to the American newspaper industry from electronic delivery of information to the home."

Newspapers had survived radio. They had survived television. According to ANPA, they would survive computer networks.

ANPA President Katharine Graham (publisher of *The Washington Post*) still expressed concern that AT&T would get involved in the online distribution or creation of information. She was even then directing the Association's efforts toward getting legislation passed to bar telephone companies from becoming information providers.

The Associated Press and United Press International would continue to supply news to CompuServe and The Source, respectively. And the *St. Louis Post-Dispatch*, *Washington Post*, *Columbus Dispatch*, and *Middlesex News* decided to carry on with supplying content to CompuServe.

The *Wall Street Journal* wasn't part of the ANPA experiment because it had been online all along—at $60 an hour—through the Dow Jones News/Retrieval Service. And DJNS was progressively experimenting with a cable-TV version, at $40 per month. It soon appeared on CompuServe and The Source's menus as a gateway service.

Separate from everything else, Mead Data Central was already presenting newspapers with its Nexis (later Vu/Text) service. The service had started out modestly with the *Philadelphia Inquirer* and the *Boston Globe* in 1980, and was soon commanding $100 per hour from its customers.

A new twist in online data products went live in March 1982. NewsNet was an online service set up to publish industry-specific newsletters in electronic form. These included newsletters such as *Energy Daily*, *Satellite Week*, *Coal Outlook*, *Job Safety*, and *Sludge Newsletter*. Some of the newsletters cost $200 to $800 per issue in hard copy.

Priced at $24 to $132 per hour, NewsNet was a one-of-a-kind product. Dialog, SDC, and BRS might have offered newsletters, but they were better suited to handling archival data. NewsNet was set up to handle the rapid dissemination of new information. It soon worked out that NewsNet was a popular gateway service from other online services; you could hop over to NewsNet from Dialog, CompuServe, DELPHI, or any of a number of other services. (Interestingly, NewsNet was hosted on Dialcom's Prime mainframe computers, which also originally hosted The Source.)

Consumer Movement

NewsNet, Dialog,[2] and the other big database services were making a killing from well-heeled corporate customers. But as Jeff Wilkins had long ago observed with CompuServe, usage fell off in the evenings and on weekends. Dialog and BRS,[3] noticing all those consumers out there willing to pay $5 to $15 per hour to access online services, decided to see if they could woo some of them.

One thing was certain: the average home computer owner wasn't going to pay $500 per hour for access, nor even $35 per hour. And the database services couldn't cut their prices for consumers and continue to charge high rates to commercial customers.

---

[2] *Dialog was acquired by Knight-Ridder in 1988. After a couple more twists in ownership it became a division of the Thomson Corporation, which it remains today.*

[3] *Today Ovid.*

Someone figured out a compromise. Dialog and BRS would each make a selected group of their databases available at a lower cost, evenings and weekends. They would offer databases that didn't have high royalty rates attached to them, a couple of popular databases (like *Books in Print*), and some that were not accessed very often. The toll for these would be more in line with what the consumer online services charged. Dialog's consumer database service was called Knowledge-Index. BRS/After Dark served up three dozen or so databases from the BRS collections

Around the same time, DJNS lowered its non-prime-time rates, attracting a larger portion of the consumer market to its unique offerings. (Some of the more popular items on the DJNS menu still carried a surcharge.) Many users had already experimented with DJNS through the growing number of gateways from other online services, and they were more than ready to sign on as customers at reduced nighttime rates.

The Ultimate Gateway

Gateways were a popular way to market database products outside their usual markets. They gave customers access to a rich variety of information without their having to set up new accounts and remember several logon procedures, user Ids, and passwords. And there were no initiation fees or monthly minimums; customers paid only for the time they used.

The ultimate in gateway services was probably a product developed by Telebase Systems called EasyNet.

EasyNet was itself a giant gateway, consisting of links to database and information-retrieval services accessible through a uniform menu system. Users could search Dialog, LegiSlate, ORBIT, Vu/Text, Questel, BRS, NewsNet, Data-Times, and hundreds of other databases—at a flat fee per search. Created by Richard Kollin of Telebase, EasyNet was among the very first menu-driven gateway systems for the end user, and was eventually equipped with a common command language that did not require searchers to learn menus and commands for the systems they were searching.

It was made available as—what else?—a gateway on various online services. EasyNet gateways resided on a dozen different partners' systems, and it went by a different name for each host. For example, on CompuServe it was known as IQuest and on Western Union's EasyLink it was called Infomaster.

While users could search and get results from only one database at a time, EasyNet offered a scan feature that would query all the databases in a category and report the number of entries related to a given search that were available in each. Today's Google News searches in historical newspaper archives are similar, although EasyNet provided no preview of hits as Google News does.

Encyclopedias Online

As noted earlier, much of the content put online by the early database services (Dialog and BRS) was information *about* information: citations and abstracts. The information provided was detailed, things like the title of an article, the name, issue number, and page number of the magazine in which it appeared. But, what people really wanted to find online was the article itself, not directions for finding it. The same was true with reference books.

But searchers had to be satisfied with learning how to find what they sought, then going elsewhere to get it. In the early 1980s, there was a lot of doubt about putting full text online. In general, publishers feared that someone would copy their publications and distribute them. And it looked doubtful that any magazine that put its content online could even make back the cost of placing it there—nor regain the readers of the print version that being online might cost it. Even the growing number of publishers that created the content of their newspapers, books, and magazines electronically were hesitant to place their product where it could easily be copied.

Database services themselves had some doubt whether enough of a market existed to make it worthwhile to have entire contents of magazines and books keyboarded (or, later, scanned and OCR'd [OCR stands for Optical Character Recognition]).

But a few people were willing to take chances. Mead Data Central,[4] purveyors of Lexis/Nexis, had already done some pioneering work in putting legal information online (Lexis, with the Ohio Code and thousands of court decisions, for the Ohio Bar Association) and then newspapers (Nexis). And in 1981, the *Encyclopedia Britannica* teamed with Lexis/Nexis to make the encyclopedia available in a full-text searchable format—meaning the search software went through all the encyclopedia entries and if the search word appeared anywhere in the text of an entry, it was a "hit."

Dow Jones News/Retrieval brought Grolier's *Academic American Encyclopedia* online in 1982. (The *Academic American Encyclopedia* turned out to be a popular gateway service. It would show up on DELPHI, GEnie, Prodigy, and BRS/After Dark, as well as other services.) Also in 1982, CompuServe offered the *World Book Encyclopedia*. Unlike the *Britannica*, these encyclopedias were searchable by subject headers or keywords only.

The same was true of yet another online encyclopedia that would become the basis for an entire consumer online service. In 1982 a Cambridge entrepreneur named Wes Kussmaul bought the electronic rights to the single-volume *Cadillac Modern Encyclopedia*, a 2,000-page tome published by Random House. It went online as DELPHI in 1983.

---

[4] *Originally Data Central before it was acquired by the Mead Corporation.*

Keyword and Full-Text Searches

There are two ways to search a textual database. One is to have the search software examine the entire contents of the database—every word in each entry. As it goes through the database, the software creates a results list of entries, or articles, that contain the keyword(s).

The other approach is to arbitrarily assign subject headings to each entry, like tags, to serve as an index. The search software looks only at the index words. As it looks through the index, it creates a list of articles that have the keyword in their subject headings.

Why bother with the second approach at all? With some of the computer systems available in the early 1980s, it might take several minutes to search the hundreds of thousands of words in an encyclopedia. Many users would object to the lengthy search times and the billing for those extra minutes. Searching only the subject headers speeds up the search, though it may miss some relevant entries because the index depended on the judgment and knowledge of the people adding them.

As would be the case with a few newspapers, certain of the encyclopedias demanded royalties or per-use fees so large that the online services hosting them had to add a surcharge when billing their customers. Access to the encyclopedia online threatened sales of hard-copy encyclopedias. High royalties or fees compensated.

This would be true of other specialized databases, such as contemporary demographic data by region, and lists of businesses sorted by type and region. (*The Reader's Guide to Periodical Literature* is still a high-priced premium service, now accessible via the Web.) The host services had no control over what these information providers charged. In most cases, prices dropped when such a database saw little use—or when a competing service went online. Gradually, the world of reference works began to move online.

More Experiments

As the database and consumer online services continued to grow, there was some uncertainty as to what to expect from Videotex. Most pundits and journalists pointed to the European services, Prestel and Minitel (see Chapter 5) as the ideal. Yet they missed the fact that CompuServe and The Source, among others, were functioning Videotex systems in their own right, lacking only color and graphics to meet the Videotex "ideal." Broadcasters missed this, too.

It's easy to see why. Using services like CompuServe and Dow Jones News/Retrieval Service meant using computers. The public didn't want computers in their homes for Videotex. Most expected a Videotex *appliance* (rather like some of the "Internet appliances" of the 1990s). And why not? Radio, television, and telephone service were each provided by specific appliances. Why not the new media?

With that in the public consciousness, some big organizations put a lot of money into experiments in Videotex and Videotex appliances. Bellsouth, NBC, Cox (INDAX), CBS, Knight-Ridder (Viewtron), *The Los Angeles Times* (Gateway), TV/Ontario, GTE, AT&T (Canada's Telidon, Gateway, Viewtron, and several more), and others would build experimental systems to make cable interactive, to put text on broadcast and cable TV signals, or to send computer-like graphics and textual data to televisions over telephone lines.

The Warner QUBE two-way cable TV system in Columbus, Ohio, almost got it right, but it was too expensive—over $30 per month in the late 1970s. The system began as a custom two-way cable system. Information (graphics, text, etc.) came in via cable, and user commands and information went back to the main computer via cable.

Then, for a while, QUBE subscribers enjoyed Videotex as a hybrid two-way cable/computer information network. Because Warner owned Atari, it lent subscribers Atari 800 computers, *and* tied them in with CompuServe. Color text and graphics. Color photographs. Email, news, weather, sports, contests, shopping! But in the end, the cost to users and to the cable supplier was too much.

Cost seems to have killed another successful 1980s Videotex test. This was the highly touted Viewtron service. One of the larger and more public of such experiments, Viewtron was operated by Viewdata, a partnership between Knight-Ridder Newspapers and AT&T. Visually stunning, it used an object-oriented graphics system based on the NAPLPS[5] standard that displayed color text and graphics on the user's television. The appearance was better than later-generation IBM DOS graphics, and similar to the later Prodigy, which also used NAPLPS. Some 15,000 pages of images and text were available to users at any one time. Many of these—especially news and advertising—were changed as circumstances dictated.

The focus was on news and news-related products, along with email, but Viewtron grew to encompass shopping, gaming, chat, bulletin boards, auctions, and more. The service was test-marketed in Coral Gables, Florida, in 1980, and expanded to much of South Florida in 1983. The monthly fee was $12, with a $1 per hour fee for telephone connection to the service.

---

[5] *NAPLPS stands for North American Presentation Level Protocol Syntax. It is a standard used in Videotex graphics presentation, co-developed by the Canadian government's Telidon Videotex service and AT&T.*

At first, users had to buy special terminals for $900 (later reduced to $600, then offered on lease). After the first year, the terminals could be rented. In a belated attempt to reach the home computer market, Viewtron developed software that enabled IBM, Commodore, and Apple computers to access the service. (Viewtron was entirely telephone line–based. Viewtron's Sceptre terminals contained 1200bps modems.) The growing number of computer users could not be ignored. Albert Gillen, president of Viewdata, was quoted in a 1984 story on Videotex as saying, "What we're really hoping for is that some manufacturer will come out with a 'black box' that allows computers to display full Videotex graphics and colors."

Viewdata also contracted with The Source to provide some of its content, probably a financial lifesaver for The Source.

Over the next few years, Viewtron expanded to include all of Florida and at least 15 cities in the eastern half of the United States, among them Baltimore, Boston, Cleveland, Detroit, Kansas City, and Philadelphia. The cities' services were not interconnected; each Viewtron service stood alone, like a walled garden—indeed, like all the online services, except for gateways.

After experimenting with varying pricing structures, the company found that it couldn't turn a profit at prices members were willing to pay. So Viewdata pulled the plug on the service in 1986, having spent $50 million on the "experiment."

Canada's Viewtron counterpart and NAPLPS co-developer, Telidon, was among the more interesting Videotex experiments of the early 1980s. Telidon was a hybrid combination of telephone lines and broadcast teletext (transmitting data during the vertical blanking interval in television broadcasts, discussed in Chapter 5). The broadcast sent data to TV receivers.[6] A terminal and modem connected to standard telephone lines carried user input and commands. The wider bandwidth of the broadcast television system allowed for extremely fast, high-quality graphics and data transfer.

Another noteworthy experiment of this era was a field test of what eventually became the Prodigy online service. Called CBS Venture One, it was a Videotex partnership between CBS and AT&T. Two hundred homes in Ridgewood and Fair Lawn, New Jersey, were chosen to be equipped with special keyboards that attached to a TV set, or a keyboard-and-monitor outfit that would be the residents' gateway to the online world.

Planning for Venture One began in 1978, but the service didn't go live until 1982, and was shut down after little more than a year, AT&T and CBS having gotten the information they wanted from the experiment. The experiment would resurface in 1984 as something called "Trintex."

---

[6] *Teletext required a converter box or a special television set with teletext capability built in. Zenith was the only North American manufacturer that made teletext-ready sets.*

Meanwhile, Back at the ARPA Ranch . . .

ARPANET had not remained in stasis while the commercial online world was developing. ARPANET evolved and grew in many directions from the late 1970s through the early 1980s. And other networks were formed—ALOHAnet (packet radio) and SATNET (satellite packet) by ARPA investigators, DECnet (Digital Equipment Company's network), CSNET (Computer Science Research Network), DDN (Defense Data Network), SPAN (NASA), BITNET (Because It's Time Network, another academic network: BITNET was set up between the City University of New York and Yale University by Ira Fuchs and Graydon Freeman, students at City and Yale, respectively, using modems and leased telephone lines; it would grow to 3,000 nodes), and, of course, Usenet, as described in Chapter 5. Further, networks similar to ARPANET were developed in other countries, and ARPANET itself had expanded to include sites in Europe and Asia.

TCP/IP

When ARPANET was first put together, a Network Control Protocol was developed to enable the IMPs (Internet message processors) to track and reassemble the data packets that made up a message. After the Hawaii-based ALOHAnet radio packet network and the SATNET packet-satellite network were successfully tested in concert with ARPANET, Vint Cerf went to work on developing an improved network protocol.

In 1973, Vint Cerf and Bob Kahn completed work on that protocol, called Transmission Control Protocol (TCP). At the instigation of Jon Postel (who, among many other ARPANET developments, helped devise the Internet domain name system), a second set of protocols for handling data between networks, called Internet Protocol (IP), was created in 1978.[7]

Together they were known as TCP/IP, the standard protocols used in inter-networking. It was now possible for a computer on any network to communicate with a computer on any other network. From this time (1978) onward, a closed network of computers would be known as an "internet," while computers in networks that communicated with other computers and networks were an Internet (capital I).

As of January 1, 1983, every Internet computer was required to switch to TCP/IP from NCP (Network Control Protocol) if it hadn't already. By spring of that year, any computers that weren't operating TCP/IP fell away from the Internet.

---

[7] *The Internet Society's Jonathan B. Postel Service Award is named in his honor, as is the Postel Center at the University of Southern California's Information Sciences Institute.*

Even with all the commercial development going on, none of the networks on the Internet were connected with online services. Only the few thousand people who had access to ARPANET—students, professors, engineers, military contractors, and various military staff—could access the Internet. It was a government project; therefore, commercial use was forbidden. All manner of pranking and horseplay, personal email, and extended discussions that had nothing to do with research (as in Usenet) were permitted, but nothing that involved making money was allowed.

In 1983, ARPANET was split into ARPANET and MILNET. MILNET consisted of 68 specific nodes of the 113 that then existed. These were integrated into the military's Defense Data Network (DDN). During the 1980s, MILNET would expand to become a worldwide network of military nets.

For security reasons, MILNET and ARPANET were linked only by email gateways. A number of new networks were linked with ARPANET, and other networks linked to some of the new networks.

Huge and isolated, the Internet was a mighty fortress. Nothing linked to it without its consent, and only on its very specific terms. Outside it were the walled cities of commercial online services and database services. A small amount of commerce moved between some of the walled cities by special gateways and under a heavy toll. But for the most part, the walled cities didn't talk to one another any more than they talked to the Internet, for many different languages were spoken, and few lines of communication existed.

Data Smuggling?

Among ARPANET techies who also had accounts on DELPHI, CompuServe, or other online services, it was a popular activity to copy portions of Usenet discussions and "port" them over to an online service. The ARPANET users would post messages on bulletin boards or share them with their less fortunate, non-ARPA friends through email.

In similar fashion, a number of home BBS hobbyists occasionally dialed up BBSs in Europe and elsewhere, saving their entire sessions on the foreign systems in text files. The online tourists then uploaded the files to share with other BBS aficionados.

The Second Wave

My biggest fear was going head-to-head with CompuServe.
—Bill Louden, founder of GEnie

Some 800,000 modems were sold in 1983, and projections were for a million modems to be shipped in 1984. Combined with the modems already out there, this made for a significant market for online services of all stripes.

MCI Telecommunications launched MCI Mail, its $100 million email service, in September 1983. MCI Mail's entry into the growing market was significant for several reasons, paramount among them the fact that it was the first large, brand-name company to establish a commercial online service. A combination business/consumer service, it had the potential to grow faster than existing online services, and perhaps even carry email to mainstream status.

The market for business email was previously served by a variety of vendors, including Dialcom (by this time owned by British Telecom), CompuServe, and other general and specialty online services. Some appealed to consumers, and others to businesses. MCI Mail was targeted at both.

MCI's system was perfect for smaller businesses and individuals who would benefit from an email-only service. But it was easily scaled up to hosting corporate email networks that functioned like private networks (as CompuServe had done for companies like General Motors in the early 1970s).

MCI Mail had every imaginable email feature. In addition to sending, replying, filing, copying, mailing lists, and delivery confirmation, MCI Mail offered more esoteric options such as project billing, fax service, and hard-copy mailing services, as well as Telex.

A unique feature was same-day hard-copy letter delivery. It was a fairly straightforward process. The user would type in or upload a multipage letter, provide the name and postal address of the recipient(s), and press Send. The letter would be printed out in the city nearest the addressee. From there a Purolator courier would hand-deliver the letter to the recipient.

This was fairly successful, and Federal Express copied the idea with a service called ZapMail.

Early on, MCI Mail offered a gateway to Dow Jones News/Retrieval Service; on its first day, MCI saw 55,000 DJNS customers use the gateway. The service also pioneered email connection to the Internet, having hired Vint Cerf to head the effort. And it would be an important part of what would become the backbone of the Internet when it built the National Science Foundation Network (NSFNet) in the late 1980s (see Chapter 5).

AT&T responded with AT&T Mail, which was marketed as a corporate communications solution. It pretty much matched MCI Mail in services, but was more complex to use. A novel feature was "Mail Talk," which allowed a user to dial a toll-free voice number and have email read aloud by a synthesized voice.

The presence of these heavy-hitters did not have a big effect on consumer online services; most computer owners were out to do more than just send and receive email. Established services continued to add new members, and a variety of entrepreneurs worked on a second wave of consumer services.

DELPHI

In 1981 Cambridge entrepreneur Wesley Kussmaul had an idea. He would buy the rights to an encyclopedia, have it keyboarded into electronic files, and then put it online in searchable format. Customers would dial in direct or via Tymnet or Telenet and pay a modest per-minute rate for access.

The encyclopedia he had in mind was the *Cadillac Modern Encyclopedia*, published in 1973 by Random House. Kussmaul negotiated for the rights, then had the encyclopedia's 1,954 pages typed into ASCII text files. He next made a deal with a time-sharing operation in Texas to host the encyclopedia files, along with a database program, a billing program, and some other simple programs. It was a textbook example of bootstrapping a business, similar to what von Meister had done with The Source, but with a unique product offering.

This consumer service was initially named the *Kussmaul Encyclopedia*, but was renamed DELPHI, after the Delphic Oracle of classic Greek myth, in March 1983. Like the Oracle, DELPHI would be a source of knowledge and, hopefully, wisdom.

Dan Bruns, later president of DELPHI's parent company, General Videotex Corp. (GVC), joined the company in 1983, when the service was beginning a rapid expansion. "We had chat and some pretty simple bulletin-board systems," Bruns remembers, "and a prototype program that was called the *Collaborative Novel*, where the idea was that people would work together to create a novel.

"As I started we were connecting to various newsfeeds and trying to hook in information providers. We were making gateways out to services like Dialog and Dialcom for external databases."

In 1984 the chat feature (called Conference on DELPHI), and a bulletin board system, were folded together with an announcement system, databases, and user tracking into SIGs. Bruns was the SIG system's primary programmer.

The SIGs were the center of DELPHI activity, as was the case with Forums on CompuServe. Also like CompuServe, each SIG manager was paid a percentage of the gross revenue his SIG generated. (By the late 1980s, the nomenclature went from SIGs to "Groups and Clubs.")

DELPHI went live in March 1983. In addition to email, the *Kussmaul Encyclopedia* (updated regularly), databases, and SIGs, a raft of services almost equal to CompuServe's offerings was added. These included AP News and Accu-Weather forecasts, classified ads, a member directory, Violette Wine Reports, Security Objective Services, a travel agency, and a raft of services equal to CompuServe's offerings. There were plenty of gateway services, including Dialog, Dialcom, OAG, North American Investment Corp. (NAICO), Comp-U-Store Online, GlobalLink Translation Services, and more.

DELPHI's Conference (chat) system was probably its most popular feature. As with CompuServe Forums and, later, GEnie RoundTables, most DELPHI SIGs held weekly chats. Among the more memorable for many was the regular Wednesday night chat in the Science Fiction Forum. Beginning in 1985, the SIG manager, KZIN, hosted the weekly chat which was frequented by several professional science fiction writers and editors, among them Lawrence Watt-Evans, Gardner Dozois, Pat Cadigan, Mike Resnick, Michael A. Banks, Jack L. Chalker, Lawrence Person, Martha Soukup, and Barbara Delaplace.

Delphi's unique offerings included an ongoing collaborative novel, private groups (GroupLink), and the aforementioned Delphi Oracle, who would provide an answer to any question (often tongue-in-cheek). The Boston Computer Exchange (also known as BCE or BoCoEx) was on DELPHI as well. BCE started in 1982 as a paper listing of computers for sale or trade. It went online as a BBS soon after starting up. In 1983 the database was uploaded to DELPHI and remained available (with regular updates) until the business closed in the 1990s. Along the way it developed what may have been the first online auction system. When CompuServe opened its Online Mall in 1989, BCE took the first online store.

Eventually DELPHI would move to a leased DEC VAX[1] minicomputer in Cambridge, Massachusetts, the location of the company headquarters. DELPHI would later add a second VAX, increasing speed and user capacity.

---

[1] The name VAX was originally an acronym for Virtual Address Extension, after the system's early use of virtual memory and the fact that it was a 32-bit extension of an earlier Digital Equipment Corporation (DEC) 16-bit com called the PDP-11 (PDP is an acronym for Programmed Data Processor).

The Original Online Novel Debut

Much has been made of writers giving away works on the Internet. Chapters from my own *Blogging Heroes* (Wiley, 2007), and the entire text of Cory Doctorow's *Down and Out in the Magic Kingdom* (published by TOR Books in 2003, and concurrently released on the Web under a limited Creative Commons license) are two examples.

But, as with so many other "new" ideas, this one isn't. The year 1984 saw the first online publication of a novel by an established author, *before* it was published. It was that year that Orson Scott Card posted *Ender's Game* on DELPHI. The novel was published in 1985, and went on to win both the Hugo and the Nebula Awards, as well as receiving great critical and popular acclaim. (Another testament to the popularity of *Ender's Game* is the fact that it remains in print over 20 years later.) It was the first example of a popular work by a professional writer being given away online.

Over the next few years well-known fiction writers such as Mike Resnick and Joel Rosenberg began putting entire novels online, again at no charge, and the practice has continued from there.

There are, of course, a number of works of fiction and nonfiction put online before 1984, but these were unpublished works (save for one that was previously published but out of print).

Part of Delphi's original business plan was to offer "local" versions of the service in major cities, beginning with Boston and Kansas City in the mid-1980s. These services would focus on local information and communications features, with some of the national service's offerings bundled in, all for a flat fee. Users would dial a local phone number, which eliminated the overhead of packet-switched network charges, small as they were. Plus, if they wished, DELPHI local users could transition to the national service through a gateway, and pay regular DELPHI rates.

Unfortunately, the Boston and Kansas City versions of DELPHI were unable to find or develop enough local content to be compelling offerings, but DELPHI continued to grow nationally. Throughout the early 1980s, it vied with The Source for the position of the second-largest consumer online service. DELPHI also licensed its service in Argentina, and maintained a link between DELPHI/Argentina and the American version.

More Regional Online Services

DELPHI had a good idea with its regional online services, even if it didn't quite work out. Or, at least, other entrepreneurs agreed that it was a good idea. A variety of regional online services popped up in cities across the United States. We'll take a quick look at some representative examples: Keycom in Chicago, Gateway in Los Angeles, Electra in Cincinnati, and Georgia OnLine in Atlanta—bearing in mind that dozens of teletext, Videotex, and other online experiments were being launched in the early 1980s, just about all of them doomed to failure.

Keycom was planned to be a hybrid service that operated like Canada's Telidon, with information from the service broadcast as teletext, and commands and other user input to the service via modem. But between the initial planning stages in 1981 and finally going online in 1984, Keycom morphed into a completely modem-based service. It could be used with a special terminal made by Honeywell (similar to AT&T's Sceptre). The terminal cost $750, but could be leased. Keycom access was not limited to the terminal; anyone with an IBM or compatible personal computer could dial up Keycom with special software. Computer users were at a disadvantage, however, because the only way a user could view the system's NAPLPS[2] graphics was using the Keycom terminal.

The majority owner of Keycom was Centel, the regional telephone services provider, with the next largest investment (30 percent) coming from Honeywell. In addition to Honeywell, *The Chicago Sun-Times* and Field Enterprises acquired interests in Keycom. And media magnate Rupert Murdoch chose Keycom as his News America Corp.'s first foray into the online world. It would not be his last.

The Los Angeles Gateway service, established under the auspices of the Times-Mirror Company, began field trials late in 1984. Gateway was similar to Viewtron, and used AT&T's Sceptre terminal. The service intended to take advantage of Sceptre's graphics capability to draw advertisers. Its business plan looked for 70 percent of the service's revenue to come from advertising, while subscribers would contribute 30 percent.

Home computers were initially left out of the service's market, until Gateway developed terminal emulation software for IBM and compatibles. As with Keycom, however, computer users could not view the graphics that appeared on terminal users' screens.

Electra was a free teletext system that was online from 1982 through 1993. It was operated by Taft Broadcasting in Cincinnati, Ohio. Despite being in operation for more than a decade, Electra never achieved a large membership, and the majority of the city's population never knew it existed. Accessing it required an expensive decoder box or a specific Zenith TV model with a teletext decoder built in. Taft did little promotion, even though Electra was available to anyone who received "Super Station" WTBS by cable, as well as to people in Cincinnati.

---

[2] *See Chapter 8.*

The First Dot-Com Bust

Another example of a local, computer and modem-based online service was Georgia OnLine in Atlanta. This service was built in 1984 by Bill Louden, Al Keener, Larry Sturtz, and several other former CompuServe executives who had left because they were disaffected by changes in management.

According to Louden, many of the 16 people who originally built CIS ". . . were getting shoved out a little bit by the corporate people at CompuServe. They saw the success in the consumer business, and a lot of them started squeezing us. We saw these commercial people coming in, and not starting at the same level we were, [yet] they were becoming our bosses. So there was some issue about that."

Things came to a head in 1984, when Louden and the others decided to pursue a new opportunity. "We all had this concept of starting a new service," Louden explained, "better than CompuServe. We wanted to build it with local information, wanted to build it with open standards—open source stuff—and we wanted to build it on UNIX, System 5 at the time. There were about eight of us. We created a company called Georgia OnLine, and tried to launch a service in Atlanta, Georgia."

Why Atlanta? "At the time, Atlanta was the largest local dialing area in the country. And of course we had Georgia Tech, too. The system was built on Convergent Technologies MegaFrames. The boxes were about $50,000, fairly cheap, solid and supposedly pretty good for the time. Unfortunately they had a lot of technical hardware problems back then, too.

"The theory was, if we built these things locally and got the content, we could franchise them out to New York City and Washington. It was like Citysearch, but ten years too early."

Georgia OnLine would offer its customers shopping, email, a local events guide, and classified ads for a flat rate of $12 per month. For an extra $6 per hour, members could access chat, bulletin boards, and online games.

It would also be the first dot-com service, built in part on Internet resources. As Louden later explained, "At the time, the dot-com domain was about six months old. We tried to build the system using dot-com resources—with Usenet and all the UNIX capabilities of the time. We spent several months building a product, and probably put three quarters of a million dollars into it, between me and the other investors."

But people weren't lining up to join. "It was," Louden remembers, "difficult to go out and talk to customers, because most people said 'Are you crazy? Dot-com? We'll never pay for this stuff!'

"The reality was that we were so early that nobody would think of paying for anything that was Usenet or Internet-based. Most potential customers were government, military, or students, and they got it all free. The attitude was pretty much, 'You want us to pay for that stuff? We'll pay for CompuServe, but if you're going to build us a service based on these open standards and UNIX, we'll never pay for it.'"

Louden and his group had problems getting local content for the service, too. In sum, Louden says, "we built some interesting product, but it wasn't going to work. In some respects I could already envision that we were going to be the first dot-com bomb, in 1984. The company eventually busted."

GEnie

Fortunately for Bill Louden, General Electric contacted him as Georgia OnLine was starting to fail. GE had gotten into time-sharing in the mid-1960s, using mainframe computers it built and operating under the name General Electric Information Services (GEIS). GEIS was a fast-growth business and by the 1980s GE had the world's largest data network. It spanned 23 time zones and had presence in 650 cities worldwide.

When Compu-Serv was founded in 1969, the biggest player in the time-sharing business was General Electric. Under the aegis of General Electric Information Services Company (GEISCO or GEIS), GE had 40 percent of the $70 million market. In operation since 1964, the company had its own worldwide communications network and built its own computers, so time-sharing was an outgrowth of something the company was already doing. There was no need to build a communications infrastructure, buy computers, hire programmers, or make deals with data networks.

Like other time-sharing operations, GEIS computers had a low load during off-peak hours in the United States. (GE had two major computing centers— one in Cleveland, the other in the Netherlands.) In 1984, a few GE marketing people decided there ought to be a market for the computing power.

Someone who knew about consumer online services decided Bill Louden was the person to help with the project.

"We have this worldwide network that's used in the daytime, and it's pretty much sitting at night doing nothing," a GE representative told Louden. "And yet we have to manage it and have people staffing it. What do you think you can do?"

He was just the person GE needed, and this was exactly the opportunity Louden wanted. "And so I went to work with them. We had two strategies," Louden recalled. "We could off-sell their bulk network to a CompuServe or a Source, like Tymnet. We could get maybe a buck an hour. Or we could build a service on top of it [the GEIS network] like CompuServe, maybe get five or six bucks per hour. And that's what I did."

Louden's team examined a couple of scenarios to make sure an online service was the best way to go, particularly since going that route meant a far greater investment in time, money, and company resources.

The World's First Online Service

"I founded within GE the first commercial online information service in the world. It quickly caught on. As one fellow said within a few years . . . if you said 'time-sharing' on Wall Street, they'd throw money at you."

So Warner Sinback, head of GE marketing operations, reminisced in an interview in 2004.

Did GE build the world's first commercial online service? History supports the idea. General Electric started manufacturing mainframe computers in 1952, when the company decided that, because it was the country's largest user of computer services, except for the federal government, it could save money by getting into the business. By 1964, GE was one of the eight largest computer manufacturers in the world.

To take advantage of its computer expertise and available hardware, GE decided to set up computer service bureaus at its four computing centers (in Schenectady, New York, Chicago, and Phoenix). The plan was to use computers at each location for batch processing jobs when they weren't being used for demonstrations. The head of computer operations, Louis Rader (formerly of Univac), decided to bring someone in to turn the business around.

Rader selected Warner Sinback, head of marketing operations at General Electric's Defense Systems Unit. Sinback had just returned from overseeing the installation of air weapons control systems in East and West Germany. Sinback was familiar with the early time-sharing experiments at Dartmouth by John Kemeny, who used a computer loaned to the school by GE to develop. He decided that time-sharing had commercial possibilities and took the idea to GE engineers.

By April 1965, the time-sharing software developed at Dartmouth had been adapted to a time-sharing system used within the company. For communications the system used GE's dedicated national telephone network. By the end of the year the General Electric Information Services Company (GEIS) had just about as many customers as it could handle. Over the next few years, GEIS built an international data network in order to offer services outside the United States.

GEnie was built on top of an existing mainframe operating system called General Comprehensive Operating System (GCOS) that Louden characterized as "arcane." Building a menu-driven system over the existing framework was quite a challenge, as was creating an email system out of an antiquated system that, according to Louden "was made for computer nuts."

They managed to camouflage most of the GCOS system with tricks like allowing a user to assign herself an email address that was not the same as her account ID. GEnie account IDs were something like this: XVY61106,xxx, similar to CompuServe's numeric code email addresses. Everyone's email address was also their online "alias," the name displayed to other users in chats, BBS posts, and so forth. The alias, which could be something like MIKEBANKS or BILL, added an extra level of security. Since a would-be hacker couldn't get a member's logon ID without the member volunteering it, there was no way to log on as someone else.

GEnie went live in October 1985, with what had come to be the basic online service offerings; email, a CB simulator called "LiveWire," bulletin boards, and personal computing SIGs ("RoundTables" in the GEnie lexicon). News, weather, and sports were the same as most of the other services offered.

The gaming offerings were basic but that would change fast. Louden had been the driving force behind the development of games at CompuServe, and online multiplayer games would become a major focus at GEnie.

The price? $5 an hour for both 1200- and 2400bps, making GEnie effectively half the cost of CompuServe at the higher speeds (CompuServe added a surcharge for access speeds higher than 300bps).

What's in a Name?

The name "GEnie" wasn't just pulled out of the air—not immediately. Louden's first approach was to pay someone to come up with a name for the service. It was the way things were usually done in corporate America.

"GE initially gave me $60,000 to start the business, and we blew a significant piece of that trying to come up with the name GEnie. It was a big fiasco. Management told me to use BBD Needham, go use the GE advertising people in New York. So we go up there and they said, 'Give us fifty thousand dollars and we'll come up with a name.'

"I gave them my requirements. I said, 'Look, this is a nighttime business, it's a service-based business, we want to have a name that has GE in it somehow. We want to convey something that's magical and technology based.'

"They came back with a list of names, and the best one was 'Albert,' for Albert Einstein."

"I came home literally in tears. I just blew fifty grand of my sixty grand. My wife and I sat down on the bed and started going through the dictionary. 'Let's just start with the Gs,' I said, 'and we'll see what we can come up with. Give me a name with GE in it, like imagine or imagination.'

"And we found the word 'genie' and said, 'Hey, there's the word!' It conveys everything we wanted to convey, but now we had to figure out what the acronym stood for.

"So we had the name GEnie, and we said it stands for the 'General Electric Network for Information Exchange.' I give my wife credit. She was the one who came up with the name. I should have given *her* the fifty grand."

The early GEnie menu looked something like this:

```
GEnie              TOP             Page 1
       GE Information Services

   1. About GEnie... 2. New on GEnie
   3. GE Mail        4. Livewire CB
   5. Computing      6. Travel
   7. Finance        8. Shopping
   9. News          10. Games
  11. Professional  12. Leisure
  13. Reference     14. Logoff


Enter #, <P>revious, or <H>elp

Command? _
```

GEnie would offer all the online basics, and then some. Over the next year the menu items would lead to an increasingly rich variety of products and services.

GEnie had the potential to become serious competition for CompuServe, but Louden was uncertain at first. "My biggest fear was going head-to-head with CompuServe," he confessed. "I'd just left them and knew Forums were their forte, and I said we're not going head-to-head with CompuServe Forums. That would be suicide, at the time. So we tried to go more for personal entertainment products, more for the game products that CompuServe wasn't as focused on after I left. And some products for the small business market.

"But after a year, we discovered that we actually made significant inroads in the RoundTable segment, more than we thought in computing. We didn't think we could get customers to switch, but a lot of customers felt like CompuServe was taking them for granted, a lot of early computer enthusiasts; and so we picked up a lot of those customers.

"We ended up doing about $260,000 by the end of the year," a figure of which Louden was particularly proud, since it came in within 90 days.

"As much as CompuServe was my alma mater," Louden said, "GEnie was my baby."

Other services lost customers to GEnie, but The Source probably lost a smaller percentage of its customers to GEnie than did CompuServe—though it could ill afford to lose any. When GEnie opened, The Source had 40,000 members, and CompuServe 130,000. (They were both left behind by DJNS, which claimed 300,000 users.)

At this point, The Source had improved hardware and some important new features—Chat and SIGs. These put the service on a more competitive footing, and it lost fewer customers than it would have otherwise.

AOL DNA, Part I

Speaking of The Source, it is often painted as the direct ancestor of America Online—AOL. As detailed in Chapter 4, The Source was founded and literally assembled by Bill von Meister—sometimes said to be the "father" of AOL.

However, The Source contributed only a portion of AOL's DNA. It would mutate through *three* forms before emerging as America Online: The Source, Control Video Corporation, and Quantum Computing.

AOL DNA, Part 2: Gameline and Control Video Corporation

William F. von Meister was becoming the Entrepreneur Who Wouldn't Go Away. Having been thwarted in his plan to create the world's first music download service, the Digital Music Company, he took a tip from a Warner Records executive and turned the idea into downloading games to owners of Atari 2600 game consoles. The market was huge: in the United States alone, there were 14 million Atari sets.

Doing what he did best, von Meister lined up $400,000 in venture capital from Kleiner, Perkins, Caufield, and Buyers, and another venture-capital firm, Hambrecht & Quist. Then he started a company called Control Video Corporation (CVC). The name was catchy; it implied the product (video games used controllers), and would seem familiar to some people because a well-known computer company had a similar name: Control Data Corporation (CDC).

CVC's game service was named Gameline. It would be based on a box called the Gameline Master Module, which looked like an oversized game cartridge and plugged right into the Atari 2600's cartridge slot. The Master Module contained a modem and circuitry that enabled it to store a game and transmit joystick and trigger movements back to Gameline's mainframe computer host as commands. It would sell for $59.95.

Von Meister touted Gameline as a way for gamers to play far more games than they might be able to buy, and to test-play games before buying. Naturally, game companies would receive royalties.

The product worked like this: the Gameline subscriber connected a telephone line to the Master Module, dialed up a toll-free number, and logged in. The system then displayed a menu of available games on her television set.

Using the joystick and trigger button, she would select a game to be down-loaded into the Master Module's memory. After a quick download, the modem disconnected and the customer was free to play the game until she turned off the console or downloaded another game. The price: $1 per game.

The system's primary designer was Mark Seriff, the engineer who had designed the first menus for The Source, and who later went to work for von Meister at GTE Telenet when von Meister was trying to convince the company to create an online service. When von Meister left Telenet to set up Digital Music, he hired Seriff to be the technical and operations director. Seriff was there when von Meister set up Gameline.

Even though there was no Gameline product to show, von Meister was getting press for the company, announcing that he had deals with all of the game cartridge producers except Atari and Activision. But those were forth-coming, he promised newspaper reporters.

"Everybody tells me it's a 'can't miss' proposition," he told *The Washington Post* in May 1983. He also explained how he planned to create a community of users to keep people coming back. There would be a *Gameline* magazine. And top local, regional, and national "Gameliners" would see their scores displayed on the logon screen. "The vanity screen," he said, "just like the ones in the arcade games, will be available on Day One."

In the background, Mark Seriff had a team of engineers working on "reverse-engineering" Atari 2600 video games. They needed the source code for the games to download them to Gameline members. But none of the video game companies would give them source code. So they worked from the out-side in, creating programming code that emulated the games.

If things went as planned, Gameline would be about more than playing games. CVC's computers would make it possible for owners of the Master Model to send email, spelling out words by maneuvering the onscreen cursor with the Atari joystick, and pressing the trigger to select letters from an alpha-bet displayed at the top of the TV screen. (If you think that sounds cumber-some, watch the average person texting with two thumbs.)

Several specialized information services were planned as well: Sportsline, Stockline, Bankline, and Newsline. "We're going to turn the videogame jockey into an information junkie," von Meister boasted. And maybe, sometime in the future, he would sell software downloads to home computer users.

It was almost as if he was trying to re-create The Source. But Control Video Corporation—soon to collide with an online service called Playnet—was destined for something bigger.

AOL DNA, Part 3: Playnet

As von Meister was setting up Gameline, two engineers in Troy, New York, were preparing to release a new online service called Playnet.

Howard S. Goldberg and David Panzl had left their positions with General Electric in Schenectady in 1982. With venture capital from Key Venture Corp., the New York State Science and Technology Foundation, and other sources, they founded Playnet, Inc. and moved into a "business incubator" associated with Rensselaer Polytechnic Institute (RPI).

The Rensselaer Business Incubator was a program for helping new high-tech businesses get started. The businesses in the program—13, all told—rented space in an old structure on RPI's campus known as the J Building. All the tenants were high-tech development companies, with names like Applied Robotics and Intermagnetics General Corp. These companies were given access to university resources and faculty, as well as management assistance and help in finding funding.

Panzl and Goldberg spent nearly two years developing special software for Playnet—both for the service itself and for its users' computers (client software). The service would be unique among national online services (as opposed to limited services like Viewtron or other NAPLPS systems) in several ways. First, it had graphics and color. The graphics were possible in part because much of what the user saw didn't have to be transmitted from the Playnet computer. Oft-used templates and a number of graphic elements were loaded from the disks and could be combined in myriad patterns. Games and other programs were also on the user's disk.

Without these elements on the user's system, graphics would have taken impossibly long to transmit with the 300- and 1200bps modems then in use.

Another extraordinary element had to do with updates. If this or that element of Playnet was changed, the disks would be updated while the member was online. It was a brilliant concept that would eventually play a role in all commercial online services. (Playnet's direct descendent, AOL, continues to do this today.)

Playnet distributed the software on three floppy disks. There was no other way to use Playnet because it employed unconventional protocols, even though it was accessed through Telenet or Tymnet.

Developing Playnet required so much time and effort that it was limited to one brand of computer. (Versions for IBM, Apple, and so forth were planned.) The Commodore was chosen to take advantage of its graphics capabilities. The fact that Commodore had an installed base of 3 million owners also played a role. And lots of Commodore owners owned Commodore-built modems (the VICmodem). According to company sources, Commodore sold more modems than any other company in 1982 and 1983.

Playnet opened regionally in April 1984. It offered email, bulletin boards and—most popular of all—chat and instant messages. Single- and multiplayer games (checkers, poker, bridge, Sea Strike, and others) were also available, and users could chat while playing. A specialized shopping service was planned but didn't get off the ground.

> ## Marketing Tokens
>
> Signup fees were largely marketing tokens, to be waived or discounted during special promotions or to provide business partners with a value-added element in exchange for the partners' promotion of the service. Most online services eventually dropped signup fees, except for The Source and Playnet. The need to continue charging signup fees was probably a result of poor cash-flow or undercapitalization.

The service went national in October, with a strategy of leaving business applications for other services and emphasizing the social element. Initially there was a signup fee of $49.95 (soon lowered to $29.95), but the three disks that came with signup made the fee sting less—psychologically, it made the user feel like he was getting more for his money. After that, there was a $6 monthly maintenance fee, and $2 per hour of usage. Compared with other services, Playnet was a bargain.

Commodore of course thought Playnet was a grand idea, too. While it didn't invest in the company, it bundled Playnet software and a free membership with its modems, alongside membership offers from CompuServe, Dow Jones News/Retrieval Service, and The Source.

One might have expected Commodore to make Playnet Commodore's official online service. But Commodore already had a very profitable deal with CompuServe, under which a CompuServe Forum served as the official Commodore Information Network. As with other Forums, Commodore received a percentage of connect-time revenue associated with the Commodore Information Network.

Still, Playnet flourished. In less than a year, several thousand Commodore computer owners had joined and were cavorting in their own private online world, chatting, gaming, downloading, and making friends.

The First Online Wedding

If you search the Web, you'll find all sorts of claims about the first online wedding. Some claim it took place on Prodigy in the 1980s. Others say AOL in the 1990s.

The first online wedding was held on CompuServe on February 14, 1983. The couple were George Stickles and Debbie Fuhrman. They met via CompuServe's CB Simulator, and decided it would be fun to get married in the same venue.

The service was conventional and the logistics were fairly simple. A minister and the couple sat at different computers in the same room in Texas. All three were logged into a CB channel, along with more than 100 other CompuServe members. The minister spoke aloud while an assistant typed in his words. Stickles and Fuhrman spoke and then repeated their vows by typing them out.

If you're broad-minded in your definition of "online," you'll be interested to know that the first long-distance, electrically enhanced wedding ceremony was held in 1876—by telegraph. (See *The Victorian Internet* by Thomas Standage [Walker & Company, 2007].)

AOL Gestation

. . . the least quotable human at the company.

—*Washington Post* reporter Michael Schrage on Steve Case

To announce Gameline to the trade, Bill von Meister headed for the Consumer Electronics Show (CES) in Las Vegas in January 1983. Unconventional as always, he didn't rent a booth in the show at the convention center. Instead, he got a suite in the Tropicana Hotel, set up demos, and hired showgirls to entertain prospective buyers and the press.

CVC also held a drawing for a one-ounce bar of gold; all you had to do was register at the suite. To make sure people knew something big was happening, von Meister spent $5,000 on a huge hot-air balloon that was shaped like a joystick and had "GAMELINE" in big letters down the sides. It was tethered above the Tropicana's entrance.

The promotion was a huge success. Lured by advertising, press releases, posters, and word of mouth, hundreds of buyers came to catch the demos, flirt with the showgirls, and enjoy free food and drink. Someone went home with a bar of gold and CVC took orders for more than 100,000 Gameline Master Module units. (Von Meister would later tell the press that CVC had sold 400,000 units.)

A young marketing man employed by Pizza Hut named Steve Case was among the crowd who came to the Tropicana to see what Gameline had to offer. Case wasn't there on Pizza Hut's behalf; he was invited by his older brother, Dan Case III, an investment banker with Hambrecht & Quist, which had put $2 million into Gameline and was looking to invest more.

Dan Case introduced Steve to "the guys" of CVC. The story is often told that Steve Case and Bill von Meister immediately bonded over a shared vision, and von Meister begged Dan Case to let them hire his little brother. This is not what happened. After the CES ended, everybody went home and no one at CVC gave any more thought to Steve Case—not until, that is, Dan Case telephoned and asked Gameline to hire his little brother.

The company hired him. They had little choice in the matter, considering all the money Case's company had put into Gameline, with the prospect of millions more.

Steve Case didn't come across as a strong candidate to help turn around a company in trouble. Quiet and standoffish, his work experience consisted of two low-profile marketing jobs after he graduated from Williams College, and he had been rejected by more than one MBA program.

His first job after college was with consumer giant Procter & Gamble. He had applied for a marketing position and was turned down after the interview. Perhaps thinking that persistence would show P&G he had mettle, Case bugged the company and was granted a second interview. He traveled to Cincinnati at his own expense and this time was hired to work as an assistant brand manager with a group developing new products.

One of his group's products was a novel approach to applying hair conditioner—a towelette called Abound. It flopped, and after two years at P&G Case moved on to PepsiCo's Pizza Hut division. There he spent most of his time researching the offerings of pizzerias large and small, in search of new toppings and other potential product variations for Pizza Hut.

Case knew little about computers beyond a college course, which he'd hated, but he was an early member of The Source and was excited about the potential for online communication and marketing.

His experience with The Source and his knowledge of P&G marketing methodologies were his major assets. Case went to work for CVC as a marketing consultant with a limited term contract at 20 bucks an hour.

One of the young consultant's first tasks at CVC was to write up a careful analysis of the company's product development and marketing—most of which agreed with von Meister's vision. He recommended strategies such as taking advantage of being first to market to lock up the category, and selling Gameline as the base of an entire home information system—which is exactly what von Meister had in his sights.

Steve Case did not lack for intelligence, but he was not a forceful personality, and therefore not regarded as a "player" in the business world. He tended to observe, evaluate, and store things away for later action or expostulation. Many thought of him as "bland." *Washington Post* reporter Michael Schrage, who covered CVC, once described Case as "the least quotable human at the company."[1]

---

[1] *Schrage ended up as a columnist for one of the magazines owned by AOL Time-Warner when Case was its president.*

As Gameline's "live" date approached, the company had burned through a significant amount of money, nearly $20 million. There were software and hardware development costs, the host system, and Master Module manufacture and packaging costs. Then there were announcements and advertisements in consumer magazines, salaries, communications, office space, and dozens of other expense items that dog any new business. Lots of spending, and nothing coming in.

At this point, Frank Caufield stepped in. He was a partner in Kleiner, Perkins, Caufield, & Byers, a company that had put at least $400,000 into Gameline. The West Point graduate sat on Gameline's board and decided that CVC's spending might be a little out of control. And he knew that von Meister's gosh-wow ideas had a history of flopping or getting into financial trouble.

Caufield asked friend and fellow West Pointer James Kimsey to come on board as a consultant. Having recently sold one of his businesses, Kimsey was relatively free, and James Caufield felt that Kimsey was just the guy to get things squared away at CVC, and that he would find the business interesting.

Kimsey's experience was, to say the least, varied. He graduated from Georgetown and West Point with honors, and as an Army Airborne Ranger attained the rank of major. Following combat tours in the Dominican Republic and Vietnam (twice), he wrapped up his Army career and found himself at loose ends in Washington, D.C. Almost on a whim, he took out a loan to buy an office building on M Street NW. He rented the top floor to a brokerage whose partners were working on opening an upscale bar on the first floor.

The would-be barkeepers ran out of money, and Kimsey took over the establishment, which he opened as "The Exchange" several months later. (The themed lounge featured a stock tickertape and matching decor.) It was an unqualified success, and Kimsey followed it with a second pub, a restaurant chain, real estate operations, and other ventures (which included founding and supporting an orphanage in Vietnam).

Kimsey's initial role at CVC was that of manufacturing consultant. Caufield had sent him in to find out why this group was going through so much money with no profit. Kimsey's real job was to babysit von Meister.

Shortly after Kimsey joined CVC (in May 1983), Atari issued a press release announcing it had lost a *billion* dollars during the first quarter of 1983—which gave it the distinction of being the first business ever to lose so much money in so short a time. This was an ill omen for CVC, as Gameline depended entirely on Atari's popularity and sales.

Atari had owned as much as 80 percent of the videogame business nation-wide, but in 1982 sales were beginning a nosedive that couldn't be reversed. The system was then several years old, and the development of a new generation of Atari's game console had been diverted into the Atari 400 personal computer. Hence, new gaming consoles were eroding sales of the now old-style Atari 2600. With adapters that could play Atari cartridges on their machines, the competing companies were also tearing into Atari's cartridge sales.

In addition, competitors were making cartridges for use with the Atari 2600, which likewise cut into the sales of Atari's cartridges—on which it was counting for profits after deep-discounting the 2600 to compete with the glamorous new game consoles.

Finally, top game programmers and designers found working conditions under the management of Warner Communications insulting at best. Most of them left for other jobs. In the end, Atari was selling outdated, low-quality products in a market that constantly demanded something *new*.

It was too late for CVC to turn back. Gameline had a host mainframe with fully operating software, and its own proprietary network. The product was announced and advertising was in place. Gameline Master Modules had started shipping to retailers. Within weeks, people would be signing up. There was really nothing to do but go through with the product launch. If nothing else, a miracle might happen; it just might catch on.

Gameline went live in July 1983. Months later, it had shipped 16,000 Master Module units, but had only 1,500 customers. Tens of thousand of Master Modules were still with CVC. It turned out that all those orders from the CES weren't really orders until the buyers gave Gameline the go-ahead to ship. And the company was still working on getting licenses for many of the videogames on the market.

Kimsey took on more and more responsibility—and a stake in the company—during this period. From consultant, he went on to become head of manufacturing. Kimsey brought in another West Point friend, Brad Johnson, to take over manufacturing while he became operations director.

Kimsey and von Meister also hired Steve Case full-time, as a marketing assistant.

By the end of the year, Gameline had 3,000 customers, but—as CVC's staff said more than once—they were burning money, and they had little to show for it. As reported in a board meeting early in 1985, Gameline's direct product proceeds totaled $25,000. The sale of the joystick hot-air balloon from the CES had netted another $15,000 (three times what von Meister had paid for it). This was the full extent of Gameline's income. Caufield remarked, "You'd have thought they'd shoplifted more than that!" Kimsey expressed the opinion that the company would have sold more units by offering them out of the back of a truck on US 1.

Eventually, a total of 40,000 Gameline Master Modules were shipped to retailers; 37,000 were returned. Another 20,000 to 30,000 units never left

Gameline's headquarters. The module manufacturer wasn't paid in full; nor were more than 100 other creditors. The company's debt—beyond the $20 million already spent—was around $10 million.

The members of CVC's board were anything but happy. Von Meister and Mark Seriff still had ideas about turning failure into triumph. Seriff's modem could be adapted to personal computers. Information and software could be sold through a computer network. It was just a matter of leaping past the game idea and going directly to von Meister's eventual goal, Mainline.

They approached BellSouth,[2] and made it to the planning stages—despite Case almost short-circuiting the deal by annoying the BellSouth contact with his withdrawn personality. The new online service was not to be; Judge Harold H. Greene (who had presided over the breakup of AT&T) issued an order that Bell telephone operating companies could not be involved in originating online information.

Suddenly CVC had no product. The fallout was a company with a handful of employees. Kimsey fired everybody with a higher salary than that of Case. Von Meister was relegated to the role of figurehead, while the board informally elevated Kimsey to president of CVC. Mark Seriff (who had years before designed The Source's menus for von Meister) remained in place as the technical chief. Kimsey soon promoted Case to vice president of marketing. He felt it worthwhile to mentor Case, as he saw a potential in the younger man that others missed.

Kimsey struggled to keep the company alive, at least on paper. There wasn't much chance that anything could be done with CVC, but Kimsey was motivated by more than a desire to save the business. About the time he joined CVC, he was involved in starting a bank holding company. A form he had to complete for the Securities & Exchange Commission included among its questions whether he had ever been part of a bankruptcy. He realized that, if CVC went bankrupt, he might be knocked out of participating in federally regulated activities. That decided it: he would do whatever he could to keep CVC out of bankruptcy.

With the idea of an online personal computer service clear in his mind, Kimsey began looking for another company with whom CVC could partner, as they had planned to do with BellSouth.

Failing that, perhaps he could find a buyer for Control Video. While it didn't have a product, it had a potential product: an online service. The real online services were no longer experiments. Successful examples—CompuServe and DJNS and others—were out there for anyone to see. They had proven the concept. (In the meantime, what was left of the Videotex experiments, like Viewtron, was fading away.)

---

[2] *BellSouth went on to go online with Transtext Universal Gateway (TUG) in 1988. TUG served as a gateway to services such as DJNS and Eaasy Sabre.*

Kimsey first approached Apple Computer, to no avail. It was not a good time, in terms of the feud between John Sculley and Steve Jobs. Besides, Apple was already planning its own internal network for the company and its dealers, to be called AppleLink.[3]

Almost incidental to everything else, von Meister was edged out of CVC just before a creditors' meeting early in 1985.[4] It was more a matter of him giving up than being asked to leave directly, but more than one CVC veteran voiced the belief that certain investors had been trying to get rid of him since they started putting representatives in the company (Case, Kimsey, and Brad Johnson).

Despite intense pressure from creditors, Kimsey warded off being forced into bankruptcy (largely by threatening to go into bankruptcy and leaving creditors with next to nothing, odd as that may seem to some). But for all practical purposes it was closed down. He retired CVC's records to a shoebox at the back of a desk drawer. But it was not gone for good; in May 1985, CVC would reemerge as "Quantum Computing."

~

While CVC drifted toward a dormant state in 1984, Playnet moved into the Rensselaer Technology Park, just outside Albany, New York. Commodore was booming, and anything to do with Commodore seemed destined for success. Commodore owners were fiercely proud of their brand (just as fiercely proud as Macintosh, Atari, and Apple owners), and welcomed an online service dedicated to their computer.

The number of members rose to nearly 3,000 in 1984, which was Playnet's first calendar year of business. Without the competition from the official Commodore Forum on Commodore, and the lure of the new GEnie service, Playnet might have drawn ten times that. But such was not to be. The year 1985 saw a sharp drop in users, as well as the amount of time those who remained members spent online.

It happened that, at this point, Commodore Computing executive Clive Smith was looking for a company to host an official online service for Commodore. (Founder Jack Tramiel had left by this time.) The company felt that it would make more money and serve its owners better with its own service, as opposed to running the Official Commodore Forum on CompuServe.

Playnet was almost the ideal candidate. The service took full advantage of the Commodore computer's sound, color, and graphics capabilities. And

---

[3] *Interestingly, Apple's network would be hosted on GEIS computers and use the GEIS network.*

[4] *The story goes that von Meister drove or had delivered an expensive BMW to CVC headquarters on the day of a meeting with creditors—to whom Kimsey hoped to demonstrate fiscal responsibility. Astounded, Kimsey told him to go home. Von Meister never came back.*

working with Commodore would be a boon for Playnet; Commodore's high profile and marketing presence would assure thousands of new members.

The only problem was Playnet's instability as a business. Commodore was skeptical of putting such a big project in the company's hands. Playnet didn't have stable backing. (The situation was similar to that of Telenet and General Motors, detailed in Chapter 3—except that Telenet was a healthy business.)

~

Having been waved off by Apple, Kimsey next went to Commodore. He offered to sell Quantum Computing to Clive Smith, but instead Smith made a deal with Kimsey to provide the hardware host, software, and content for Commodore's planned online service.

There was one important stipulation: Smith required that the software be based on Playnet. In a complicated deal, Kimsey licensed Playnet's software, apparently for an initial payment of $50,000, with royalties down the line.

Playnet itself remained in business as a Commodore-only service. The competition was too great and resources too low to consider developing and marketing IBM and other versions of the service. Playnet filed for bankruptcy protection in March 1986, and stayed in business until late 1988, when Quantum stopped paying royalties. When the service closed for good, it was operating at a loss with 1,329 subscribers. That Playnet remained in operation so long is a monument to the enthusiasm of those few members and to David Panzl's technical skills and tenacity.

Even though it went down in flames, Playnet was truly a trailblazer. In addition to its then-stunning graphics, the service pioneered multiplayer games. At the time of its closing, Playnet programmers were working on Poker and a Dungeons & Dragons game similar to *Neverwinter Nights*, AOL's first graphical MMORPG (massively multiplayer online role-playing game).

For a brilliant product that was the literal foundation of the world's largest online service, Playnet's end was a sad one.

The Third Wave

*. . . like a New York cockroach, Control Video simply couldn't be
killed off.*

—Michael Schrage in *The Washington Post*

During the period when CVC and Playnet (the companies that would become
AOL) rose and fell, several new consumer online services showed up. Their
themes and sources were varied.

American People/Link (Plink)

GEnie would not be the only direct competitor for CompuServe. In 1983, two
CompuServe Forum sysops left to build an online service dubbed American
People/Link, better-known to its members as "Plink."[1]

   Located in Chicago, Plink was an engaging service that targeted a young
demographic and presented itself as more of a "social" service than
CompuServe. The founders wanted to make it clear that Plink was not for
"techies" only, a reputation that plagued CompuServe for years, even though
CIS was dedicated to any and all interests.

   Chat (called "PartyLine") was heavily promoted, as were Plink "Clubs,"
which were Plink's version of CompuServe's Forums. Plink's emphasis was not
on computing, but on hobbies and other personal interests, though computing
was not ignored completely in Plink's collection of clubs. There was, for example, a Commodore Business Machines Club, as well as clubs for IBM and
Macintosh. But overall, Plink was more likely to advertise the possibilities for
online romance than the number of programs in its club databases.

---

[1] *An alternate story claims that American People/Link was started by two CIS members who were so
discouraged by their huge CompuServe bills that they decided to start their own service.*

Plink's menus were not unlike CompuServe's:

```
PEOPLE/LINK Main Menu

    1    Party/Line                        /PARTY
    2    Clubs and Forums         /CLUBS
    3    Online Shops               /SHOPS
    4    Mail                                  /MAIL
    5    Tavel                             /TRAV
    6    User Directory              /UD
    7    Bulletin Boards             /BB
    8    Information                   /GO 411
    9    News and Publications    /GO NEWS

Enter command or HELP
MAIN MENU>
```

From the beginning, the service offered "slash commands" (also known as command characters) for direct navigation to any page on the service, as did DELPHI.[2] Each of those services also required that a command character be used in chat rooms. The same was true of CompuServe's CB Simulator. So, those who had used the CB Simulator (which required that commands in a chat room be preceded by a hyphen, -) would feel at home in a Plink chat room.

Having to preface a command with a special character was fraught with danger, especially if you were trying to send a private IM to another member. If you mistyped and left out the command characters—or if you put another character in front of the command character (which line noise sometimes did for you), the entire chat room could see your "private" message. It could be very embarrassing!

Plink offered rates two dollars an hour less than CompuServe, which included packet-switched network (PSN) access. This gave the service a big boost from the beginning. Interestingly, the majority of Plinkers (what Plink members called themselves) had experience with other online services, and many had memberships with CompuServe, DELPHI, or other services.

---

[2] *The slash (/) preceding a command was made necessary by the operating system of Plink's host. On some online services you didn't have to type anything for a command. For example, on CompuServe,* **GO MAIL** *would get you there. The / told the system that what followed was a command. This was used extensively within chat systems on various services, too, to enable users to check mail, carry on side conversations with individuals, and so forth.*

VCO: Adding Another Dimension to Chat

Just about everyone online today is acquainted with emoticons, those sideways representations of faces created with keyboard characters. :-) is a smile, :-(a sad face, and so on. No one can say for certain where and when these began, though many have tried to claim their invention. It's most likely that the idea was developed spontaneously by a number of different individuals in the early 1980s. Considering the fact that people were using typewriter characters to create "graphics" as far back as the 1940s, emoticons may well predate the online world.

A few people tried to popularize vertical emoticons based on some different keyboard characters, but the basic approach of using characters like : -) { prevailed. There are dozens of possible "faces" to be made with these and a few other characters. Google "emoticons" and you'll find plenty of examples.

A different approach to putting faces to words was undertaken by a couple of pioneering programmers in 1985, when they created two programs called VCO (for Voice COnferencing) that enabled users to create graphical representations of their own faces and share them with others in a chat room. VCO was available in a Macintosh version, written by Harry Chesley,[3] and a PC version, by Richard L. McGinnis.

VCO operated as a front end[4] to chats on CompuServe, GEnie, People/Link, The WELL, and DELPHI. It provided a graphics program with which the user could create a graphic image that seemed reasonably representative of his or her face. Several versions were created, each representing a different emotion. The graphics were stored as GIF files, and all the VCO user had to do was upload or email the images to other VCO users.

In a chat room with other VCO users, the program would map each user's ID with the graphics she or he created, and expressions as the speaker directed. It also offered a voice-messaging mode. Everything was accomplished by transmitting coded instructions through the chat room to other chatters' copies of VCO. As with Playnet and Business*Talk and their descendents, almost all the action was on the users' disks.

VCO was a very clever approach to bringing just a taste of reality to the early online world. Chesley later created a version of VCO for Internet chat rooms, called V-Chat. Microsoft also explored this realm with Microsoft Chat and an "authored social environment" called Lead Line.

---

[3] *Harry Chesley was also lead developer for Macromedia's Flash.*

[4] *A front end is a program that enhances and simplifies another, more complex program. See Chapter 12 for other examples of and more information about front ends.*

BIX (Byte Information eXchange)

In 1984, *BYTE* magazine decided to open an online service primarily for its readers, and for those who shared its readers' interests—leading-edge personal computing technology and applications, programming, and related topics such as home networks.

It was almost required that BIX use a Unix-based system, a techie favorite. Though BIX began development with another system, when it went into beta late in 1984 BIX was based on the CoSy conferencing system ("conferencing" in this case meaning a bulletin board–like system) with elaborate features.[5] This was the same software that *BYTE*'s publisher, McGraw-Hill, used internally. It was also implemented on an English system called CIX (Compulink Information eXchange) and one in Japan named MIX (Multi-user Information eXchange). Initially set up on an Arete multiprocessor system, BIX ran on a Pyramid minicomputer for most of its early life. In its final few years, it was moved to a DEC server.

BIX was initially very straightforward. Rather than try to be every kind of online service for everyone, BIX focused on communication between *BYTE* and its readers, with various hardware and software vendors, and among BIX members (who referred to themselves collectively as "BIXen").

Like PARTI (see Chapter 4), CoSy conferencing offered conversation threads, tracking, endless categorization into topics and subtopics, and more features than many BIXen could use. There was also an email program. But it would be several years before BIX added other features.

BIX was famous for the online activities of its columnists (including Jerry Pournelle and Hugh Kenner, among others) and staff. And it soon went beyond technical topics, to include relationships, the arts (writing, in particular, with conference topics hosting Rick Cook, Mike Banks, and G. Harry Stine), space exploration, women's conferences, current events, and just about everything else.

Access was via the usual PSNs (packet-switching networks) and was basically a command-driven system, appropriately for *BYTE*. Costs were compatible with CompuServe and The Source, and it would eventually add a file exchange and a chat system.

---

[5] *CoSy was developed by a team headed by Alistair J.W. Mayer at the University of Guelph. The name CoSy is based on "collaboration system," "conferencing system," and other appropriate two-word phrases. Many viewed it as a vast improvement over Usenet.*

USA Today Sports Center

Probably the first online service dedicated to a single subject, USA Today Sports Center went live in 1985. It was produced by LINC Networks, in cooperation with *USA Today*, and was located in Washington, D.C.

Accessible via direct-dial or PSNs, the service offered everything the sports nut—any kind of sports nut—could want: box scores, team and player stats, and schedules for professional, minor-league, and college baseball, soccer, golf, football, hockey, and basketball games. Reports on sporting events sometimes ignored by other media, such as chess and target shooting, were also included.

As with newscasts and game broadcasts on today's cable and broadcast TV channels, this 1985 service offered a ticker at the bottom of the member's computer monitor that reported the latest scores and news from recently completed and ongoing games. This was unique to online services at the time.

To get the ticker, you had to use the service's special software, called SportsWare. This *front-end software*[6] was available for IBM, Macintosh, and Commodore from the beginning. USA Today wasn't an elaborate, dedicated system like Playnet, and didn't require the use of SportsWare. What SportsWare did was provide color frames and make use of certain graphical elements unique to each brand of computer. And it made the sports ticker possible.

The WELL

The WELL (an acronym for Whole Earth 'Lectronic Link) began life in 1985 as a bulletin board system based on a DEC VAX minicomputer, in Sausalito, California. Its founders referred to it as a "conferencing" system, using the term in its older application, but it was a bulletin board system and not a chat service (see Chapter 6 for a more detailed explanation of the distinction in usages). It also offered email.

The WELL, co-founded by Stewart Brand and Larry Brilliant, is one of the few early services still in existence today, having made the successful transition to Internet service provider (ISP). The name alludes to Brand's famous

---

[6] *The functions of front-end programs for online services were to make the service easier to use—often providing a unified series of menus and shortcuts—and to give the online service in question a different appearance, providing color where the online service was not in color. Front ends also automated tasks such as sending and receiving email, and allowed users to do much of their online activities offline, thus saving money at time when online services charged by the hour. Front ends were made for specific kinds of computers by CompuServe, GEnie, DELPHI, BIX, Dialog, MCI Mail, The Source, and even Prodigy. In essence, Playnet's software and later that of Q-Link, AOL, and related services, were all front ends, the differences in the services being that with these services you had to use the front-end software.*

earlier project, *The Whole Earth Catalog*. The WELL charged a reasonable rate—$3 per hour—and by 1988 it would grow to 3,000 members and purchase a Sequent Unix-based computer to replace the VAX (financed largely by member contributions). In the mid-1990s, The WELL expanded to become an ISP.

The WELL was regarded as a counter- or alternative-cultural meeting place, and many have made claims for it being first virtual community. However, virtual communities existed as long as five years before The WELL's founding. Scores of virtual communities sprang up on CompuServe and other online services, and especially on BBSs around the world. Some of these were mainstream, and some were counter-cultural. (On the online services, virtual communities sprouted in special-interest groups, while a virtual community would take over an entire BBS.)

One thing The WELL did that was unique to its community was serve as an nonthreatening introduction to the online world for many people who might not have been drawn to telecommunications so soon, if ever. The nature of pre-Web online services and BBSs was such that the only way you could understand the online world was to try it out. Many early WELL members hesitated because getting online involved technology. The cultural essence of a service like The WELL enabled many "newbies" to see beyond the technology to the benefits to be had.

Another element that made The WELL stand out and get noticed by both the alternative and mainstream press was the sorts of people it attracted, in part by association with Brand's "Whole Earth" projects, and in part by providing free memberships. These were given to a good number of journalists of repute, who tended to spread the idea of The WELL around public media. The presence of a few celebrities helped, and The WELL was also known as a meeting place for Grateful Dead fans, and a conference (again, in this usage, a bulletin board topic) is dedicated to them.

Its conference (BBS) topics include hobbies, spirituality, music, politics, and dozens more, as well as personal conferences controlled by individuals or groups and accessible only by certain members. Each conference topic was facilitated by one or more people whose job was to moderate conversations and enforce the few rules The WELL imposes.

The WELL would eventually add IM and chat capabilities, along with access via CompuServe's network (with a surcharge).

Quantum Link (Q-Link)

CVC came out of the shoebox as Quantum Computer Services on May 25, 1985. Like von Meister's TDX, the words in the company name had no special meaning (aside from "computing"), but it sounded good.

With just the beginnings of a product—the deal with Commodore for an online service—Quantum Computer Services received a new round of financing in June 1985. *The Washington Post* noted the deal and commented, ". . . like a New York cockroach, Control Video simply couldn't be killed off."

This was a critical time for Commodore as well as for Quantum. Commodore's sales were on the wane as potential customers waited for the long-promised Commodore Amiga, while other computer manufacturers grabbed large pieces of the market.

After an unsuccessful run at producing software for the Commodore service, Quantum made the deal with Playnet. Mark Seriff and his programmers worked with Playnet's PL/1 code throughout the summer, and developed customized floppy disk software for Commodore to bundle with its $39.95 modem. The new service would be hosted on Stratus minicomputers, the same kind of computer system that hosted Playnet.

Quantum was down to 10 employees after Kimsey—now CEO—fired everyone who made more money than Steve Case. As the effort to build the Commodore service ramped up, Quantum hired 15 new employees, most of them destined for customer service positions. The company could have used several more people, but Kimsey wasn't going to spend any more than he had to.

With everyone pulling together and no doubt a lot of late-night work, it took less than six months to get Q-Link up and running. At 6:00 PM on Friday, November 1, 1985, Q-Link went live from Quantum's second-rate business park headquarters in Vienna, Virginia. The system had been in beta test for some time, and people began logging on immediately. Soon there were more than just the usual beta-testers. At one point, nearly 100 users were signed on.

Members could avail themselves of all the important features offered by other online services: email, games, bulletin boards, file downloads, shopping, IMs, chat, news, special-interest areas, and gaming. Q-Link's games included solo and multiplayer games like hangman, backgammon, bingo, and poker; slot machines; blackjack; and other casino-type diversions in an area called "RabbitJack's Casino." Rabbitjack's featured animated graphics and multiple players.

Quantum looked a lot like Playnet, offering a graphic menu that had the same look and feel as most other Commodore applications. Instead of a text menu, a three-by-three block of boxes met the user at logon, each carrying text that explained what you were selecting by pressing the button: Commodore Software Showcase, People Connection (gateway to chat rooms), Commodore Information Network (Commodore's online presence), Just for Fun, Quantum Link, Learning Center, Customer Service Center, The Mall, and News & Information. Each box was a different color, and some minor animation spiced up the menu. To navigate a menu, members used Tab or arrow keys and pressed Enter to select the menu item. There were also keyboard commands for certain selections and actions.

The First Virtual Reality GUI

By the time Q-Link came along, there had been several attempts to create a more realistic online experience. Typing and reading, even enhanced by emoticons or nonmoving computer graphics, wasn't quite enough. Some computers could record voice, and brief messages could be exchanged that way. And after the GIF breakthrough, people could exchange photos, but that was about the limit. These were the same tools people had used in postal correspondence for years. The only real advantage over postal mail that online chat brought to communication was its immediacy. VCO was as advanced as it got—until Q-Link put the virtual world of *Club Caribe* online.

Created by Lucasfilm Games, *Club Caribe* was originally called *Habitat*, but it was renamed before it went live. Q-Link members created avatars[7] in what were then high-resolution graphics. Once a member completed her avatar, she could take it into an imaginary graphic world and interact with other Q-Link members' avatars.

The background for *Club Caribe* was a Caribbean island resort in a virtual world. A member's avatar could not only chat with other avatars, but also pick up and manipulate objects. All of the action was faithfully reproduced in the onscreen graphics environment.

After Q-Link was taken down, *Club Caribe* was sold to Fujitsu, which turned it into an online playground/game called *Worlds Away*.

Behind the screens a good deal of Playnet architecture was retained. The client software (on the members' computers) was a multitasking environment like Playnet. And as with Playnet, Q-Link members were restricted to a 10-character name to make it possible to fit four names to a Commodore 40-column line. (This carried over to AOL until the late 1990s.) Games were programmed in BASIC and assembler.

Members used packet-switching networks for access at 300- to 1200bps, and the service was online only after 6:00 PM weekdays, and all day on weekends. The schedule was a luxury for the technical support people, because they could work on the system eight hours a day if they needed to.

When it opened, Q-Link charged $9.95 per month, plus 6 cents per minute for what were called "plus" areas and services. These included games, mail, chat, and most other popular services. The per-minute rate increased to 8 cents as soon as Quantum determined that users would stick around after a rate increase.

---

[7] *The word "avatar" has several possible meanings, but as used in the online world an avatar is a visual representation of a computer user. An avatar may be a crude drawing or a highly detailed graphic image.*

A couple of months later, in January 1986, Q-Link had a bit over 10,000 members. It could handle only 247 connections simultaneously, a problem that was being worked on. Both Quantum and Commodore were disappointed. They had expected the huge installed base of Commodore 64 and 128[8] owners to gravitate to the service in larger numbers, especially because Commodore endorsed Q-Link and maintained a presence on the service.

In truth, this was not a bad beginning. So it was decided that Q-Link would stay in business and develop more features. Money was tight. Kimsey made a pitch to Alan Patricof for Quantum financing. Patricof put up $750,000, enough to keep Q-Link going and growing for a few more months.

Kimsey promoted Steve Case to vice president of marketing. By December 1986, Q-Link had 55 employees, and nearly 50,000 members. Despite this rapid growth, or perhaps because of it, money was still tight.

For now, Q-Link would remain a Commodore-only service, but forward-looking minds at Quantum were already considering how they could work the same deal with another manufacturer. Catering to just one brand of computer was putting all the eggs in one unsteady basket.

~

The new competitors were optimistic. With the exception of The WELL and possibly BIX, each dreamed of having tens of thousands of members like CompuServe or The Source. And each had its own idea of the image it should present to the world.

The Source had something over 60,000 members, but the Reader's Digest Association was beginning to think twice about this business. The growth wasn't as fast as it had anticipated, and it was proving difficult to translate print products into online products.

The Source's advertising seemed to present a bland face to the world. Perhaps this was because it had tried to define itself as a serious, business-oriented online service, without the hullabaloo of SIGs and chat. The service had also worked hard to divest itself of a reputation as an online meeting spot for singles looking for sex, the unfortunate result of several somewhat sensationalistic magazine and newspaper stories a few years earlier. Growth was slow, but The Source got the staid reputation it wanted. (Interestingly, Q-Link was beginning to get the same reputation for sex. Members could name chat rooms, and there were always names like M4F, SWF, or just SEX.)

CompuServe was still the leader. The technical staff constantly worked on increasing system efficiency and reliability, and developing new products. The Electronic Mall was rolled out, and major brand names took out virtual space in it. Marketing shifted heavily to bundling membership offers with software

---

[8] *Commodore's new 128 could be run in emulation of the Commodore 64.*

and hardware manufacturers, while retail promotions (as with Radio Shack) were cut back. General-interest magazines were included in advertising, and the service experimented successfully with placing subscription kits in bookstores. Weekly and monthly billing processes were revamped. Parts of the service—all first- and second-level menus in particular—were redesigned. User manuals were rewritten. A new graphics standard (GIF) was created, with versions for all types of personal computers. New file transfer protocols were developed. More nodes were added to the CompuServe network. The first CompuServe television commercials were aired on cable television. Financial products were cleaned up to create a more professional look. All of these things, and more, were accomplished between 1984 and 1988.

Several years earlier, the company's management decided that CompuServe needed a more professional image. Perhaps they wanted to pull in some of that group that The Source's staid image attracted. Certainly, CompuServe didn't want to be regarded as just for computer geeks. Nor did it want people to think you had to be a computer whiz to use it. Some of the redesign and a lot of the marketing were directed toward these issues.

Intersystem Email

With all the new services popping up, many people maintained accounts on a second or even a third online service, just to keep in touch with friends, family, or business associates who didn't use the same "home" service. Recognizing the need for intersystem email delivery, in 1987 a company named DASnet[9] started a service that carried email between online services.

The logistics involved were straightforward. DASnet maintained accounts on all the online services it served. DASnet subscribers who wanted to send an email message from, for example, DELPHI, to an MCI Mail user addressed the message to DASnet on the local system (on DELPHI, DASnet's address was DASnet). In the subject header, the sender entered the system (MCI MAIL) and the recipient's address on that service. DASnet's computer checked email addressed to it several times daily, and sorted out the messages to be resent to other systems, readdressed them, and logged onto the other services and sent them.

The cost to send a message depended on the addressee's service and the size of a message. Most messages sent within the United States could be transmitted for a fee of 59 cents, while a Telex to England cost $5, and a Telemail message to Japan cost $2.18. The service became outdated as online services began offering Internet email.

---

[9] *The name was formed from the company name,* DA Systems, *and* net.

CompuServe's strategy of continuously improving and refining the quality of both technical and nontechnical elements of the service worked. It also worked on advanced projects, like object-oriented protocol for gaming, and graphics—for several years, CompuServe engineers and product designers had known that graphics were the next big step in online gaming.

CompuServe also took careful note of the new competition, especially GEnie (which a CompuServe employee called a "CompuServe clone" in an internal report), Q-Link, and People/Link.

Trin-what?

Even before GEnie went online, there had been rumors about Sears, IBM, and CBS putting together an online service for consumers. Few believed it. On May 11, 1984, those who followed business news were informed that the trio had chosen a name for the "broadly based Videotex service that can be used by people with home and personal computers." The name would be "Trintex."

Trintex. It sounded a new window cleaner. Break the word down as "Mr. Know-It-All" used to do, and you had something like *"Trin* for *Trinity* and *Tex* for *Videotex: Trintex!"* That made as much sense as anything else.

Trintex carefully pointed out that the inauguration of the service was two years away, and that the companies would spend $250 million on the project.

A few months after that news broke, rumors of still more new online services backed by commercial giants popped. AT&T (using what it learned from Venture One, no doubt) was to team with Chemical Bank, which had its own banking service, Covidea, in operation. Time, Inc., and the Bank of America might be minority participants, along with Nynex. A "source" in *The New York Times* opined that, "Chemical and AT&T feel they need a joint venture because of Trintex."

Another group, composed of RCA, Citicorp, JC Penney—and maybe NBC—was making noises about an online service.

Neither of those ventures went anywhere. AT&T and Nynex would need permission from Judge Harold Greene, who had already ruled that telephone companies could not originate information. And the "source" was probably correct about the ventures being a reaction to Trintex.

But Trintex—there just might be something to it. In 1986, the public was treated to what a Trintex screen *might* look like. It went like this:

```
SEARS                                              SR-1
               WELCOME TO SEARS!
1 TOP SEARS VALUES
2 BACK TO SCHOOL
3 SEARS ELECTRONIC SHOWPLACE
4 COMPUTERWARE
```

```
 5 ELECTRONIC BARGAIN DIRECTORY
 6 ORDER CATALOGS AND SPECIALOGS
 7 HOW TO ORDER FROM
   OUR PRINTED CATALOGS
 8 SEARS FACTS
 9 TO APPLY FOR SEARS CREDIT
10 WARRANTIES, REQUEST FREE COPY
```

Very interesting! The simulated menu made you want to enter **5** and see just what those electronic bargains might be. The newspaper story illustrated by the menu discussed how text-only services compared with Videotex. In the end, all one learned about Trintex was that it had a mock-up menu.

Trintex broke a lengthy silence in mid-1987 to announce that MCI would provide the data lines for its service. In the meantime, CBS had dropped out of the project. In December, Sears and IBM showed they were hanging tough by promising that they would introduce their Videotex service "next year in San Francisco."

Most people had never seen a Videotex screen, or even a photo of one. So the general consensus was that Trintex would look like CompuServe. If it ever came to be. After four years, it seemed a lot like online vaporware.

In with the New, Out with the Old

You've got mail!
—Elwood Edwards, the voice of AOL

The online world was stable, for now. It looked as if Prodigy was never going to happen, and there were no newcomers on the horizon. Some small operations were still making noises about Minitel. A Canadian service called the NABU Network had tried to get an online service going in Washington, D.C., and quickly failed. A few other companies tried to develop local information and email services, but they were doomed to failure, having lost most of their potential market to CompuServe or one of the other established services even before they began.

Although there was no room for newcomers, it would turn out that there was plenty of room for the existing players to expand, in several directions. While CIS and the rest concentrated on introducing new products for existing services and drawing new members, Quantum was creating a new market. No one at the company realized it at the time, but Q-Link was a precursor to an online service empire.

Great Product, Great Customers— Where's the Money?

Q-Link had all the other services beat in ease of use, hands-down. The Playnet/Q-Link graphical user interface (GUI) was the most pleasant online environment anywhere. It was difficult to make the wrong selection or get lost. Members were enthusiastic, and lauded Q-Link as superior to all the other services. Color, graphics, sounds, and a spark of animation kept things lively, and made some people think that Videotex might actually be on the way—if not, then at least online services with a decent GUI.

Best of all for some, no one argued that their brand of computer was better than yours: everyone had a Commodore.

Behind the screens, Quantum the company was still tight for money. Their 50,000 members were not enough. Both Quantum and Commodore expected tens of thousands more by mid-1986. Things were so bad that Kimsey had everyone move from the upper floors of the building to the basement, to save money. They cut back on promotional efforts, scaling back advertising and canceling a deal with an ad agency to make video demos.

Great Expectations

Apparently, some things had been left unsaid between Quantum and Commodore during and after the negotiations for the new online service. Quantum counted on Commodore's name—and Commodore's advertising and promotion of the service—to bring in tens of thousands of new members immediately. At the same time, Commodore didn't do much advertising or promotion, and expected Q-Link to reverse the downturn in Commodore computer sales. Q-Link, it was hoped, would be the new killer app that would make everybody rush out to buy Commodore computers so they could use Q-Link. So much for computer-enhanced communications, at least within the industry.

Neither side got exactly what it wanted. Each blamed the other for the slow rise in revenues.

Steve Case decided that, since Quantum had proven itself adept at creating a proprietary online service with advanced features for one brand of computer, it could do the same for other brands. Quantum would bring color and graphics and ease of use to everyone, one brand at a time. And per the lesson learned from Gameline, it would not be dependent on one product.

The Entrepreneur Who Wouldn't Go Away, Redux

Steve Case went after Apple first, in part because Quantum was already working on a service that could do for Apple owners what Q-Link did for Commodore owners. It was a tough play. Quantum had already been turned down once, and Apple's internal AppleLink service was still hosted by (and had been developed by) GEIS, GEnie's parent. But unlike the last time, when Kimsey approached Apple, Case had a product to show: Q-Link. And Apple's thoughts had by now turned to offering a consumer online service to help reduced customer support expenses and to generate income. GEIS was charging Apple $300,000 a month just to host and maintain the service. Plus, it charged customers $15 per hour to access AppleLink. Apple wanted out of that deal, but was sure it would cost them much more than they were paying GEIS.

Case knew none of this. He did know that Apple was going to be a tough nut to crack. So he decided to use a brute-force approach. Rather than waste time with proposals and phone calls, Case camped out on Apple's doorstep for three months. He flew to California late in 1986 and rented an apartment in Cupertino, near Apple's headquarters, and settled in for a campaign intended to wear down the resistance.

Every day Case traveled from his apartment to Apple, meeting with people from different divisions, making presentations, talking up the future of consumer online for Apple. He brushed aside the fact that Apple already had an online presence with CompuServe. He played up using the Apple II's and Apple IIgs's color and sound capabilities to draw Apple owners to Quantum's service, where they would generate royalties and help sell computers for Apple. He talked about how the Macintosh version would seamlessly blend in with the Mac's look and feel.

Every day. For months. He must have learned something about persistence from Bill von Meister.

Apple's customer service division eventually gave in—out of annoyance, weariness, disgust, enthusiasm, curiosity, or some combination thereof. In 1987, Case returned to Quantum Computer's Virginia headquarters with a signed deal that included a 10 percent royalty for Apple.

AppleLink–Personal Edition

Quantum Computer Services would build AppleLink–Personal Edition, a consumer service for owners of Apple IIgs and Mac computers, complete with a GUI. Apple fans rejoiced.

Speculation was rife among members of the online community. Was a PC version in the works? How about versions for other brands of computers? Would Quantum's services share resources, so that a Q-Link member could exchange email and files with AppleLink users?

"No," came the answer to each question.

Equally important questions in other circles were, "Is this the future of the online world? Will consumers abandon CompuServe, DELPHI, GEnie, The Source, and other services for glitzy GUIs?"

No one could say for certain.

GEnie and AOL: Cousins?

According to well-placed sources, the original AppleLink GUI was developed largely by GEIS, whose mainframe computers also hosted the AppleLink service that Apple used internally. The GE product on which it was based was called Business*Talk—a GUI front end for both IBM and Macintosh computers. Through Apple or otherwise, Quantum Computer obtained a copy of the software after they made the deal with Apple. This was used to create AppleLink–Personal Edition and Quantum's own Apple service and Macintosh service.

The roots in Business*Talk were traceable by "Easter Eggs"[1] that were hidden in Business*Talk and turned up in early versions of AppleLink–Personal Edition and AOL's Apple software.

Ironically, in 1986 Apple had put GEnie on a list of companies that could not have access to the Business*Talk software. GEIS honored their agreement and did not allow GEnie developers to have the software source code. Thus, GEnie went online as a text-based service, and would have to develop its own GUI programs, independent of Business*Talk. As GEnie founder Bill Louden saw it, "GEnie was more like the bastard step-child when it came to leveraging the GEIS Business*Talk GUI."

AppleLink–Personal Edition went live in May 1988, at the annual Apple Fest in San Francisco. It might have been available sooner, but Apple was very particular about the design and how the service operated. The folks at Quantum thought they had done an excellent job—and they had—but Apple demanded that AppleLink have an absolute Apple "look and feel," in line with other Apple products. The same general look and the fonts used by the Apple systems weren't enough.

There were other points of friction. Quantum wanted to bundle the user software with new Apple computers and modems, and were astonished when Apple said no to this obviously beneficial marketing move. Apple was against giving away software (or anything else) in any form. The software would be purchased by customers, like any other Apple software. Apple further placed additional rules and limits on how AppleLink–Personal Edition could be marketed by Quantum. They demanded a certain elegant and costly approach to advertising, and a large customer service department underwritten by Quantum.

AppleLink–Personal Edition started out with a $35 annual fee, and a $6-per-hour evening rate ($15 daytime). There were no surcharges for higher

---

[1] An "Easter Egg" is a hidden message, image, or feature in a computer program, placed there by the original programmer. An Easter Egg is revealed only when a program's user follows an unusual sequence of commands or operations.

speeds. Thanks to Apple actually doing some marketing of the service (and the interest in online GUIs created by Playnet and Q-Link), tens of thousands of Apple II owners climbed on board.

Quantum did some marketing of its own, placing ads and disks with AppleLink software in relevant computer magazines (foreshadowing AOL's free disk distribution campaigns to come). It also offered one month free, along with a 20 percent lifetime discount, for the first 25,000 members.

The new service offered everything that Q-Link offered: file downloads, email, bulletin boards, chat, forums, news, travel, stock prices, games—and it looked great. Users were quite enamored of AppleLink. But Apple was less than happy; it had expected a far greater number of users, and faster. The company completely missed the fact that its restrictive marketing hampered the recruitment of new customers and blamed everything on Q-Link, one way or another.

PC-Link

Fresh from the Apple deal in Cupertino, Steve Case must've felt like a conquering hero, and he was ready for more. So while AppleLink–Personal Edition was still in the works, he made some appointments with Tandy in Texas.

Tandy was then preparing to bring out DeskMate 3, which would battle Windows 3 for the graphical operating system market (even as those same graphical operating systems were rapidly gobbling up task-switching environments like DesqVIEW). The early versions of DeskMate and Windows were glitchy and awkward.[2] But DeskMate 3 and Windows 3 were different. They were appealing, and one could do serious work with them. DeskMate tried to be user-friendly—and succeeded, although it was perhaps oversimplified in some respects. Windows, on the other hand, went for a smooth, "professional" look and feel that was intimidating to some users.

When Case showed up at Tandy's Ft. Worth headquarters, Tandy was working overtime, signing up software companies to make DeskMate versions of their programs, and building the DeskMate operating system into ROM so there would be almost zero load time.

The reaction was pretty much, "A DeskMate-specific online service? Why, that's a perfect addition to DeskMate. Windows is offering nothing like this, just a little terminal program. Show us where to sign!"

In keeping with Quantum's "link" theme, the new service would be called PC-Link. As with Apple, Tandy wanted PC-Link to have the DeskMate look and feel throughout. Not a problem! Quantum and Tandy did a truly superb

---

[2] *Enough so that half or more of MS-DOS users continued to employ pop-up and task-switching programs to do what DeskMate and Windows 1 and 2 were supposed to do.*

job of seamlessly integrating PC-Link and DeskMate. A new user could log on and start doing things right away, and glean more subtle and powerful tricks from the DeskMate 3 documentation later.[3]

DeskMate 3 could run on nearly any IBM-compatible computer. This meant that IBM-PC and clone users at last had a shot at trying out a colorful graphic online interface like Commodore and Apple users enjoyed, as long as they were willing to use DeskMate.

PC-Link went online in August 1989, just in time for Christmas. It had Tandy's full backing, including heavy marketing support.

Two levels of service were available: PC-Link and PC-Link Plus. The basic PC-Link cost $9.95 per month and allowed the member one hour of access to what were known as "Plus Features." As with Q-Link, Plus encompassed games, email, chat, and several more popular services, like computer forums, but basic PC-Link included free access to News and Reference services. After using the free hour, the member was billed 15 cents per minute to access the Plus services.

The Quantum staff worked to develop new ideas, such as chat- or download-based classes in various computing subjects. At the same time, features were copied over from Q-Link and AppleLink–Personal Edition, and vice versa. This resulted in the content producers having to do everything three times because of the nature of the online tools behind the services. This duplication would eventually be eliminated by all of Quantum's services being drawn together into one entity with common resources and content.

Sour Apples

When Apple heard about PC-Link, they were more than a little annoyed. Apple had expected Quantum to devote all of its time and energy (outside of Q-Link) to AppleLink–Personal Edition.

Quantum's contract with Apple did not guarantee Apple that kind of exclusivity, so Quantum was not moved by their client's expectations. In fact, back in Virginia, Kimsey and the rest of the crew at Quantum were tiring of dealing with Apple. The computer-maker was complaining about minutiae and asking for major changes in certain elements of the service. And Apple wanted Quantum to do still more marketing that it couldn't afford.

For all that, Quantum was still planning on moving ahead with new services, Apple be damned.

---

[3] *The only extended documentation for PC-Link was part of my book,* Getting the Most Out of DeskMate 3 *(Brady/Simon & Schuster, 1989, 1990).*

Tensions grew. Someone breached the contract. One story says Apple did it. Another says it was Quantum. According to CEO Kimsey, ". . . it cost us about five million bucks." Kimsey ended up telling John Sculley that dealing with Apple was worse than dealing with the Pentagon, a strong invective from the ex-military officer, indeed.

Before the end of 1989, just as the Macintosh version was to go online, the plug was pulled on AppleLink–Personal Edition, and it joined Playnet on the online casualty list.

But there was an odd paragraph in the Apple/Quantum deal that left Quantum with the right to use the Apple logo with an online service. Apple wanted that right for itself, and Quantum sold it back to them for $2.5 million.

However, the contract did not prohibit Quantum from running an Apple online service—and it did, retooling the AppleLink–Personal Edition software to excise the Apple logo.

Since Quantum's Apple-oriented online service was no longer an official Apple Computer operation, a name change was indicated. "AppleLink–Personal Edition" could not be used.

An employee contest was held to generate possible names. Case was the judge. He chose his own idea: America Online. Some people didn't like it, but from then on they were stuck with it.[4]

Case decided that the service should seem friendlier, and the users more like members of something than customers, just like they were part of America. To that end, he came up with the idea of an online greeting and other voice files to add to the friendliness. Broadcaster and voiceover actor Elwood Edwards, whose wife, Karen, worked at AOL, recorded four quick lines: "Welcome," "You've got mail," "File's done," and "Goodbye." These are among the most-often heard phrases in the Western world.[5]

The revamped Apple service became America Online on October 2, 1989. It was more commonly referred to as "AOL," Case having noticed that most well-known companies have three letters in their abbreviations (IBM, MTV, GMC, etc.).[6] The company continued operating officially as Quantum Computer, Inc., and went to work on the aborted Macintosh version of AppleLink, which would become part of AOL.

---

[4] *One of the three top choices from employee submissions was "Odyssey," which at that time was the name of a small pornographic online service.*

[5] *America Online software allows users to turn off the phrases or substitute other sounds. It wasn't long before AOL members were creating their own versions of Elwood Edwards' words and sharing them. There are versions with British, Scottish, and Irish accents, as well as in other languages.*

[6] *There was some contention inside AOL over what the acronym should be. Many people were of the opinion that "AO" was the best representation of the two words that made up the service's name. But as the company's president was behind "AOL," that's the way it went.*

The Competition Wakes

Quantum's innovations and deals had not gone unnoticed. With graphical
online services now available for three major computer brands (and, presumably, more to come), there was concern at GEnie, CompuServe, DELPHI,
and other services over how many people would fall for a pretty face and move
to one of Quantum/AOL's computer-specific services. Each of the online services offered Forums or SIGs and other products devoted to the major computer brands, but they lacked the "look and feel" that was becoming a factor
of growing importance in computer products of all kinds.

Equally important were the hundreds of thousands of people who would
buy computers or modems for the first time over the next few years. Would
they sign up and stay with an online service that looked like just another computer program, with menus and prompts and command lines—and nothing
but text to look at? Or would they prefer one with color, sound, and button-
pressing simplicity?

Jokes were made about cartoon-like online services, and people were saying that using Q-Link and AOL was like going online with training wheels. But
the big services were looking over their shoulders.

It would be difficult to match Q-Link, AOL, or PC-Link in appearance and
operation. Everyone knew they had to change to compete. Each service was
working to improve reliability and response time, and some were adding new
features. But with hundreds of thousands of new computer users about to go
online, appearance and ease of use meant as much as features. Q-Link and
now AOL proved that.

The fastest way to change an online service's appearance would be a
front end.

Front Ends

Generally speaking, a front end is a program that enhances and simplifies
another program, be it an offline database or word processor, or an online
service. Online service front ends often enhanced text-based online services
by changing their appearance. The techniques to accomplish this ranged from
simple frames constructed by ASCII (keyboard) characters to colors and lines
generated by the user's computer. Where an online service presented just a
few lines of text, a front end might change the color of the characters and
enclose them in a red box—using colors and lines that weren't transmitted by
the online service, but created by a small front-end program on the user's
computer.

With more graphic-oriented computers, a front-end program could alter
the online service's appearance dramatically through the native graphic capabilities of the user's system. Where Windows was involved, an operating

system front end could make an online service like CompuServe look like any another Windowed application. The point was to create graphics without transmitting graphics.

Of course, front ends went beyond changing appearance. They could completely automate such tasks as reading and replying to email and BBS messages as well as software uploads and downloads. Reading and composing messages would be done offline. With most front ends, the user could set the system to sign on, send and collect messages, and sign off at a predetermined time of day.[7]

Some front ends would let the user replace commands with words that made more sense to them, like "Erase" instead of "Delete."

A sophisticated terminal program, like Procomm Plus or Crosstalk, could be customized to an extent by automating tasks and changing commands, but a front end designed by the host online service was usually superior to home-made front ends.[8]

In truth, Playnet, Q-Link, and AOL software were examples of extreme front ends, in that what the user saw was built up using his computer's capabilities. Each permitted customization and automation on some level as well.

CompuServe had a long history of building front ends for various kinds of computers. The earliest front ends (Vidtex and TAPCIS) did not focus on changing CompuServe's appearance. They were designed to automate CompuServe tasks. TAPCIS was oriented toward CompuServe Forums, and its users were almost evangelistic about the program's benefits. Eventually, CompuServe developed front ends for nearly every major brand of personal computer, including Commodore, IBM, Apple, Macintosh, CP/M, Atari, and others. There was little emphasis on giving the service a flashy appearance, though each front end had a different look. The main focus, and what the users were after, was automation and ease of use.

CompuServe engineers created its *Host Micro Interface* (HMI) so CompuServe could interact with faster, more advanced front ends (like WinCIM) to achieve things that weren't originally built into the system. It was almost as if the custom program on the client (user's) computer was talking with a server-based front end for CompuServe.

---

[7] *This aspect of a front end could benefit the online service, at well. Each had a maximum user limits, and some might not be able to log on if the system was maxed. Automated front ends minimized online time for some users, and reduced complaints from others about not being able to log on.*

[8] *Personal computer hobbyists had been making their own front ends for years, and functions built into some of the terminal programs allowed them to make pretty elaborate front ends.*

Quality

Interestingly, CompuServe was already a step or two ahead of all the other online services in terms of hardware, networks, operational quality, and keeping systems running. Unlike AOL, which put its money into carpet-bombing the country with diskettes and ads, CompuServe put a major emphasis on quality.

Sandy Trevor describes some of CompuServe's quality-oriented efforts: "We had huge UPS systems, dual diesel generators, backup sites, redundant geographically diverse communications, tornado-proof computer rooms, etc., long before most people thought of such stuff. We incented all our tech people based on uptime. And it worked! We never had a major outage, though of course there were some local network outages in individual cities, such as during hurricanes.

"During the stock market crash of 1987, many of CompuServe's competitors crashed due to overloads, but CompuServe stayed fully operational. This was such a big deal that CompuServe ran ads afterwards to the effect, 'CompuServe was UP when the Dow was DOWN.'"

CompuServe was thus able to remain the top player long after it would have otherwise. While AOL suffered significant crashes due to new users overloading the system, CompuServe never paused, no matter how many users it had. This undoubtedly influenced many modem users to avoid or move from AOL to CompuServe.

GEnie's front end, developed by David Kozin in 1988, was called Aladdin. It gave GEnie a much more pleasant appearance than a simple terminal program could, and was particularly adept at handling mail and RoundTable BBS postings. It also generated a menu layout that most users found superior to GEnie's.

GEnie bought the program from its developer for $60,000 in 1989. The reason that happened is explained by GEnie founder Bill Louden: "Buying Aladdin was supposed to be a stopgap measure until we got a full GUI-application like AOL." But GEIS was slow to spend money on development, so the GUI version of GEnie was never finished. And of course the almost-ready-to-use GUI that GEnie's parent company had developed, Business*Talk, remained untouchable.

Earthquake Proof!

GEnie's worldwide network (GEIS' network) had been in development long before CompuServe or any other consumer online service went online. It tended to use the latest technology, including satellite links.

It was because of its satellite links that it was almost the only link to the outside world immediately after the 1987 San Francisco earthquake. Links to all telephone lines (surface and underground, wire and fiber-optic) were broken by the earthquake. But somehow, GEnie members were logging on and visiting chat rooms to let concerned people know what the situation was.

The GEIS network had a major satellite uplink in San Francisco for trans-Pacific communication. This link was able to carry traffic from GEnie via an alternate route until San Francisco's land-line telephone links to the outside world were reestablished.

The Source showed up with a front end that was too little, too late. It was named re:Source, and did a fine job of saving members money by allowing them to handle communications offline. It navigated the system direct, from one service to another without bothering with menus. And more. But it still presented a text face to the world, and The Source was losing a lot of members who may or may not have been influenced by re:Source.

BIX had two front ends, JBLink[9] for MS-DOS machines and BIXNAV (BIX NAVigator) for Windows. Both lightened the workload involved in going through BIX's myriad conference topics and email, and reduced online time. Front ends were also developed for DELPHI (ONCALL), and for database services like Dialog (DialogLink) as well as AT&T Mail and MCI Mail. All of these were designed more for improving functionality and efficiency than appearance.

One clever but overworked programmer, Philippe Rabergrau, developed *two* front ends to simplify Prodigy. One automated email and bulletin boards, while the other gathered and archived information on stocks.

These front ends were available, variously, as commercial packages, shareware, and for free.

---

[9] *The BIX lingo for an automated front in was "blinker." The "J" in JBLink represented the name of the creator.*

Another Online Casualty

By 1989, CompuServe was still leading the pack in number of users, the universal measure for online services used by the press and public. It had a half million members. AOL (still officially operating as Quantum) had perhaps 100,000 customers. GEnie was close to that. The Source carried 50,000 members on its rolls (down from a peak of 80,000). DELPHI had a virtual population of 60,000, and BIX around 40,000. People/Link had broken 10,000, and The WELL had a significant membership.

It came as a surprise to many when CompuServe bought The Source. Others were not surprised. Ownership had changed a couple of times over the preceding two years. The Reader's Digest Association sold 30 percent ownership to Control Data Corporation (CDC) in 1983, but bought them back in 1987, a year after the service became profitable. The Source was sold to a venture capital group that same year. CompuServe bought the company in June 1989. No price was released, and it was never said which side initiated the deal.

There were hopes that CompuServe might operate The Source as a separate company. But it didn't happen. The Source was terminated on August 1, 1989. Source members received CompuServe memberships and free time. Many became CompuServe users. Many others, angry at having The Source yanked out from under them after all those years, headed for GEnie or another service.

CompuServe did for a time maintain the popular PARTI (the Usenet-like bulletin board conferencing system), which drew a good number of Source members to CompuServe. These were the serious PARTI users, a unique culture that had evolved into a tight community over two decades.

CompuServe eventually dropped PARTI, but original PARTI conferences from The Source were replicated on Patricia Niehoff's UNISON (a VAX-based online service).[10] This gave die-hard PARTI users (and there were many) a place to continue their favorite pursuit.

UNISON went out of business in the mid-1990s, and that was it for the last vestige of the original Source. Bill von Meister had passed away by then. His grand ideas for a wireless Internet, downloadable music, downloadable games, and security devices were all gone. The only legacy of his career as an entrepreneur was AOL. As Steve Case said at von Meister's funeral, "Without Bill von Meister, there would have been no AOL."

---

[10] *UNISON also served as a communications provider in the third world, setting up telecommunications services on behalf of the Anglican Church.*

AOL Evolves: Expansion, Integration, and Success

We could be bigger than AT&T.

—Steve Case to a reporter, 1995

It is interesting to consider how the early development of Quantum Computer/AOL echoed that of the first online database providers. As with Dialog, SDC, and others, Quantum was paid by a client to develop and manage a product. In each instance, much of the product development work was already done. The content (massive quantities of textual data) that database providers put online was compiled for them by their clients. Quantum was given the software and some of the content that would be the basis for Q-Link and, later, AppleLink.

Database providers expanded their content through partnerships with other data providers, and found new customers through gateways. Quantum did something similar with its Apple and Tandy partnerships.

Eventually, the online database providers evolved into independent entities. So did Quantum Computer, as America Online/AOL. But the process of AOL's independence began almost accidentally, when Apple pulled the plug on AppleLink–Personal Edition.

Independence

When Apple Computer dropped AppleLink–Personal Edition (shown in Figure 13-1), it was not unlike when Commodore withdrew its support from Q-Link. In both cases, the computer makers simply walked away from their investments, asserting no further claim on the intellectual property involved. (One wonders whether this was explicit in the contract between the computer manufacturers and Quantum.)

The main difference in the two situations was that Apple wasn't approaching its demise as Commodore was. Apple was healthy and producing more potential customers every day.

Figure 13-1. AppleLink for the Apple II, before it became AOL for Apple

What's more, a second market would soon open: the Macintosh version was nearly ready for release when Apple pulled out. And all that needed to be done for it to go public was to remove the official Apple logos and tweak a few things, as had been done with the Apple II version. Then America Online for Macintosh would go online, right alongside America Online for the Apple II. (They were the same service on AOL's end, but the software came in a version for Apple II and a version for Macintosh that looked quite similar.)

It was nice to be in charge, but Quantum wasn't looking to drop clients in exchange for independence. In fact, it still operated PC-Link for Tandy, and was about to get into a new private label deal, with IBM.

Promenade

With America Online for Apple and Macintosh online and growing, AOL was approached by IBM to start what it thought would be the last of its private-brand deals. IBM was planning to introduce a new computer, the PS/1, in 1990.

The PS/1 had a built-in modem, at a time when most personal computers came without modems. To increase customer awareness of this value-added item, IBM wanted to create an online service dedicated to the PS/1. The service would also provide an owner-support channel.

To this end, the computer giant contracted with Quantum to build an online service called Promenade. Potential PS/1 buyers would hopefully view the free modem and the private service as bonus features. From IBM's perspective, Promenade would be a marketing tool, one for which the users would pay if all went as planned.

Promenade went online in June 1990. Promenade was based on GeoWorks, like AOL for MS-DOS. The software was packaged with every IBM PS/1. On the same principle as the other private label services, Promenade looked and operated like other computer applications, drop-down menus and all. The product offerings were in line with other online services—email, software downloads, bulletin boards, games, chat, travel, news and other information.[1]

IBM paid Quantum the better part of two million dollars to set up the service, but Promenade did not last long, for two reasons. First, the conservatism of IBM permeated it, which meant monitored chat rooms and other restrictions.

Second, IBM promoted Promenade almost exclusively to PS/1 owners, which made for a limited audience—a lot more limited than anyone had expected. Personal computing professionals were suspicious of the machine from the beginning. Its design, which placed the motherboard and other circuits inside the monitor, handicapped the PS/1 from the start: it was impossible to use any monitor but IBM's. Other faults included limited memory expansion and difficulties with upgrading. IBM released several new versions of the PS/1 over the next three years, but didn't get rid of all the bad features. The PS/1 sold poorly, and as the PS/1 went, so went Promenade—in part kept alive by IBM's support.

PC (IBM-compatible computer, that is) users were a market that couldn't be ignored. Creating a version of America Online for PCs was the obvious next step. In fact, PC owners and elements of the computer press were already wondering when—not if—America Online would provide software for them.

As it turned out, this was a job that would have to be done in two stages: one for MS-DOS and one for Windows. Before that, however, America Online would address the issue of running multiple services with duplicate resources—and bring together nearly all the members of its services.

The Great Commingling

Even as AOL was setting up Promenade, the revenues from Q-Link and PC-Link were falling off. Commodore Computing was losing market share to PC clones and Macintosh. Windows 3 would soon knock DeskMate out of the game, and Tandy would slowly withdraw from the computer market. All this had strong implications for the future.

---

[1] *One element that Quantum's online services did not include early on was gateways to database services. The thinking was that adding this dimension might make a service too complicated for someone who had never been online before.*

The future aside, running one Apple and two PC-oriented services meant three times the work for content producers and customer service. Because of the way the content-management tools were set up, the staff had to make additions to one service at a time, even if the changes were the same.

In March 1991, AOL decided to "commingle" nearly all of its online services: PC-Link, Promenade, AOL for Apple II, and AOL for Macintosh. Commodore would have to remain off to one side, because the client-side and server software did not share directly the common heritage of the Apple and DeskMate services (GEIS Business°Talk). Commodore was taking a beating in the market, and some people wondered how long it would stay in business.

The other services were gathered under the banner of America Online. Members saw pretty much the same version for their machines as they had been seeing, but there were suddenly a lot of "new" members.

Before commingling, each service was in its own little universe. Now members of all three services could meet in the same chat rooms, exchange email, play the same games, and more.

The initial changeover created some confusion, before new client software was available to present each separate service simply as America Online for Apple, Macintosh, or PCs. Email was tagged with the name of the service it was from, as well as the sender, which caused some to do double-takes. In chat rooms members meeting for the first time confused one another by referring to themselves as "on PC-Link" or "on America Online for Apple." Some members who had been around for a while talked about "AppleLink," which left a lot of people scratching their heads.

In October 1991, Quantum Computer Services legally changed its name to America Online, but was more commonly known as AOL, as explained in Chapter 12. It was by then the third-largest online service in the United States, having nearly 300,000 members. It was surpassed by newcomer Prodigy (see Chapter 14), which had accumulated 465,000 users to CompuServe's 600,000.

Barbarians at the Gates

AOL, Q-Link, PC-Link, AppleLink, and Promenade gave hundreds of thousands of people their first view of the online world. When members of these services began exploring other online services, they were met with a rude surprise: much of the online population treated them as if they were somehow handicapped or underdeveloped.

The general opinion was that AOL (as well as its relatives) was not a "real" online service because it was so easy to use. AOLers didn't have to know anything about computers, and therefore were somehow inferior. They were using the equivalent of training wheels to get online.

Pretty soon, some newcomers came to resent the old hands as online geeks. Chat rooms, message boards, and email were venues for discussion of "us" and "them."

Prodigy members were met with the same scorn when the service went national in 1988. And when Internet and web access became available in the 1990s, anyone who used either AOL or Prodigy faced renewed contempt. Members of both services were derided and browbeaten to join a real ISP or an online service like CompuServe, The Source, or DELPHI.

This was at a time when membership in online services was growing faster than ever. Online veterans feared that the systems would be overloaded and online offerings diluted. And there were so many newbies and so few who had the knowledge to help, and who knew how to diagnose and explain problems.

This situation didn't exist in the early days of consumer online services. The online experts were more than happy to help the amateurs. Sharing their superior knowledge was an ego boost, and there was the warm glow of having helped someone else. But when things got crowded, the load was just too great. Some tried, creating message board topics for modem Q&A, writing postings, emailing detailed instructions on overcoming the most commonly faced difficulties, and patiently talking new members through their problems in chat rooms. (It didn't help that most of the people selling computers and modems knew little about operating them.)

The anti-AOL and -Prodigy sentiments spread, and spilled over into the real world. In addition to journalists reporting on it, there were magazine articles that tried to smooth over the rift, and demonstrations such as individuals wearing "Prodigy Sucks" T-shirts at COMDEX and other trade shows and consumer events.

Prodigy is long gone, but a large group of online experts remains who view AOL as "the Internet with training wheels."

AOL for PCs: DOS and Windows

AOL came out with a version for DOS before Windows. This was because it had help from the GeoWorks Corporation. GeoWorks was a direct competitor for Windows, and had quite a following. AOL approached GeoWorks with the idea of using the system's kernel as the basis for the DOS version of AOL, according to AOL Vice-President Audrey Weil, "because we wanted something small, and Geoworks' kernel was very small." The small system left more room on subscribers' disks for the elements of AOL, and made for faster development.

The DOS version, which came out in February 1991, is shown in Figure 13-2.

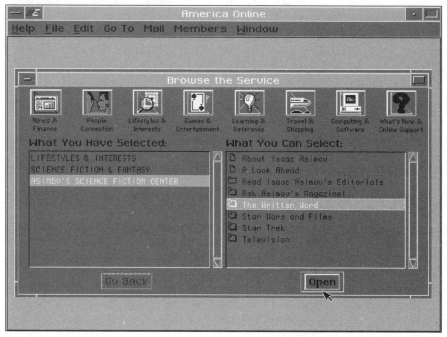

Figure 13-2. AOL GeoWorks interface for MS-DOS computers

The Windows version would not be ready until January 1993. The delay was not so much the development time as it was the fact that IBM considered Microsoft a heavy competitor and was reluctant to provide the Windows version. Until they had their own version of AOL, quite a few Windows users went back to DOS or experimented with running the GeoWorks version of AOL under Windows.

CompuServe Makes an Offer

As Quantum/AOL was transforming itself in 1991, CompuServe approached James Kimsey with an offer to buy the company. Kimsey, who had been with the company from its beginnings, was still looking for a buyer.

CompuServe's offer was $50 million. Still CEO of the company, Kimsey seriously considered the offer against Quantum's $20 million annual gross and its growth potential. He later said he would have folded for $60 million, even though Steve Case was against it.

Not incidentally, AOL for Windows (Figure 13-3) was developed independently of Microsoft. Steve Case and James Kimsey did not want to be a part of Microsoft. In illustration of that fact, Kimsey and Case would later fend off a takeover bid by Microsoft co-founder Paul Allen and turn down offers from Bill Gates. (Gates was already planning the Microsoft Network.)

Figure 13-3. AOL for Windows today

Case was not, as history shows, against merging with another megacorporation, Time Warner.

Planning Ahead

CompuServe remained ahead of AOL in number of members. Each had its own unique offerings, including the look and feel of their front ends. Each had certain products that were unique—specific databases or games, and the character and nature of forums and online events (like celebrity chats). And of course there were communities and cliques on each service that existed nowhere else.

One thing that CompuServe had that AOL couldn't offer was access to a wide variety of computers. To connect with AOL, you had to have an Apple, a Macintosh, or a PC. But you could log on to CompuServe with Apple, IBM,

Mac, or your high-mileage Atari computer, or Commodore, Apple, or TRS-80—with or without a front end. If you had a home-built UNIX box you could log on, as long as you had a modem and terminal program. Some people dialed into CompuServe with DEC VAXs. The same was true for GEnie and DELPHI.

But the classic computer users were a market that diminished daily. By the early 1990s, it was easy to see that the overwhelming majority of personal computer users would go with either Macintosh or PC/Windows computers. This being the case, AOL really did itself no harm in creating services for those platforms only.

Marketing AOL

AOL now had all the advantages. It could serve the most popular computer brands. It was the most colorful and easy-to-use online service in North America (yes, it had expanded to Canada, like its competitors).

In marketing itself, AOL did the same things that CompuServe, DELPHI, GEnie, and other services had always done. It advertised in computer magazines, and a few general-interest publications now and then. It maintained a presence at industry events.

AOL software was bundled with new computers and peripherals, and with software. Sometimes it was included with computer magazines. Computer books often had free signups with free online time printed in their back pages.

AOL established partnerships with magazine and software publishers as well as computer manufacturers, bringing them online to provide online support, sales, and customer service areas. Some signed up as "content providers" and were paid royalties for the time members spent in their areas. Others were charged to maintain a presence. Those who set up to sell merchandise directly to consumers were usually charged a monthly fee and a percentage of sales.

These promotional, advertising, and partnership techniques were common to all the consumer online services.

Then AOL came up with something different: direct mail.

Carpet-Bombing America

AOL began a small direct mail campaign in 1993. It was the idea of AOL marketer Jan Brandt, who had developed a highly successful direct mail marketing campaign for a children's book in her previous job. The book was unusual in its illustrations and other elements; you really did have to see it to appreciate it. And thousands of customers appreciated and bought the book, once they saw it. It was a matter of putting the product in the customers' hands.

The same concept was behind bundling software with original equipment manufacturer (OEM) products, something begun by CompuServe in the early 1980s. The idea was to put the product literally into the hands of the most likely potential customers.

Brandt's approach differed in that the disks went to general mailing lists, rather than targeted groups like computer hardware and software buyers, and computer magazine readers. Essentially, every address in a given zip code was sent a disk, town by town, region by region. (The addresses were probably obtained from the U.S. Postal Service, which sells American addresses in database form.)

In fact, thousands of the recipients would not be computer owners. Those who did own computers might or might not own modems. More than a few had the equipment, but had not ever thought about signing up for an online service. The mailings reached for a cross section of the entire American demographic—techies, women, blue-collar workers, men, professionals, Luddites, everyone in America, no matter what their background or belief.

Conventional marketing wisdom had it that between 1 and 1.5 percent of recipients of untargeted direct mail would "convert," or buy the product. That wasn't strictly true, because there were categories of products and services that just didn't draw that kind of response. Nobody knew whether a consumer online service fit in the category.

But Brandt wasn't playing the percentages. She planned to get people thinking about AOL by putting it in their hands, explaining how an online service worked with an accompanying insert or booklet, and showing what AOL had to offer. (Market research had revealed that many people had no idea of what an online service was. And in all truth AOL was something that most people had to see to understand.)

Brandt asked Steve Case for permission to do a small mailing to fewer than 200,000 people, at a cost of $250,000. Case gave her the go-ahead, but told her it wouldn't work.

The conversion rate on that first mailing was nearly 10 percent. That came to about $12.50 per new member, a good deal.

Encouraged, the company did more and larger mailings to similar effect. Some lists were hit with mailings a second time. The mailings continued to pay off with high conversion rates.

Each disk included an offer of free time on AOL, in order to give the consumers a hands-on sample of the service. At first it was 5 or 10 hours, but as the mail campaign grew over the next several years, the free time grew to 100 hours, then 1,000 hours. The increase in free time was inspired in part by competing services making similar offers.

The direct mail campaigns proved Brandt's thesis: if you put the product in the hands of customers, enough of them would subscribe to make the distribution profitable.

The key, then, was putting the disks or CDs in consumers' hands. It was decided to try other forms of distribution. AOL disks and CDs were handed out by marketing companies at concerts and other events. They started showing up at Wal-Mart and other chain retailers' checkout counters, and on special racks with FREE! signs.

Already old hands at bundling AOL with computer products, AOL marketers decided to try including disks or CDs with other kinds of merchandise. The pitch to the manufacturer was that here was a value-added element that would distinguish their product from those of their competitors.

It was an easy sell. You could include a shrink-wrapped AOL disk and its paper insert in all sorts of packaging. AOL software was given away with toys, cereal, by airlines, and (this one really wowed journalists) in frozen boxes of Omaha steaks.

Shutting Down Online Services

It may seem odd to think of being emotionally attached to an online service, but when an institution is part of your life for a number of years—like high school or college—it is only natural that you have some feelings about it. Just as with school, consumer services put one in touch with other people, and communities were created. (See "The WELL" in Chapter 11.)

When AOL shut down Q-link in 1994, it was pulling the plug on the communities that made up the service. Many of the members had been online with Q-Link from the beginning—nearly ten years. By 1994, they had other types of computers, but they kept their old Commodores so they could continue logging on to Q-Link. They relied on the service for computer support and updates, software, entertainment, news, and—most of all—communication and interaction with thousands of like-minded people. For many, the communities of Q-Link—and the greater community of the service itself—were as important as home, school, and work. *Club Caribe* was sorely missed, and its successor, *WorldAway*, has gone away.

Quite a few Q-Linkers blamed Steve Case personally for the cessation of the service. Maybe it was because he was the one who told them about it. Q-Link stopped taking new members in August 1994, and Case sent a systemwide email shortly after that to announce that Q-Link would cease to exist on November 1, 1991.

Q-Link members were uncommonly loyal. They put up websites devoted to the service, and shared screen shots and videos of Q-Link. For a time, there was a website dedicated to re-creating the service through reverse engineering, called "Q-Link Reloaded," and it may return. PC-Link and Promenade were also shut down in 1991. From this point on, AOL would offer a single, unified service.

Even before AOL disks started showing up in local grocery stores and convenience markets, the campaign was famously referred to as "carpet-bombing America with disks." Most people were hard-pressed to find anyone who hadn't received an AOL disk in the mail. The ubiquitous disks soon became a joke. Columnists were writing about them, and word quickly spread all over the online world. Even late-night television entertainers were working them into comedy monologues. Such mentions were worth millions of dollars in exposure.

The carpet-bombing had one unpleasant side effect. AOL grew rapidly to 500,000 members—more than anyone had anticipated. It got to the point that many members couldn't log on. Those who got on experienced slowdowns. Some subscribers started calling it "America On Hold," but still new members signed up. AOL raced to add new hardware and software as its membership approached one million.

The unbridled growth would result in a catastrophe, but that was still several years in the future. In the meantime, AOL—and the other online services—had something more important than quality of service to worry about: the long-rumored Prodigy online service had gone live across the country and was sucking up veteran and new online services alike with an absurdly low flat rate for access.

14

Prodigy: The Flat-Rate Pioneer Who Just Didn't Get It

Eleven years ago, the Internet was just an intangible dream that Prodigy brought to life. Now it is a force to be reckoned with.
—Bill Kirkner, Prodigy Communications' Chief Technology Officer, 1999

From the beginning, Prodigy portrayed itself as what everyone was seeking in an online service. Although it was lacking some elements considered standard for online services, Prodigy offered several spectacular innovations, first among them flat-rate pricing. Backed by two of the nation's largest corporations, IBM and Sears, Prodigy promised to bring the best of home information service and shopping convenience to home computer users in a fast and easy-to-use graphic package.

On first glance, Prodigy looked able to deliver on its promise. But in less than two years it was inciting revolt among its subscribers. Lawsuits and threats of lawsuits were flying, and thousands of members were banded together into an underground intent on undermining Prodigy in every way possible.

How did a commercial entity get into so much trouble? To understand that, you need to know the story from the beginning.

In the Beginning . . .

Prodigy's beginning can be found in a project conceived by AT&T and CBS in 1978. The two industry giants decided to build an information service for the masses, one that anyone could use.

Research and planning commenced. Four years later—in 1982—the results manifested themselves as a cable-based Videotex service named "Venture One." Two hundred homes in a development in Ridgewood,

New Jersey, were outfitted for the service.[1] (One has to wonder whether some of those homes had computers and were signed up for The Source or CompuServe.)

To tap in, some of the homeowners were equipped with a keyboard that plugged into a set-top box. According to *The New York Times*, others were given "an integrated unit made up of a color monitor and an attached keyboard." The latter was a terminal built by AT&T that would turn up in other Videotex experiments. With cable pumping text and NAPLPS[2] graphics into households, Venture One was fast and impressive.

Hundreds of screens of text and graphics were available. Each screen was identified by a three-digit number, and an online index (displayed by pressing a button) listed the pages' contents and their numbers. A hard-copy reference backed it up. To view a specific screen, you entered its number with the keyboard.

Most pages contained fixed text and graphics, but were easily changed when necessary, as with news and weather updates, and advertisements. Email and online purchases were handled through online forms, as were bulletin board postings.

The master plan for the future was to generate income by selling terminals or software, charging users a "small monthly fee," and selling advertising.[3] During the Ridgewood test, neither users nor advertisers were charged.

Among the products Venture One offered were email, shopping, a travel service, stock exchange reports, and a primitive chat. An editorial staff fed information from *The Record of Hackensack* and CBS network radio and TV news reports. Some content came from CBS-affiliated properties like *Woman's Day* magazine. It was all swathed in color NAPLPS graphics.

Venture One was shut down in 1983, after just seven months. As with the closings of QUBE and Viewtron,[4] the reactions of many of the users was probably "Bring it back—we'll pay!" But Venture One was just a limited test, never intended to go public.

AT&T was enthusiastic about the test results. Company spokesman Edward Langsam told the press that a full-blown market test of Videotex would get under way in 1983. "And by 1984," he added, "we're hoping to provide a fully on-line Videotex service."

This was an odd statement, coming from the company that had passed on its chance to own the original information highway a decade earlier, saying that it was "incompatble with our future."[5] It just goes to show that anyone can change.

---

[1] See Chapters 8 and 11 for more information.

[2] NAPLPS was a standard developed for Videotex graphics. See Chapter 8 for details.

[3] The "small monthly fee" for cable-based information services always seemed to be around $40—or, if not, it soon crept up to $40. It was enough to make you think twice at the time—especially when you took into consideration the money that the services were making on terminals.

[4] See Chapters 4, 5, and 8 for more information on Videotex, NAPLPS, QUBE, and Viewtron.

[5] AT&T's refusal to buy the rights to ARPA's networking technology is detailed in Chapter 3.

CBS remained close-mouthed about its online plans. But the television network intended to do something with all the information it had gathered.

~

The AT&T service did not materialize.[6] CBS found two new partners with whom to create an online service. The partners were national icons Sears and IBM. The trio spent over two years planning the new venture and dropping hints in the press before they made a formal announcement late in 1987: Sears, IBM, and CBS were opening a new consumer online service called "Trintex" that would be available in 1988.

Videotex *Again?*

And it was available in 1988, sort of. On April 11, 1988, the service—now named "Prodigy" (see Figure 14-1)—had a limited rollout in San Francisco, Atlanta, and Hartford, Connecticut. The national introduction was September 6, 1990, following a massive advertising campaign.

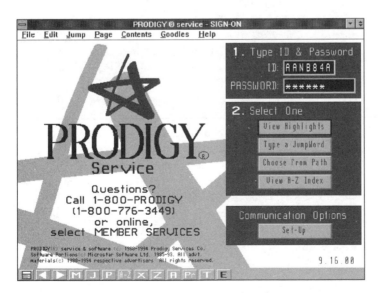

Figure 14-1. Prodigy sign-on screen

---

[6] *AT&T was forced to drop out when Judge Greene said the company couldn't participate in creating online information. When Greene reversed his ruling in 1987, AT&T teamed up with Citibank, Nynex, and RCA to study Videotex. Nothing came of that partnership.*

Meanwhile, the partnership had shrunk to two. CBS was experiencing hard times, and divesting itself of all nonbroadcast ventures. Sears and IBM bought out the CBS share.

One of the most anticipated communication and information services in history turned out to be Videotex, via personal computer. It made sense; there were already so many personal computers in households that the idea of trying to sell users on Minitel sets or other Videotex terminals was as silly as trying to sell telegraph keys. And although Time Warner and others tried to revive the idea of a cable-television-based information service, people just weren't buying.

In any event, with IBM backing this venture it had to be based on personal computers. So, MS-DOS–based software was bundled with IBM PS/1s and PS/2s, and distributed through computer stores, including Radio Shack. It was given away in magazines, too. (Windows and Apple Macintosh would be accommodated later. IBM dragged its feet over Windows, adding to the delay.)

The idea was to create an online service for people who knew nothing about computers, as well as for computer techies. You wouldn't have to figure out software or hardware settings. All you had to do was start the software (after connecting your computer and modem to a telephone line, of course) and go.

Part of Prodigy's marketing superseded the competition; people who had never seen an online service were a major target. (This was before AOL's massive direct-mail campaigns, described in Chapter 13.) Prodigy found the target through magazines, newspapers, and network television. It was expensive. Industry estimates were that it cost Prodigy $1,500 to acquire a customer. In contrast, Bill Louden stated that during that period GEnie was spending just $35 for each new customer. CompuServe spent less than half that. Louden also noted that Prodigy spent almost nothing to retain customers. (This was the opposite of AOL later in the 1990s, when there was a minor scandal over apparently underhanded methods to keep members on the rolls.)

The information and interactive nature of the service were novel ideas for those new to the online world. Enhanced by the graphical interface, the whole package could be related to television, something people understood.

Hopefully, the pretty face of NAPLPS graphics would take some of the fear out of using computers. It *looked* like television, after all—color television–quality images on computer screens. Not even AOL could match it. The smooth graphics with sharp color boundaries, and the large, easy-to-read text were exactly what people had hoped to see in this kind of service.

True Videotex on a large scale had come to America at last.

New & Improved

Prodigy Videotex was Videotex with improvements. In more than two decades of experiments (counting those in France, England, Canada, and other countries), most of the kinks in Videotex had been ironed out. Screen-loading was smooth, and there were no visual artifacts to ruin an otherwise perfect image. Response to user input was fast.

Boldly proclaiming itself the "first consumer online service," Prodigy promised to blend the power and simplicity of IBM's computers with the mechandising might of Sears.

Online Disinformation

When Prodigy went online, it managed to mystify most of us modem users by claiming to be the world's *first consumer online service.*

Magazine and newspaper reporters who weren't technically oriented bought into this idea and validated it by repeating it in print. Some reports seemed to be spun out of Prodigy press releases. For example, a report in *The New York Times* on April 12, 1988, opened with the hilarious statement that Prodigy "will try this year what others have failed to do—to make a success of a home electronic information service." CompuServe and AOL, to name two, were immensely successful home electronic information services—and still are.

This sort of disinformation confused the public, most of whom had never used an online service.

It also confused other writers. Undoubtedly still reeling from the stunning revelation that there were no successful online services in America, one information trade journal columnist trebled the confusion by telling his readers some months later that a "brand-new" service called AOL was on the way and would give Prodigy a run for its money. A few other scribes were confused enough to present AOL, CompuServe, and Prodigy as "BBSs."

Newspaper stories wished Prodigy the best, but did not neglect to point out that other Videotex products, like Viewtron and Gateway, had spent millions of dollars and then failed.

But Prodigy membership grew quickly, and by 1991 it claimed more than 600,000 subscribers, second only to CompuServe's 750,000.[7]

One reason for the rapid growth was the mainstreaming of personal computers. But the biggest reason was that Prodigy charged a flat rate of just $9.95 per month for unlimited access to its services.[8] This alone earned Prodigy

---

[7] *Some reports held that Prodigy's user numbers were based on the six screen names issued to each subscriber, or household. Not all of them were used, so Prodigy may have been multiplying its user base far beyond what it really was. Some accused Prodigy of counting members who had left.*

[8] *The initial subscription fee was $9.95. Prodigy raised the flat monthly rate to $12.95 when it went national.*

loads of press, industry, and public notice. Had the service gone online with an hourly rate, it would have gotten nowhere near the attention it did, and probably would have had fewer signups.

Online Advertising?

Prodigy's content was pretty much the usual for an online service, though it lacked chat and file downloads. Features included news from AP, business news, and stock quotes from Dow Jones. Banking and an online brokerage service were planned, along with grocery shopping for home delivery, *Consumer Reports* features, airline reservations, and more. Other features included games and trivia quizzes, email, and bulletin boards. Howard Cosell and Jane Fonda, or their surrogates, would answer questions about sports and fitness on a special bulletin board.

And there were games. One was a particularly addictive maze game called MadMaze (see Figure 14-2), created by science fiction writer and game designer Greg Costykian. (A devotee maintains a screen-by-screen re-creation of MadMaze on the Web.)

Figure 14-2. MadMaze game on Prodigy

And there would be shopping—shopping like no one had ever seen online. In addition to Sears, names like Neiman-Marcus, Polaroid, Levi Strauss, JC Penney, Ford, Columbia Record/CD Club, Broderbund Software, and many more had signed on. Each organization was prepared for sales, but a major benefit of being online was the exposure gained by maintaining a presence. That had been established in the early 1980s, when a major book publisher paid $4,000 per month just to list its books online, without any provision for sales.

Advertising and the shopping it supported were major elements of the Prodigy business plan; they would make their profit from advertising, and from a percentage on sales made online. Perhaps this is why Prodigy felt that it was a consumer medium—and that CompuServe and the other online services were not—because it carried advertising like the conventional media: television, magazines, and newspapers.

This was not, however, a total distinction. GEnie, CompuServe, DELPHI, and AOL had carried ads in selected areas for years. There was also indirect advertising on the online services, through companies sponsoring forums or other online areas.

But Prodigy went all out: with very few exceptions, every screen on Prodigy carried a graphic ad that took up three lines near the bottom of an MS-DOS screen (Figure 14-3), and a similar area on Windows and Macintosh displays.

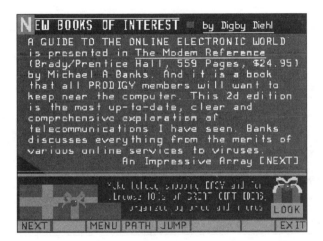

Figure 14-3. Prodigy text screen with an ad at the bottom

Users could click on an ad to get full screens with more information from the advertiser, at which point the advertiser was charged (Figure 14-4).[9] Sponsors who provided online ordering and payment also paid a percentage of each sale.

---

[9] *Online advertisers paid by the click in those days, too.*

The purpose of Chrysler has always been to produce cars and trucks that people will want to buy, will enjoy driving, and will want to buy again. Judging from customer response, we're succeeding. But you are your own judge. That's why we've got every car and truck Chrysler Corporation makes right here for you. Check out Chrysler,

Figure 14-4. Full-page ad on Prodigy

The ads were not really intrusive. The Google Adsense ads that pepper some web pages nowadays are more annoying. Some Prodigy ads were pleasing to the eye, but no matter what their appearance, the ads were easy to ignore. And if you really wanted to, you could page back and forth through ads while retaining the game or email screen or whatever you were looking at.

Was It Really That Different?

Prodigy *was* different. It had smooth graphics. The monthly charge was a flat rate; no minutes to worry about. It was the first service to offer multiple IDs to members. And it carried advertising.

But some elements were missing; it was impossible to capture or save anything to disk, not even email or bulletin board text. Prodigy did not have software or other files to download, and it did not offer chat.

Those were the distinctions between Prodigy and other online services, as far as the public could see—hardly enough to rate a "first consumer online service" ranking. The first online service to carry advertising on every screen, and the first to charge a flat monthly fee, yes—but not the first of its kind.

Prodigy Call Home

In terms of technology, Prodigy did have one important new element. The system was designed with "points of presence" (POP) in the various cities where it was offered. Each POP was a computer that held most of Prodigy's content—the elements that Prodigy figured would be most in demand.[10] Users would receive the content direct from their local POP computer, with no transmission delays.

If new data was requested by a member (email for example), the POP would dial up the Prodigy mainframe in White Plains, New York, and retrieve it. This way, Prodigy would not have to keep dedicated lines open; the plan was that most content would be delivered to the 120 POP sites only once.[11] Members would access it again and again from POP caches, but via local telephone lines.

The POP configuration was intended to save a tremendous amount of money by eliminating having to transmit and retransmit data to individual members' computers. Unfortunately, the plan was based on the uninformed or overly optimistic assumption that its membership would use the service in a passive mode, mostly reading. Prodigy's planners had missed or ignored the main element that drove online services: interactivity. Email and bulletin boards were used far more heavily than anyone had imagined. In 1990, 5 percent of Prodigy's membership sent or posted 3.7 million messages (95 percent sent or posted 360,000 messages). This was far more than Prodigy had counted on.

Okay, so it was a minority interacting, but it was a *busy* minority. That 5 percent was costing Prodigy plenty. Leased lines for the service's POP computers were carrying over 40 million messages per year. The leased lines cost around two dollars per hour, but the cumulative bill was several million dollars per year.

Censored!

It got worse when Prodigy began censoring content on bulletin boards early in 1991. The censorship seems to have been inspired by a post containing anti-Semitic comments copied from a private email message, and the reply to those remarks. The post was deleted from a public board by Prodigy staff. The fellow trying to post the offensive material attempted to post his reply more than a dozen times. Each time it was deleted.

The would-be poster complained to the Anti-Defamation League (ADL), and suddenly it was like virtual Keystone Cops. Facts were garbled, and the ADL jumped to the conclusion that an anti-Semitic post had been made, and the press picked up the story. The ACLU rushed to get in on this high-profile dispute—all over messages that two people had seen.

---

[10] This is called "caching."

[11] Prodigy built a system of 250 minicomputers at 120 sites around the country.

By the time the press sorted out what was posted and what was not, Prodigy was censoring *all* bulletin boards. Staffers previewed everything— every single message—and blocked posts that might contain *anything* offensive to *anyone*. It was a Sisyphean labor, and they overdid it. Messages containing the world "beaver" were deleted because it was used in sexual slang. Notes on a dog breeders' board that contained the word "bitch" were likewise deleted.

Many brand names were prohibited, out of consideration for Prodigy's advertisers. You couldn't even use another member's full name in a post, lest you defame or insult him.

"My Name Is Dime . . . Roosevelt Dime"

The online rumor mills went wild when word got out that Prodigy was practicing censorship. A frequently repeated story—likely to be apocryphal— had to do with an attempted discussion in a coin collectors' bulletin board about the Roosevelt Dime—that is, the ten-cent American coin that has Franklin Delano Roosevelt's profile stamped on the obverse (front), minted from 1946 through the present.

The story goes that posts containing the phrase "Roosevelt Dime" were deleted by Prodigy's bulletin board patrol, supposedly because there was a Prodigy member named Roosevelt Dime.

Apparently, no one bothered to ask Mr. Dime whether he was offended. Or maybe his own posts were deleted because they contained the name "Roosevelt Dime." Did Roosevelt Dime really exist? He has yet to come forward.

Prodigy would have done better to stay in hands-off mode. Someone should have at least examined how other services handled such issues. As it was, trying to control messages on public bulletin boards incited some members to post even more offensive material.

Members complained to the attorney general of Texas, among other states, and before long class-action and other lawsuits were organized. The matter was eventually settled, to no one's satisfaction, least of all Prodigy's. Prodigy spent thousands of dollars to pay the salaries of the censors. The costs of the ill will and damage to Prodigy's reputation were incalcuable.

"Of Course You Realize . . . This Means War!"

Prodigy members were incensed. A Cooperative Defense Committee was organized among the membership, the leaders preparing for war. Some online activists claimed that more than 20,000 members were involved.

Members retaliated by organizing bulletin board users into underground email groups. Conversation threads were picked up from the boards and circulated via email in listserv fashion. Each member added her comments, then passed them on to everyone else. The email traffic grew to staggering proportions, given the sending and re-sending of messages hundreds and even thousands of times.

It was like having to transmit Usenet newsgroups to hordes of computer users several times a day. Prodigy's telecommunications charges were out of control.

Prodigy returned fire with a limit on free email. Prodigy executives claimed that the volume of email was increasing at a rate of 20 percent per month, and that the cost was intolerable. So, beginning January 1, 1991, members would be allowed to send 30 messages per month free; after that, their accounts were charged 25 cents for each message. CC'ing a message to other members also cost 25 cents a pop.

At the same time, Prodigy raised its rate from $12.95 to $14.95.

These measures did not have the desired effect. Dissatisfied subscribers protested with posts on Prodigy's bulletin boards. These were usually caught by the censors.[12] Some of the protesters emailed several advertisers to let them know that they were sponsoring a service that curtailed freedom of speech.

The members who wrote to Prodigy advertisers (8, according to some stories, or 12, according to others) had their accounts cancelled, but were later invited to return on the condition that they follow Prodigy's rules—including a new rule that prohibited members from writing to advertisers for any reason other than to ask about a product or an order.

The mood in some quarters bordered on hysteria. Rumors flew that Prodigy was reading everyone's email. But there was no proof (and, really, no motivation for Prodigy to read members' mail), so all irate members could do was spread discontent and look for other problems on Prodigy to use as ammo.

---

[12] *It was against Prodigy's rules to say anything that put Prodigy in a bad light, or that might cause people to change to another service.*

No, Not Spyware!

Problems were found. The next Prodigy crisis (Prodigy couldn't seem to avoid them) had to do with Prodigy software. Prodigy's setup was akin to a sealed system. Users could not upload or download files (there were none to download) or save anything to disk, not even email. The only way to get something from Prodigy was to memorize it, copy it with a pencil, or print it out—and printing didn't work everywhere on the service. As you saw in Figure 14-3 earlier, some screen-capture software could grab an image, but it would not always get all the detail in a screen.

That aspect of Prodigy (rationalized by fears of violating copyrights) led to the discovery of what looked like evidence that Prodigy was collecting data from members' disks.

Prodigy worked like GEIS, Playnet, and AOL in that it built part of the service on members' systems. On the MS-DOS system, this involved writing temporary data to their disks, specifically to two files called `stage.dat` and `cache.dat`. (Various versions of AOL make a file and folder with the same names.) The files were deleted when members logged off.

Several people working independently to hack a way to save Prodigy elements to disk found what was left of these files and examined their contents. They discovered that the files sometimes contained information created by other applications, like word processors.

Whoa! It didn't take long for word of that to spread. "Something I created with my word processor [or database, spreadsheet, etc.] is in a file created by Prodigy? That means that they are spying on me—collecting information from my disk. Stone them!"

Thus was a conspiracy spun from a few stray data bytes.

As it worked out, the reason there was material from other programs in the files' disk areas was because the areas were actually deleted file space, and other applications were writing new data to the empty space, just as they were supposed to do.

There were lots of excitable folks who didn't want to believe that, so Prodigy was forced to revise some of its software. Prodigy members were sent new disks that would zero out the areas used by `stage.dat` and `cache.dat`. A lot of people were disappointed that something more sinister wasn't going on. After all, this was corporate America on their disks; they *had* to be up to something, didn't they?

Despite this attitude, the controversy eventually died out, not to return until the Web came along and *real* spyware was developed.

Prodigy Picnic

Prodigy was strong on public relations and image. The service was presented as a family place, friendly and open to everyone. And Prodigy was eager to show members a friendly face after the scandals. To that end, the company sponsored huge Prodigy summer picnics in cities across the country. The company rented out entire amusement parks in some cities (like Coney Island in Cincinnati) and invited all members to come out and enjoy free food, tug-o-war games, prizes, and more.

This was not the first time that online service members held a meeting. But it was the first systemwide event. But the goodwill generated meant nothing when Prodigy killed chat.

"Didn't Prodigy Invent the Internet?"

As if all this wasn't enough, Prodigy members venturing out to other online services—and, after early 1994, to the Internet—got the same contempt and cold-shoulder treatment as AOL users had received. It was a bit worse for Prodigy-ites because Prodigy let users think that it *was* the Internet, or had invented the Internet.

The quote that opens this chapter is one example of how these ideas were perpetuated. The same 1999 press release from which the quote is excerpted also offered these paragraphs, which certainly surprised those of us who had been online with CompuServe and other online services for years *before* 1989:

> *Many Prodigy Classic[13] members have been with Prodigy since the beginning—1989—when the Internet was still in its infancy. The general public didn't know about e-mail, e-commerce didn't exist and there was no "Internet" as we know it today.*

> *Prodigy was the first to bring these early-adopters services such as a World Wide Web browser, e-mail and online airline reservations and banking.*

Um . . . what about Mosaic and Netscape, Internet and DELPHI email, and Eaasy Sabre? Of course, the statements were erroneous, the result of

---

[13] *"Prodigy Classic" was used to designate the online service after Prodigy began providing Internet services separately as "Prodigy Internet."*

hyperbole or possibly ignorance.[14] Fortunately, most newspapers and magazines knew better. But Prodigy members suffered scorn and derision wherever they went online. It didn't help that Prodigy's president and CEO, Theodore C. Papes, remarked during a 1991 newspaper interview, "Our approach is to try to get as many different types of people as you can. *When you are fundamentally engaged in making a new medium*, you don't know what people will react to." (Italics are the author's.)

"Making a new medium?" Enough said.

Files, Anyone?

In 1992, Prodigy beefed up its stock market services and set up a file download area. However, since it was co-sponsored by Ziff-Davis, the download area carried a price. There was a charge of $14.95 per month in addition to Prodigy's charges, plus $6 per hour after the first three hours of downloading each month. Prodigy probably got a little kickback on it all. (Aren't you glad the Internet offers so many free downloads?) The files were mostly shareware and freeware, and were at least in one area so you didn't have to trudge around the system to find them.

Although Ziff-Davis was making money by offering shareware files, it did not give the creators of the drawing cards—the shareware authors—a split. It did encourage downloaders to pay shareware authors a licensing fee if they really liked the programs. But the shareware users who paid the fee were a minority.

Prodigy's download system did offer a nice little extra; it told you if you had already downloaded a particular file. (Some other services kept download records, but you had to find and open a download log, then go through it manually.)

In another cooperative effort, Prodigy began offering the Yellow Pages with Nynex.

The New York Times, *Online at Last*

While Prodigy was grabbing headlines, *The New York Times* finally got its online service going. Top news stories and leisure, entertainment, news, sports and other content would be offered on AOL.

AOL members could read the *Times* five hours per month for $9.95 per month.

---

[14] *I sometimes wonder if the motivation behind statements like this wasn't to encourage such thinking. It would certainly make Prodigy more alluring to those who didn't know better.*

Turning On the Meter

In an online world accustomed to paying by the minute (bills for some services were broken down to fractions of a minute), the thought of a flat rate for unlimited usage was almost unbelievable.

This challenged the competition; how could they match unlimited usage for such a low price? How was Prodigy making money charging so little? The task was figuring out the magic numbers that would draw customers and not lose money.

While Prodigy was dealing with its various controversies, CompuServe, GEnie, DELPHI, AOL, and other services worked up competitive pricing plans, offering access to selected services for a flat rate. More popular products, like chat and file downloads, were still charged by the minute.

At AOL, a flat rate for unlimited access to all the service's offerings was, in the words of Steve Case, "highly unlikely." He told journalists, "To offer unlimited use, we'd have to charge a fairly high monthly fee, and that would price AOL out of the range of many people. We think a low monthly fee including a certain amount of usage is a better approach."

Of course, the amount of free usage set by an online service under this sort of pricing plan would be below the average time a typical member spent online, after which the per-minute charge kicked in.

GEnie, on the other hand, took the approach that most of its members could be retained if they got a break on at least part of the service. And new members might find GEnie's plan more attractive than other services' price structures.

Bill Louden came up with a two-tier approach, somewhat akin to the early pricing structure at Q-Link. Under the Star°Services plan, launched in October 1989, GEnie offered a set of basic services that included email as well as shopping, news, and information features. (GEnie changed the name to GEnie°Basic after Prodigy threatened a lawsuit over the use of their star trademark.) Unlimited access to GEnie°Basic services was only $4.95 per month.

Email was among the most valuable elements of an online service in the eyes of its users, so offering it gave GEnie°Basic extra value. Users would still pay by the minute for chat, downloads, RoundTable bulletin boards, and gaming.

GEIS management was dubious, but Louden was confident in this lower-cost plan. "When we launched Star°Services in October 1989," said Louden, "the deal I had with my management was that, if my financial forecasts were correct, our flat pricing model of $4.95 for Basic Services would double revenue in 6 months. If GEnie achieved those numbers by June 1990, we would have nearly $20 Million in new revenues—not booked with GE corporate—for the year.

"The deal with my GEIS management, was that since this would be revenue, and profits Corporate GE was not expecting, we could apply this to build new products, a GUI (like Apple°Link), and perhaps even our own client-server systems as mainframes.

"GEIS agreed to split the additional proceeds fifty-fifty—I would get nearly $10 million of the new-found profits to invest in GEnie and they would get $10 million to invest in other GEIS projects."

GEnie was able to provide such a wide range of services at such a low price in part because it operated its own network, which reduced overhead that most other online services couldn't. CompuServe ran its own network, too, but it would be some time before it offered a flat-rate plan.

DELPHI, BIX, and other services would spend much of the new decade experimenting with alternative pricing policies to stay in the competition. DELPHI rolled out its "20/20 Plan," which gave members 20 hours a month for $20, with per-minute charges after 20 hours. Most online services also worked to improve quality and develop new products, but pricing was too sensitive an issue to neglect for long.

Customers naturally benefited from the pricing competition. So did the online service business as a whole, because lower pricing attracted more and more new members at all the services. "The flat-rate pricing model spurred the real growth of the industry," according to DELPHI President Dan Bruns. "When people didn't have to worry about paying 10 cents a minute or 20 cents a minute, the prospect of going online was suddenly more attractive."

In the end, all the consumer services would go to unlimited usage for day and nighttime access—but that was still several years in the future. It would require the Internet to make it work.

Ironically, while the other services were pondering how to cut their rates without cutting profits, Prodigy was coming to the realization that it would have to go to per-minute billing for at least some of its services. The 25-cent surcharge on email that had so angered members did not make up the cost of the message traffic over its leased lines. Nor would unit charges on other services solve their problems.

Reluctantly, Prodigy gave in and began offering a basic/premium services billing arrangement similar to GEnie's. Email carried no extra time-usage charges, but bulletin boards were surcharged. (This inspired the creation of yet another Prodigy front end to take most of the bulletin board functions offline: Bulletin Board Manager.)

Announced in 1993, the new charges met with the predictable uproar, along with reissues of "Prodigy Sucks!" T-shirts. But Prodigy wasn't exactly getting rich on its members; it would not turn a profit for over a year.

A variety of experiments in pricing followed, including the partner/ surcharge deals described in this chapter. Prodigy also tried a $25 per month flat rate that granted members access to everything but services like Ziff-Davis' files for 25 hours. The changes in charges were like a fish flopping around out of water. Prodigy's growth flattened for a while as many people left for other services offering various incentives. (AOL, for example, *lowered* its flat rate to $9.95 and picked up a lot of Prodigy subscribers.)

Esther Dyson probably hit the nail on the head when she summed up Prodigy's rate problems. "They thought they'd make revenues from people making purchases," she told *The New York Times*. "But they discovered people were less interested in shopping on the service than communicating. And they don't know how to charge for communications."

That simple statement precisely defined the appeal of online services: communication. This wasn't a big revelation. Online service members had known this for years, as had many of the people who ran online services. But this basic truth somehow eluded the people who ran Prodigy.

Chat, at Last

Prodigy began life without chat rooms, having ignored the examples of other online services, who knew that the biggest draw was user interactivity. One look at CompuServe's CB Simulator should have been enough to convince TPTB (the powers that be) at Prodigy that it would need a chat system. But this fact was somehow missed.

Prodigy decided to make up for it and add chat in 1994.

Prodigy also stopped acting (for a while) like it was the only online service. A press release announcing Prodigy's chat service, issued on February 22, 1994, said, in part:

> *Most of Prodigy's rivals in the on-line industry have long offered chat. In the last year the service, which is a joint venture between IBM and Sears, has made a number of moves aimed at making Prodigy more like its rivals, allowing some file downloads, for instance.*

Prodigy Chat, as it was known, was offered as an unlimited service with no surcharge.

The company had not learned its lesson from the bulletin board and email wars. Telecommunications charges went through the roof as thousands and thousands of members logged on to chat for 5, 10, and even 12 hours per day. Some just signed on and left their computers connected to chat while they did other things.

As Esther Dyson said, ". . . they don't know how to charge for communications."

Horrified by the cost and the goings-on in chat rooms, Prodigy shut down chat, and out came the "Prodigy Sucks!" T-shirts. People were enraged and hundreds waged nonstop wars against the service with BBS postings and email on Prodigy and other services.

Many of us knew that the unlimited chat couldn't last. I and others wrote to Prodigy executives and told them what would happen when they first announced that they were adding chat. Apparently they didn't believe that people were capable of spending so much time in chat. A little time spent in chat rooms on CompuServe, GEnie, AOL, or DELPHI would have convinced Prodigy's management that it could not support unlimited chat with the system arcitecture it employed.

Prodigy would survive this and other blunders, and go on to introduce Internet services like Usenet and FTP (though it was *not* the first online service to do so, despite its claims). It also tried creating its own web browser, but that flopped.

The Prodigy company and brand went through several iterations, building an ISP business in 1997 and maintaining the online service aspect ("Prodigy Classic") until 1999, when Y2K issues forced the company to choose between investing more money or closing the online service. It chose the latter.

Since 1999, it has gone through a number of owners. Among other things, it provided ISP services in Mexico for several years, and it is active on a limited basis in the United States. Sears and IBM are no longer involved.

In retrospect, Prodigy had several good ideas behind it. The refined NAPLPS graphics and speedy response time made possible by its POP servers were tremendous advantages. The bulletin board structure was well-thought-out. Even the sale of advertising was a good thing. It shifted part of the load of generating revenue away from the membership. (The idea of turning a good profit with online advertising would be perfected by AOL and the Web.)

Several other clever ideas were implemented on the service, but poor management and ignoring the competition and the results of its research eventually knocked it out of the business.

And, if nothing else, Prodigy introduced several million people to the online world, and made consumer online services get serious about competing on pricing, which eventually led to flat-rate pricing for everyone—the template for Internet access.

∼

AOL, BIX, CompuServe, DELPHI, Genie, Prodigy, The WELL, and their counterparts in other countries prepared the world for the Web. But most disappeared on the way to the Web. So did ARPANET. What happened to these pioneering efforts? On to the next chapter!

Moving to the Net

Ninety percent of all good things that I can think of that have been done in computer science have been funded by that agency [ARPA]. Chances that they would have been funded elsewhere are very low. The basic ARPA idea is that you find good people and you give them a lot of money and then you step back. If they don't do good things in three years they get dropped—where "good" is very much related to new or interesting.

—Alan Kay, personal computing pioneer

If I had to sum up the story of the Internet and online services through the end of the twentieth century in as few words as possible, I might write the following:

ARPANET was decommissioned in 1989, replaced by a new Internet backbone called NSFNET[1] that connected scores of universities and would soon carry commercial traffic.[2] Prodigy, CompuServe, and AOL brought tens of millions of new members online. DELPHI, the smallest of the remaining online services, broke 100,000 in membership.

Then came the Web. All of the consumer online services in the United States, except for AOL, The WELL, and CompuServe, went out of business after failing as ISPs and/or losing most of their membership to conventional Internet Service Providers (ISPs). And here we are today.

---

[1] *National Science Foundation NETwork, detailed later in this chapter.*

[2] *Though the original ARPANET was officially offline, several of its Internet message processors (IMPs) remained in service, connecting their computers with the Internet.*

That's overly simplistic, of course. There's so much more to it than that: international expansion of online services, the opening up of the Internet, the end of consumer online services as you've read about them in these pages, and much more, including a few twists and surprises. Hence, this chapter.

International Expansion

It is interesting to note that, when American online services reached across the oceans, personal computer BBS networks were already there. Networks like FidoNET carried netmail (private messages) and echomail (entire bulletin board topics)[3] internationally. Similar networks existed on other continents, and some still serve in lieu of online services, as has been the case with Fido BBSs in Russia.

ARPANET was there ahead of everyone, of course, with network links to England and Norway in 1973, and many more thereafter.

CompuServe, as noted in earlier chapters, began to expand internationally in the 1980s, with CompuServe UK and Germany, and NIFTY-Serve in Japan (Figure 15-1). There was CompuServe for the Latin world, too.

Figure 15-1. NIFTY-Serve

---

[3] *To move netmail and echomail quickly, and thus keep long-distance bills low, the Fido system compresses the data to be relayed.*

AOL began expanding in Europe in partnership with the Bertelsmann Group, launching AOL Germany in November 1995. AOL UK, AOL France, and AOL Canada were all rolled out in 1996.

In 1998, AOL and Bertelsmann would put AOL Australia online. AOL for Japan was a natural next step in 1999. That service was a joint venture between AOL and Mitsui.

GEnie moved into Europe in the late 1990s, courtesy of the globe-girdling GEIS network.

DELPHI partnered with ASCII Corporation in 1991 to create Japanese online services, and it developed a Spanish-language service in Argentina. (The most important elements of DELPHI—menus, prompts, help, and so forth—were translated into Spanish.)

Long-Distance News

Before international versions of CompuServe, DELPHI, and so forth were available, a fairly large number of Europeans and Japanese used their local Tymnet or Telenet nodes to reach American online services. (Some used other networks, native to their countries.) Billing for the overseas link was sometimes handled by the online service, but often the modem user had to set up a separate account with the packet-switching network she used.

These transoceanic networkers were spending $35 per hour or more, and some of them spent hours in chat. We figured these fellows were either wealthy or really, *really* into connecting with America. (This was during the mid- and late-1980s.)

Sometimes it was possible get news of world events before the news media broke the story. This happened with the Tiananmen Square Massacre in 1989. I was chatting on DELPHI with my friend Akira in Tokyo when he asked me to wait for four or five minutes. When he started typing again, it was to tell me that he was listening to a Chinese radio station, which had just reported the massacre. I checked my watch and counted 22 minutes between Akira telling me the news and CNN breaking the story.

Each of the countries penetrated by American online services had their own online services and BBSs, but nothing really like CompuServe or AOL. Among the more popular dialup services in the United Kingdom was CIX, still in service today. Japan's dialup services were a mix of BBSs and small consumer services like Nikkei-MIX and JIX. For a time, dedicated word processors (*wah-paroo*) outfitted with modems were popular as terminals for dialing up BBSs and online services.

Nearly every country with online services had versions of Minitel or Videotex or teletext. In England, for example there were Oracle (Figure 15-2), Viewdata, and Prestel, among others. France had the original Minitel

(Figure 15-3), which was first demonstrated as Teletel in 1980. In Brazil, Minitel was popular in the 1980s and 1990s. Canada had Telidon, as well as Minitel clone Alec in limited use. In Japan, an experimental system called CAPTAIN,[4] in operation from 1979 through 1981, could transmit not only graphics and ASCII characters, but also Kanji and other shaped or drawn characters.

Figure 15-2. ORACLE screen

Figure 15-3. Minitel screen

---

[4] *CAPTAIN is an acronym derived from "Character and Pattern Telephone Access Information Network."*

Apple Replay

Back in the United States, Apple returned to AOL in 1993, all but begging the company to set up a new online service for them. AOL management and staff refused, protesting that they were too busy. Apple persisted and finally persuaded AOL to set up a network for their Macintosh. It was named *eWorld*.

The cartoon-like virtual electronic world opened in June 1994. It was very compelling with its graphical metaphor—a town in which doorways into shops, newsstands, and the like served as links to various products and services. Figure 15-4 shows the eWorld "town." Members used GUI software provided by AOL It had the same ancestry as AOL's other Apple products, the original GEIS GUI.

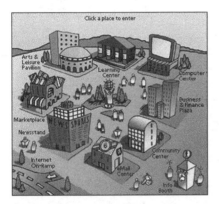

Figure 15-4. Apple/AOL's eWorld

Although the emphasis was on Macintosh, a Windows version was promised. Disappointing response from the Macintosh community led Apple to shut down eWorld in 1996, just as preparations were being made for Internet access. AOL salvaged some of the content and most of the members for the Mac version of its service.

Opening Up the Internet

As the Internet backbone and organizer—and the nearest thing to "authority" that the Internet had—NSFNET maintained a certain status quo and established rules for access to and use of the Internet.[5]

---

[5] *Other entities managed specific elements, such as the administration of domain names.*

The NSFNET went online in 1986 as a backbone to which regional and academic networks would connect. It experienced exponential growth in its network traffic. The original 56Kbps links were upgraded to 1.5Mbps in 1988 and again to 45Mbps in 1991.

Computer Science Net, the National Science Foundation, and the Internet

As large as it was, ARPANET was limited. For a commercial entity or a university's computer science department to connect with ARPANET, it had to be involved in some kind of government project, usually military. This— or the annual cost of $100,000 or more to maintain a site—excluded about 88 percent of university computer science departments nationwide.

The National Science Foundation (created in 1950 to promote scientific progress by funding basic research and science education) resolved to remedy this situation by creating a network open to all computer science departments. In 1981 Computer Science Net (CSNET) went online, funded by the NSF with the proviso that it be self-supporting in five years.

The network's infrastructure was based on Telenet X.25 communications, which enabled CSNET to connect more than 100 sites at a fifth of the cost of ARPANET. (Some departments used an email-only portion of the network called PhoneNet that cost even less.) It could also communicate with ARPANET using TCP/IP.

By 1986, CSNET was self-supporting and the NSF had turned to building a network to connect five university supercomputer sites.[6] Dubbed the National Science Foundation Network (NSFNET), it used TCP/IP protocols and was compatible with ARPANET.

Commercial organizations could sign on to use NSFNET at no charge.

In 1987, a nonprofit consortium of public universities called Merit Network, Inc. took over management of NSFNET. The consortium included MCI, IBM, and several Michigan Universities. Connected to ARPANET and other networks it had created, NSFNET became a "network of networks," the true Internet.

NSF's acceptable-use policy precluded using the Internet for commercial endeavors. The ban covered selling access to the Internet. As things had always been, any entity that connected with the Internet had to have a reason to be there. Universities, researchers, and government contractors were

---

[6] *The sites were Princeton University, Cornell University, the University of California at San Diego, the University of Illinois at Urbana-Champaign, and the University of Pittsburgh.*

typical Internet users. Individuals and businesses without any proper affiliation were not. (You could not just dial up "the Internet" with your home computer and modem, in any event: it couldn't speak the language of TCP/IP. Just as today, you had to dial up a computer equipped to communicate with the Internet, and properly connect to it.)

At the same time, a growing number of online service users were asking about Internet access. They'd read or heard about this vast, worldwide network, and wondered what they could do with it. Some had seen samples of Usenet or BITNET discussions, and wanted in on the conversations. Having neither motivation nor permission, commercial online services did not connect with the Internet.

Still, there were ways to access portions of the Internet. In 1988, "civilians" were given a public link to the Internet via the FidoNET BBS network. FidoNET linked with the Internet and started relaying Usenet newsgroups in 1988.[7] A relatively small number of people knew about the FidoNET link. The newer generations of modem users knew nothing of BBSs. They were far fewer in number than they had been in the early 1980s, and the majority of online service users had no idea how to find and access microcomputer bulletin boards.

In the late 1980s, several more public links to the Internet were created. UUNET began operating as a nonprofit commercial source of Usenet newsgroups 1987. In 1988, the online service CIX in the United Kingdom began providing Internet email and Usenet newsgroups to its members. (Not bad for a service that began as a FidoNET BBS in 1983.)

In 1989, MCI Mail became the first commercial email system to connect with the Internet. It had already pioneered intersystem email with CompuServe, using what was called an X.400 connection.[8] Within months, CompuServe, Telemail (Sprintmail, shown in Figure 15-5), and On Tyme (Tymnet) also had email links to the Internet (and via the Internet, with one another).

Three commercial ISPs were created that year as well: UUNET, PSINET, and CERFNET. In 1990, UUNET opened a commercial ISP service called AlterNet.

Users of these early services had email and newsgroup access, and varying levels of access to other Internet services. Access to the World Wide Web was available with gopher, but it was not until the introduction of the Mosaic web browser in 1993 that great numbers of people became interested in web access.

---

[7] *FidoNET used a system called* echomail *to transfer postings on member BBSs' bulletin boards before it started carrying Usenet newsgroups.*

[8] *X.400 is the name for a set of protocols for addressing and exchanging email messages between disparate message-handling systems, just as X.25 is a set of protocols for handling messages on a packet-switched network.*

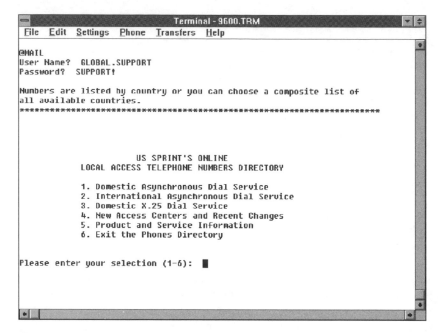

Figure 15-5. SprintNet

Decommissioning ARPANET

In the mid-1980s, the National Science Foundation (NSF) commissioned a high-performance, high-capacity data network built on TCP/IP as developed by ARPANET. MCI and IBM were the contractors for this network, which was called NSFNET.

NSFNET became the backbone of ARPANET, at the same time connecting to new networks. MCI Mail was the first "outside" commercial interest to link up with the new Internet backbone. ARPANET was decommissioned in 1990, and NSFNET became the backbone of the Internet.

Then ISPs PSINET and UUNET were connected, followed by others. The National Information Infrastructure Act of 1993 was passed, and the NSF relaxed its rules about commercial access. The commercial viability of the Internet was evident.

In 1995, the NSF ended its support of NSFNET. Today, MCI and CompuServe's network are the major Internet backbone.

Online Services and the Internet

Although the NSF forbade overt commercial use of the Internet, in 1992 DELPHI found a legitimate reason to include the Internet in its offerings. One of its clients, an environmental group with its own forum, had an affiliation that entitled it to Internet access.

DELPHI first provided Internet email in November 1992. Shortly after, DELPHI members had access to Usenet, telnet for file transfers, FTP, finger, MUDs,[9] and gopher, as well as text-based web access. Figure 15-6 shows a DELPHI front end. The surcharge for Internet access was just three dollars per month.

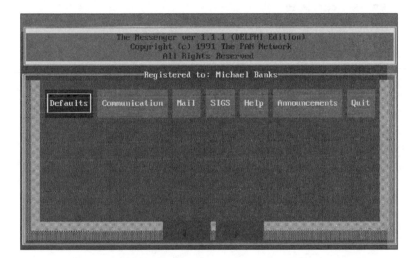

Figure 15-6. DELPHI's Messenger front end

DELPHI's advantage was somewhat diminished after the National Information Infrastructure Act of 1993 was passed. The Act's stated intentions included making the Internet as widely available to the public as possible, and moving the Internet into the commercial sphere to encourage public investment. This led NSFNET to decide to relax its acceptable-use policy.

Not everyone understood the ramifications of NSFNET's decision. There was much speculation and argument among those online as to whether it was legitimate and legal to advertise goods for sale on online services. Certainly some commercial entities were active on the online services, but CompuServe and the rest were not regulated common carriers like telephone companies and broadcasters. They made their own rules. But the Internet was different. The government was involved.

---

[9] *Multi-User Dungeons, an online gaming environment.*

It was the beginning of a trend. Internet geeks were shocked—many predicted that the Internet would be "ruined" by business. (Some would say that it has been ruined, forgetting that if it were not for commercial development the Internet would be smaller and far less efficient than it is today.)

Most online services, of course, had no problem understanding the new acceptable-use policy. DELPHI's Internet services caught some off-guard, but when the National Information Infrastructure Act of 1993 was signed into law, everyone knew it was only a matter of time before all the online services offered Internet access. Some services would add surcharges to certain Internet services, and limit the use of others.

AOL offered Internet access in a piecemeal fashion. A special front end for Usenet newsgroups was set up in 1994, and FTP access was added about the same time. (The newsgroup `alt.aol.sucks` was not on the list of available groups, but if you knew the name you could read it.)

AOL bought Spry, Inc. for its Global Network Navigator (GNN) and a foundation for an ISP business in 1995. It announced web access via "Mosaic in a Box" software designed by Spry, but a year later closed GNN and AOL became an ISP, with Microsoft Internet Explorer as its primary web browser.[10]

AOL was among the first online services to make certain features (like email) available through the Web.

BIX added full Internet access in 1993. DELPHI had acquired BIX in 1992, and Internet access followed DELPHI's Internet upgrade.

CompuServe (which had pioneered intersystem email with MCI Mail) opened its Internet email gateway in 1993, with surcharges for email over a certain amount. At the time, FTP and telnet were "under study."

In November 1994, CompuServe brought FTP and telnet to its members. The Internet was blended into its CIM (CompuServe Information Manager) front ends as well. A Usenet reader was available late in 1995. And, like AOL, CompuServe made some services available from the Internet.

The First Online Mall

From 1992 on, there were endless discussions as to the legality, legitimacy, and desirability of commercial activities on the Internet and the Web. What would happen if you set up a commercial website and offered to sell, say, model rockets or used computers? Would your ISP cut off access? Were you courting a visit from guys in black suits? Could you be arrested and charged for violating some obscure law?

---

[10] *Netscape was originally chosen by AOL, but when Microsoft offered to put AOL on the Windows desktop, AOL switched to Microsoft Internet Explorer. Later AOL announced that Netscape would be the official browser for* aol.com.

These concerns existed even after the National Information Infrastructure Act of 1993 and NSFNET's subsequent decision to relax its acceptable-use policy for the Internet. In February 1994, author and consultant Dave Taylor was assigned to write a magazine article about companies doing business on the Internet. He started by looking for a registry of such operations, and was surprised to find that there was no such list anywhere. So, he put together his own roster (in conjunction with the magazine article) and began publishing it as "a monthly list of commercial services available via the Internet."

The text-only document, titled *The Internet Mall*, started with a modest 34 entries. Distributed to a mailing list, it rapidly grew in size and popularity as more online services opened Internet email access. (Note that *The Internet Mall* was not spam; recipients heard about the list or received a copy from friends, then requested it.)

The Internet Mall document was organized as a virtual multistory department store, with each "floor's" merchants offering a different category of merchandise—books, music, and video on the first floor; personal items on the second, and so on. Individual retailer listings consisted of breezy descriptions, with instructions on how to connect to online stores using such arcane methods as gopher and telnet, and later via the Web. Email addresses were also supplied.

The list was financed by corporate underwriting.

The Internet Mall was simple, effective, and a first for the Internet. (CompuServe and other services hosted their own online merchants, but were not then accessible through the Internet.) At a time when commercial activity on the Internet was of dubious legitimacy and frowned on by purists, it was downright radical.

Taylor sold the Internet mall concept and trademark to TechWave. A couple of years later he put together another startup called iTrack.com, the first third-party auction search system (which has since been sold). *The Internet Mall* itself was supplanted by search engines and mainstream advertising, but was the template on which online malls have been created ever since.

The first *online mall* (with merchants displaying their wares and interacting with the public) of any note was probably the Electronic Mall, which CompuServe established in 1984 with the L.M. Berry Company. The Electronic Mall attract quite a few big names, including Bantam Books, Sears, Waldenbooks, AT&T, and others. As for the identity of the first web-based retailer and the first web shopping mall ... those are matters of contention among the many who claim to have been first.

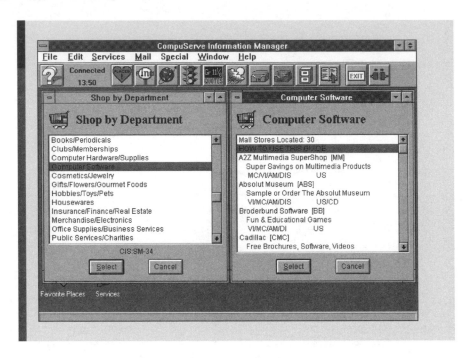

GEnie's email link to the Net also went online in 1993. Care was taken to make sure no viruses made it through with email. The same motivation slowed and limited Usenet access. Selected newsgroups were posted twice weekly. Gopher and FTP were also implemented.

Despite all evidence to the contrary, Prodigy strove mightily to stake its claim as the first online service to offer the Internet. Early in 1993 it added Internet email access to only the DOS version of its software. Windows and Mac would take longer. In 1994 Prodigy created its own integrated browser (Figure 15-7) and used it to provide FTP and gopher access. The Prodigy browser was not up to par compared to other browsers, and the company eventually abandoned it.

Prodigy did not bring in Usenet newsgroups until 1995. There was a predictable, though mild, uproar when it did not allow the newsgroup `alt.prodigy.sucks`.

The WELL was offering Internet access before the end of 1993. Thousands of Usenet newsgroups were available, along with telnet and other services. And outsiders could access some of The WELL's files via gopher.

Database services such as Dialog and Lexis/Nexis were quick to offer access through the Internet with telnet, at their standard per-minute rates. Sometimes a surcharge was added for coming in through the Net. Once the Web became commonplace, it was standard operating procedure to offer database services through websites.

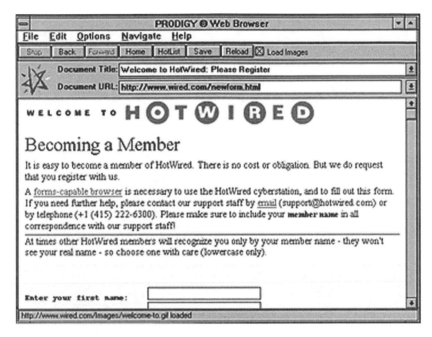

Figure 15-7. Prodigy web browser

One Step Forward, Two Steps Back

Even with Internet access in place and ISPs popping up everywhere, it took several years for the majority of modem users to get involved with the Internet and the Web. The online services offered limited front ends for the pre-Web Internet. With online services or conventional ISPs, you had to learn quite a bit (or memorize lots of steps) to get much done on the Internet. Gopher, WAIS, FTP, telnet, Archie, and other mysterious programs or tools had to be put to work—which in itself was a lot of work. Figure 15-8 shows one of the more simplified Internet front ends.

It was almost as difficult for the newcomer as logging on to The Source or CompuServe had been in 1980.

The Web was a whole new learning experience. First, you had to penetrate all the flack and buzz and argument to figure out which browser to use (unless your ISP did that for you). Then you had to figure out what you could and could not do with or through your browser, how to collect your email, how to find the great graphics and programs you downloaded, where and how to find what online, and lots more!

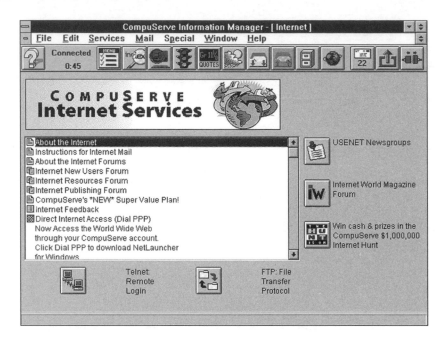

Figure 15-8. CompuServe's front end for Internet services

Fortunately, it took a lot less time for the Web to evolve to relative simplicity than it did for online services. But there's always something new to learn on the Web, and there always will be.

Where Are They Now?

So, what happened to the online services that survived the late 1980s shake-out? Let's have a look.

AOL is . . . well, it's AOL, the largest ISP on the planet, unique in being a content-intensive service as well as an ISP. It merged with Time Warner in 2000, and books are still being written about that event.[11] The company is engaged in a complex range of online services in addition to being an ISP and offering its own proprietary content. Figure 15-9 shows the contemporary AOL sign-on screen, the gateway to AOL services.

---

[11] *There are several books about the continuing saga of the merger. It's best to read them all if you want the full story, as each has multiple errors and omissions.*

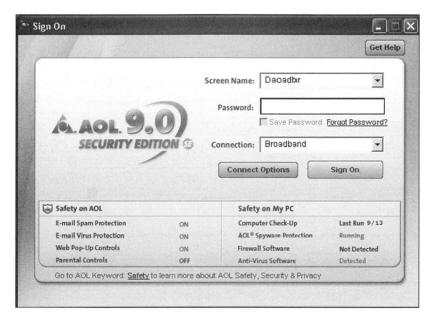

Figure 15-9. AOL today

BIX was bought by DELPHI in 1992, and DELPHI closed it down in 2001. Before that, several front ends were developed for it, including "blinking" software designed to sign on, download entire conferences, post messages, and sign off in minimal time. BIXnav for Windows, shown in Figure 15-10, was just the finishing touch BIX needed to bring it up to par with other services, but the service ceased to exist all too soon after it was introduced.

```
Terminal - 9600.TRM
File  Edit  Settings  Phone  Transfers  Help


   BIX Main Menu

 1  Electronic Mail
 2  Conference Subsystem
 3  Listings (file upload/download areas)
 4  NewsBytes - Industry News Briefs
 5  Subscriber Information
 6  Individual Options
 7  Quick Download
 8  Command Mode (abandon menus)
 9  Logoff (bye)
10  Internet Services (ftp, telnet, Usenet news, etc.)

Enter a menu option or ? for help: █
```

Figure 15-10. BIX in its final incarnation

Yahoo! now owns the `bix.com` domain and `http://www.bix.com` will take you to `bix.yahoo.com`, a music site. Former BIX member G. Armour van Horn and others formed the NLZ (Noise Level Zero) website to continue BIX's conferences in spirit as well as fact. (See `http://www.nlz.com`.) NLZ is a threaded and moderated conference system among whose primary goals is to keep the "noise level" (irrelevant talk) at an absolute minimum, while keeping useful content at a maximum. Topics range from computers and space, to religion and music, and a lot in between.

CompuServe would continue refining its content and various front ends throughout the 1990s. In 1996, it attempted to meet AOL and Prodigy head-on with a GUI-based online service called WOW! (Figure 15-11), but that service failed within a year.

Figure 15-11. CompuServe's ill-fated WOW! service

AOL acquired CompuServe in 1998, as a part of a complicated deal involving WorldComm (now Verizon). Today, CompuServe (Figure 15-12) remains in business as an ISP, advertising platform, and information provider.

In 1993, DELPHI became "DELPHI Internet," and was sold to Rupert Murdoch's News Corporation. (Talk about mainstreaming!) Sophisticated front ends were developed for it, including DELPHI InterNav (Figure 15-13), and it grew to more than 100,000 subscribers by 1995, but that wasn't quite the growth Murdoch anticipated. Some of DELPHI's original management bought the company back in 1996.

The new management, led by Dan Bruns and including Bill Louden (who had left GEnie by this time) rebuilt DELPHI into an Internet-based service, with managed content and advertising. It eventually evolved into a community site. Prospero Technologies (`http://www.prosperotechnologies.com`) is the direct descendent of DELPHI. A DELPHI Forums project remains active at `http://www.delphiforums.com`.

Figure 15-12. CompuServe today

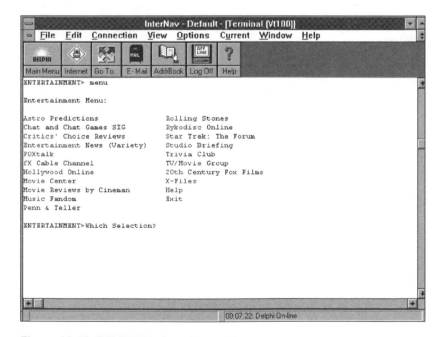

Figure 15-13. DELPHI Windows front end

Handicapped by the lack of a GUI, GEnie lost ground to the rest of the online services throughout the 1990s. Louden achieved his goal of generating millions of dollars of new revenue with GEnie's flat-rate pricing plan (see Chapter 13), but GEIS did not follow up on giving GEnie its share of the revenue—which would have enabled GEnie to create GUIs for its service.

"This was probably the beginning of the end for GEnie," Bill Louden later related. "It was now obvious to me that GEnie would never be taken seriously by GEIS. Although we were #1 in Europe and #2 in the US at that time, we would always be the tail wagging the dog.

"With Star°Services, by the end of 1990, we closed closer to $50 million in revenues, but we were being managed like a cash cow business, not a growth business. As such, we were never going to get a GUI to compete with CIS or the emerging AOL threat. I left GEnie in early 1991 and came to US Videotel in Houston. AOL went public in the summer of 1991, I believe, and rightly so left everyone in the dust."

GEnie did get a reasonably functional and good-looking front end, as shown in Figure 15-14, but it was too late to turn the service into a competitor for CompuServe or AOL.

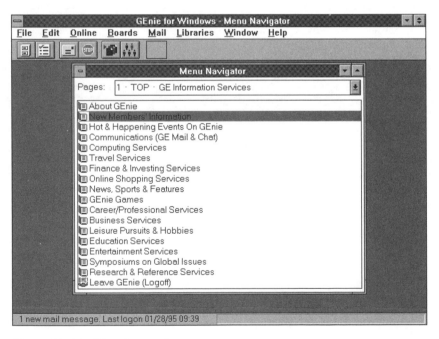

Figure 15-14. GEnie front end

GEIS sold GEnie to a company called IDT Corp., but not before Louden tried to buy it—twice. IDT developed a Macintosh GUI for it, but this couldn't revive GEnie. It shut down on December 27, 1999. GEIS was sold by GE to two technology investment firms and today operates as GXS, providing electronic data interchange (EDI).

In 1997 Prodigy would remake itself as a true Internet service provider. But for a time it would retain its original form in a separate service called Prodigy Classic. The service tried to integrate Prodigy Classic's content with the Web, but that didn't fly. The company just sort of limped along for the next two years, trying to compete with price and features, and online "events" such as celebrity interviews. Citing potential problems in dealing with the year 2000 changeover, Prodigy Classic shut down in December 1999.

The company—trade name, assets, and so forth—went through a series of owners, and was an ISP in Mexico for several years. Elements of Prodigy continue to function today under various banners.

Sears and IBM have returned to their respective roots.

The WELL remains in operation as an ISP, with its conferences available to subscribers. A few can be sampled by nonsubscribers. Its unique appeal has helped it outlast most competitors, and it's likely to be around, as an ISP and a Web presence, for a long time.

~

Which brings us well into the twenty-first century. The Web is ubiquitous, available with or without wires. You don't even have to own a computer to get online; the right cell phone will do, or you can pop into your local library and use their computers to check your email and browse the Web.

Current experiments and product development promise take the Web to a new level before the end of the decade. Forget Web 2.0—the New Web is on the way—with the Intergalactic Computer Network close on its heels!

Log On to History!

You can log on to *On the Way to the Web: The Secret History of the Internet and Its Founders* at this URL:

`http://www.onthewaytotheweb.com`

If you find that bothersome to type, a Google search on "Michael A. Banks" will turn up a link.

What's at this site? It's almost certain that a book of this kind will have errors and omissions, so you'll find a page for corrections and additions.

In addition, links to sites, people, companies, and organizations mentioned in this book are at the site. You'll also find links to additional resources.

Finally, there's a collection of images from various online services.

Afterword: Omissions, Additions, and Corrections

The astute reader will notice that I've omitted a few online services. Some were so short-lived or of so little consequence that they would be meaningless to most readers. Others are beyond the theme or time frame of this book.

Some of the omissions:

- ABI/INFORM (Abstracted Business Information), a database of abstracted information from selected business publications, hosted by ORBIT, Dialog, and eventually UMI/ProQuest

- Data Courier, a small online service hosted by the *Louisville Courier-Journal* (the owners of which bought ABI/INFORM under the company name "Data Courier")

- EasyLink, Western Union's now-defunct email/FAX/mail system

- Easynet, a front end for more than 700 database services

- EasyPlex, a specialized CompuServe email service

- E-COM, the United States Postal Service's electronic messaging service (EMS)

- Freenet, free BBSs in cities such as Cleveland and Rochester that used the same software and were designed to serve as community centers

- Info-Look, a gateway to online services hosted by Nynex

- Internet Relay Chat (IRC), the first implementation of real-time chatting via the Internet (Jarkko Oikarinen, 1988)

- Knowledge Index (KI), a subset of Dialog databases

- The Microsoft Network (MSN), more an ISP than online service that started after Bill Gates decided that the Internet was going to be important, after all

- MIX, the McGraw-Hill Information Exchange, a CoSy-based service for educators

- NABU Network, a Canadian online service that operated a short-lived online service in the Washington, DC, area

- Official Airline Guide (OAG), publisher of the Official Airline Guide

- On Tyme, Tymnet's email service

- Portal, an early BBS-based service

- Quali-Comm, General Electric Information Service's commercial email service

- The Sierra On-Line Network, a graphic online gaming service, initially called ImaginNation

- Telidon, Canadian Videotex service

- Telemail/SprintMail, email services hosted by Telenet (later SprintNet)

- WIX (Windows Information eXchange), a short-lived service, hosted by *Byte*, for Windows users and developers

- ZiffNet, a collection of services (downloads, magazine articles) originally hosted on several online services (including Prodigy) and now a web-based service

Events after 1994 are generally not detailed because after that year the Web was well established, and we were no longer "on the way to the Web."

Thus the great AOL outage of 1998 isn't chronicled here. Nor are online scams, stock manipulation, pornography, the CIA investigation of weapons dealing that involved CompuServe, ruined marriages, murders, and other crimes involving the Internet. Maybe in another book.

In the meantime, I have extended this book with a website. The site offers additions and corrections that may come up after publication, clickable links to companies and institutions mentioned herein, more graphics, and other relevant resources. The URL is easy to remember—it's the book's title:
`http://www.onthewaytotheweb.com`

Online Timeline

1945

Vannevar Bush publishes his famous essay, "As We May Think" in *The Atlantic Monthly*. This breakthrough paper provides a new way to control and access information, which even then threatened to overload humanity's ability to manage it. Bush proposes a device called a *memex*, which will not only manage information, but will also create associative trails through knowledge, not unlike the system of hyperlinks that drive the World Wide Web.

1957

Soviet rocketeers successfully orbit the first artificial Earth satellite, Sputnik. This inspires the US government to form and fund the Advanced Research Projects Agency (ARPA) under the auspices of the Department of Defense.

1960

J.C.R. Licklider publishes the famous paper, "Man-Computer Symbiosis," on the theme of using computers to augment thinking and facilitate human communication. Paul Baran at RAND develops the concept of distributed communication and message blocks for telephone networks.

1961

The first paper on packet-switching theory is presented by Leonard Kleinrock ("Information Flow in Large Communication Nets").

1962

J.C.R. Licklider is appointed ARPA's fourth director, and director of ARPA's Information Processing Techniques Office (IPTO), and introduces his Intergalactic Network, the first presentation of the concept behind the Internet. The first paper on the concept of the Internet is presented by J.C.R. Licklider and Welden Clark ("On-Line Man Computer Communication"). At RAND, Paul Baran develops the concept and design for a decentralized voice telephone network that would be capable of surviving a nationwide nuclear attack; Baran later worked as an informal consultant to the ARPANET group.

1963

Government and industry representatives develop the ASCII (American Standard Code for Information Interchange). The ASCII code specifies 128 unique 7-bit data strings, each representing a letter of the English alphabet, an Arabic numeral, a punctuation mark, or special symbol. ASCII provides the *lingua franca* for communication between different kinds of computers.

1964

Kleinrock accepts a faculty position at UCLA; his book *Communications Nets* is published. Licklider returns to MIT and is replaced by Robert Herzfield. Ivan Sutherland becomes director of ARPA's Information Processing Techniques Office (IPTO) and hires Bob Taylor, a mathematician and psychologist, as deputy director. The first paper on secure packetized voice communication is written by Paul Baran ("On Distributed Communications Networks"). The existence of this paper generated the erroneous rumor that the Internet was created to survive nuclear war. A meeting between Licklider and Roberts inspires Roberts to undertake the creation of the Internet. Writing in *The Atlantic Monthly,* Martin Greenberger of MIT posits the development of computer-based "information utilities."

1965

Under contract from ARPA, Larry Roberts of MIT and Thomas Marrill of SDC carry out the first long-distance computer communications experiment in February. A TX-2 computer at MIT's Lincoln Lab is connected with a Q-32 system at SDC in Santa Barbara. It's the first wide area network (WAN), and the first time computers communicate using data packets. General Electric opens the first online service—a time-sharing business serving commercial customers; clients use teletypewriters to communicate with GE's computers via telephone hookups. In England, Donald Watts Davies at the National Physical Laboratory develops his concept of a distributed computer network and independently invents packet switching. (He also coins the term.) One of the first email systems is set up on time-sharing mainframe computers. It consisted of users transmitting files to other users.

1966

The first paper on network experiments is published by Larry Roberts and Thomas Marrill ("Toward a Cooperative Network of Time-Shared Computers"). Robert Taylor of NASA succeeds Sutherland as head of ARPA. He hires Larry Roberts to head IPTO.

1967

Roberts and Taylor present the idea for a decentralized computer data network at a meeting of ARPA's principle investigators in Ann Arbor, Michigan. During an ARPANET design session, Wes Clark suggests the use of mini-computers for network packet switching.

1968

Larry Roberts circulates a request for proposal (RFP) among manufacturers for network hardware for ARPANET. The contract is won by Bolt, Beranek, and Neuman (BBN). Tymshare time-sharing service begins building a circuit-switched network to serve its business clients. President Lyndon Johnson mandates that all computers purchased by the US government support ASCII.

1969

BBN delivers the first Internet message processors (IMPs) to ARPA experimenters at UCLA and Stanford. On October 29, the first-ever computer message is transmitted between the two. By year's end, two more nodes (University of California, Santa Barbara and the University of Utah) are added to the network, now called ARPANET. Compu-Serv is founded in Columbus, Ohio, as a time-sharing service.

1970

The National Library of Medicine experiments with public access to its MEDLARS database via teletypewriters. ARPANET spans the continent with a connection to BBN in Cambridge, Massachusetts. This enables BBN engineers to monitor and troubleshoot ARPANET from their headquarters. Nodes are being added to the network at the rate of one per month.

1971

Bunker Ramo puts the Dow Jones-Bunker Ramo News Retrieval Service (later Dow Jones News/Retrieval Service, or DJNS) online. Lockheed's Dialog goes online. Underwritten by the NSF, the Mitre Corporation begins a 12-month teletext experiment that involves cable TV subscribers in Reston, Virginia. The British Broadcasting Corporation (BBC) applies for a patent on a teletext system it calls "Teledata."

1972

Tymshare announces it will make its data network publicly available. Ray Tomlinson of BBN creates the first network program for sending email. He specifies @ as the net address indicator. ARPA (Advanced Research Projects Agency) is renamed DARPA (Defense Advanced Research Projects Agency). The first public demonstration of the Internet takes place in Washington, DC. (At this point, ARPANET is using NCP, Network Control Protocol, to enable communications between hosts on the network. It will be replaced by TCP/IP.) Roberts writes the first email management program (RD), enabling users to send direct replies to email, and file and delete messages. The BBC announces public trials of its Teledata system, which it has renamed "CEEFAX" (see Figure A-1).

```
P100    CEEFAX 100   Mon  3 Oct  20:49/50

BBC  CEEFAX
ONE

NEWS HEADLINES  ....101    THE DEAF ..169
NEWS IN DETAIL 102-119    SUBTITLES  170
NEWS FLASH .......150
NEWS INDEX .......190    TV/RADIO 171-4
NEWSREEL .........199    TV CHOICE .177
                         TOMORROW. ..178
FINANCE HEADLINES .120    DAY AFTER .179
CITYNEWS .....121-139
                         WEATHER/TRAVEL
SPORT HEADLINES ...140    INDEX .....180
SPORT PAGES ...130-159
                         GENERAL INDEX
FOOD GUIDE .......161     ........193-5

BBC RADIO FOR SCHOOLS.........BBC2 276
```

Figure A-1. CEEFAX

1973

In an effort to take packet-switching technology to the public sphere, Larry Roberts of IPTO offers to sell it to AT&T. The telephone monopoly responds that it is not compatible with their future. Work on new network protocol (Transmission Control Protocol/Internet Protocol, or TPC/IP) is begun by Vint Cerf, Bob Kahn, and others. The first European connections to ARPANET are established in Norway and England. WGBH-TV in Boston uses teletext to caption news programs. Larry Roberts leaves ARPA to join Telenet, the first public packet-switching network.

1974

The Altair microcomputer kit is introduced in an article in *Popular Electronics*. Imsai and other systems for electronics hobbyists follow. ITV (Britain's Independent Television) begins commercial teletext broadcasts under the name "Oracle" (an acronym for Optional Reception of Announcements by Coded Line Electronics). Having worked on its development for three years, the BBC launches CEEFAX, the world's first teletext system. The first use of the term "Internet" appears in a conference paper by Vinton Cerf and Robert Kahn. Viewdata, a two-channel Videotex system (one for user requests/data, and the other for transmission from the host system) is announced by the British Post Office. It is the precursor to Prestel. The term *information super-highway* is used for the first time.

1975

Telenet goes online; along with Tymnet, it is the first public information super-highway. Compu-Serv goes public (NASDAQ: CMPU SRV). The CBS television network begins experiments with European-style Videotex systems. ARPANET is turned over to the Defense Communication Agency (DCA). Developed and hosted by GEIS, AppleLink goes online as Apple's internal network for employees and dealers. Work begins on the Antiope teletext system in France. Antiope differs from CEEFAX in that it has definable text shapes. Research on the Telidon Canadian Videotex system begins; Telidon later evolves into NAPLPS.

1976

Japan's NHK (Japan Broadcasting Corporation) begins research into a text system for transmitting data to televisions. Apple is founded to sell the Apple 1 computer. Robert Metcalf begins work on Ethernet.

1977

The first TRS-80 Model I's are offered via catalog at Radio Shack's 3,500 stores; 10,000 are sold in the first year. Apple Computer is incorporated. Warner Cable's QUBE two-way cable TV experiment begins in Columbus, Ohio. Compu-Serv's name is changed to CompuServe. Bunker Ramo is dropped from Dow Jones News/Retrieval Service. Canadian Telidon and AT&T introduce the NAPLPS Videotex protocol, later used by Minitel, Prestel, Viewtron, and Prodigy. A Videotex system called Ibertex opens in Spain.

1978

At CompuServe, Jeff Wilkins, Sandy Trevor, Russ Ranshaw, Rich Baker, and 13 others develop a small service aimed at putting the company's mainframe computers to work in the evenings. The plan is to allow microcomputer owners access to the mainframes. The service is called MicroNET. Failed entrepreneur Bill von Meister begins assembling computer, network, and data resources in Virginia to create a similar service, called Compucom (later, The Source). Japanese broadcaster NHK experiments with teletext, and the CAPTAIN modified Videotex system begins tests. In Chicago, Ward Christensen and

Randy Seuss experiment with the first microcomputer bulletin board system (BBS). Planning for Venture One (which will become Prodigy in 10 years) begins. In Germany, British Telecom begins work on a Prestel clone called *Bildschirmtext* (literally, "picture screen text") or BTX. Austria will also employ BTX, and in the Netherlands a Videotex system based on Prestel is introduced.

1979

MicroNET (soon to be called CompuServe Information Service, as in Figure A-2) and The Source (Figure A-3) finish beta testing and open for paying customers. The first Usenet newsgroups are started with two hosts (Duke University and the University of North Carolina). In five years it will have 900 hosts. The first BITNET link (between City University of New York and Yale) is made. SDC, Dialog, and other database companies extend service to European markets. The Christensen/Seuss BBS, named CBBS (for "computer bulletin board system") is opened to the public. At CompuServe, Sandy Trevor creates the "CB Simulator," the first online chat system. The Japanese Ministry of Post and Telecommunications unveils CAPTAIN, a Videotex system based on Japanese characters. In Sweden, a teletext system called Test-TV and Televerket Videotex system are in development. Invented by Sam Fedida of the British Post Office, Prestel is launched in London, Birmingham, and Nottingham.

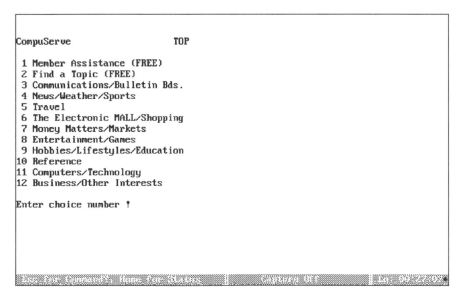

```
CompuServe                    TOP

 1 Member Assistance (FREE)
 2 Find a Topic (FREE)
 3 Communications/Bulletin Bds.
 4 News/Weather/Sports
 5 Travel
 6 The Electronic MALL/Shopping
 7 Money Matters/Markets
 8 Entertainment/Games
 9 Hobbies/Lifestyles/Education
10 Reference
11 Computers/Technology
12 Business/Other Interests

Enter choice number !
```

Figure A-2. Early CompuServe menu

INFORMATION NETWORK

The Source.

The most powerful resource
any personal computer can have.

Figure A-3. The Source member manual

1980

IBM introduces its personal computer. CompuServe's CB simulator is opened
to the public. It quickly becomes the service's highest-billing product.
CompuServe develops special-interest groups (SIGs), later given the name
Forums. H&R Block acquires CompuServe. Germany's *Bildschirmtext* is
opened to the public. The Reader's Digest Association buys majority interest
in The Source. A dozen big-city newspapers go online with CompuServe in a
yearlong experiment. Viewtron begins test marketing in Florida. In France,
Teletel, which will become the Minitel Videotex system, is demonstrated by
France Telecom.

1981

"Gateways" to database services such as Dialog. BRS, and Orbit debut on
CompuServe, The Source, and DJNS. Online services add encyclopedias to
their already profuse information offerings. Entrepreneur Wes Kussmaul puts

The Kussmaul Encyclopedia online; with the addition of email and other features, it later becomes DELPHI (Figure A-4). MUPID, a Videotex system based on Prestel, is introduced in Austria. France, Canada, and CBS begin work on an Antiope-based standard that eventually becomes NAPLPS. CSNET (Computer Science Network) goes online as a low-cost alternative to ARPANET, to be used by those universities that do not qualify for ARPANET access. Funded by the National Science Foundation, it operates at 56.6Kbps. Vinton Cerf proposes an internetwork connection between ARPANET and CSNET to create "a network of networks." Radio Shack begins selling the TRS-80 Videotex terminal.

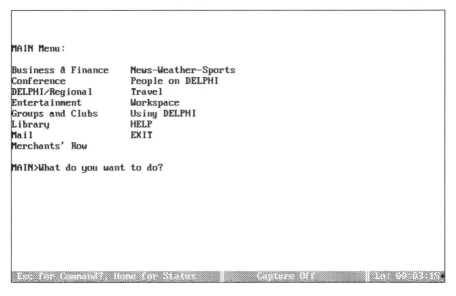

```
MAIN Menu:

Business & Finance     News-Weather-Sports
Conference             People on DELPHI
DELPHI/Regional        Travel
Entertainment          Workspace
Groups and Clubs       Using DELPHI
Library                HELP
Mail                   EXIT
Merchants' Row

MAIN>What do you want to do?
```

Figure A-4. DELPHI goes online.

1982

The US Postal Service starts E-COM (Electronic Computer Originated Mail) service. The Source's banished founder, Bill von Meister, develops Gameline to deliver Atari video games via modem (Figure A-5). A privately owned Videotex system called *Telset* goes online in Finland. In Hong Kong, a Videotex system based on the British Prestel model goes online. EUnet (European Unix Network) is established in four countries to provide Usenet access and email service. In Italy, Videotel begins testing Videotex with 2,000 terminals. The Gateway Videotex service opens in San Francisco. Cox Cable Company initiates its INDAX interactive cable TV service.

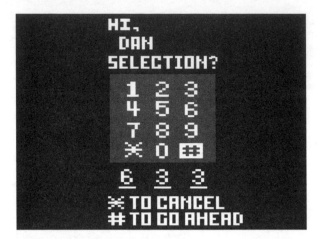

Figure A-5. Gameline screen

1983

MCI Telecommunications launches MCI Mail, followed closely by AT&T Mail. The DELPHI online service goes live. Atari loses a billion dollars during the first quarter, and Gameline, dependent on the success of Atari, crashes. ARPANET makes TCP/IP mandatory. The Internet Activities Board (IAB) is formed. The University of Wisconsin creates the Domain Name System (DNS), which allows people to use names like Apress.com instead of having to enter complicated strings of numerals to address a web service. The name extensions .com, .edu, .gov, .mil, .org, .net, and .int are created for this purpose. Tom Jennings develops the FidoNet BBS network. Tests begin for the first Russian Videotex system, based on Minitel and built by a French company. American People/Link (Plink, Figure A-6) goes online. (It was originally named "Protocol.") Deutsch Telekom opens Videotex with a service called T-Online. In Miami, Viewtron goes public. Several television stations around the country add regular teletext reports (subtitling) to their programming.

Figure A-6. American People/Link

1984

Orson Scott Card puts his award-winning novel, *Ender's Game*, on DELPHI as a free download *before* it is published in book form (TOR books publishes the novel in 1985). Several local online services (Georgia OnLine in Atlanta, Keycom in Chicago, and Electra in Cincinnati among them) go online, but most fail within a year. Near Albany, New York, the first consumer online service with a GUI goes live; named Playnet, it is limited to Commodore computers (Figure A-7). Sears, IBM, and CBS announce plans for an online service, using the name "Trintex." JUNET is established in Japan. USPS discontinues E-COM. ARPANET is divided into two networks: MILNET and ARPANET, to serve the military and the research establishment, respectively. CSNET is upgraded to 1.5Mbps T-1 lines (25 times faster than 56.6Kbps). MCI Mail, IBM, and Merit Networks (Figure A-8) are the primary contractors, and the new network is called NSFNET.

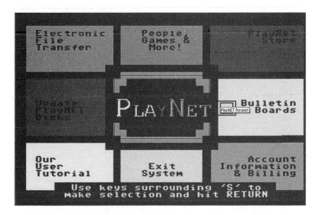

Figure A-7. Playnet main menu

Figure A-8. Merit Networks

1985

Developed by former CompuServe manager Bill Louden, the GEnie service (Figure A-9) goes online, backed by General Electric Information Services. Quantum Computer Services is incorporated. *Byte* magazine's online service, BIX, goes public, along with USA Today Sports Center, The WELL, and Quantum Link (Q-Link). In the UK, Compulink Information eXchange (CIX), a UNIX box running the CoSy conferencing system, goes online and quickly grows to be the most popular online service in the country. The first registered Internet domain name, `symbolics.com`, goes online. NSFNET begins deploying T-1 lines. VCO, an online chat graphical front end, is introduced. Q-Link debuts Lucasfilms Games' *Club Caribe*, the first online virtual world. CompuServe experiments with television commercials.

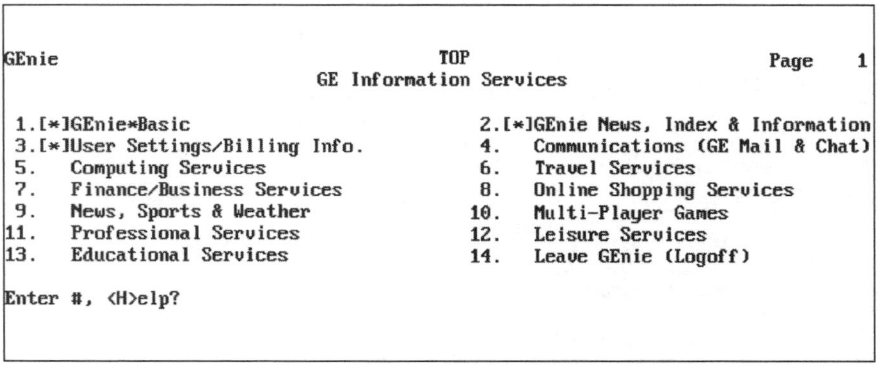

```
GEnie                              TOP                        Page    1
                          GE Information Services

 1.[*]GEnie*Basic                        2.[*]GEnie News, Index & Information
 3.[*]User Settings/Billing Info.        4.   Communications (GE Mail & Chat)
 5.    Computing Services                6.   Travel Services
 7.    Finance/Business Services         8.   Online Shopping Services
 9.    News, Sports & Weather           10.   Multi-Player Games
11.    Professional Services            12.   Leisure Services
13.    Educational Services             14.   Leave GEnie (Logoff)

Enter #, <H>elp?
```

Figure A-9. GEnie

1986

Times Mirror Company ends its Gateway Videotex service. Viewtron shuts down. CompuServe begins international expansion. NSFNET high-speed backbone (56.6Kbps) is created. NSF builds five supercomputing centers and links them with the network. CompuServe introduces the GIF graphics format.

1987

NSFNET begins upgrade to T1 speed (1.544Mbps). The number of Internet hosts passes 30,000. BITNET and CSNET merge to form CREN (Corporation for Research and Educational Networking). Source bought by venture capital firm. DASnet begins inter-system email service. The first CompuServe commercials air on cable TV. The GIF graphics format is introduced by CompuServe. Development of Beltel, a Videotex system, begins in South Africa. Sears, IBM, and CBS announce that the long-awaited Trintex service will be available in 1988. (The name is later changed to "Prodigy.")

1988

After operating under bankruptcy protection for two years, Playnet shuts down. Prodigy is introduced in San Francisco, then Atlanta and Hartford, Connecticut. CBS drops out of the Prodigy partnership. The infamous "Internet Worm" burrows through 10 percent of the Internet's 60,000 hosts. NSFNET prepares to increase its speed to accommodate the rapid increase in users. CIX (Figure A-10) provides the first commercial Internet email and Usenet access in the UK.

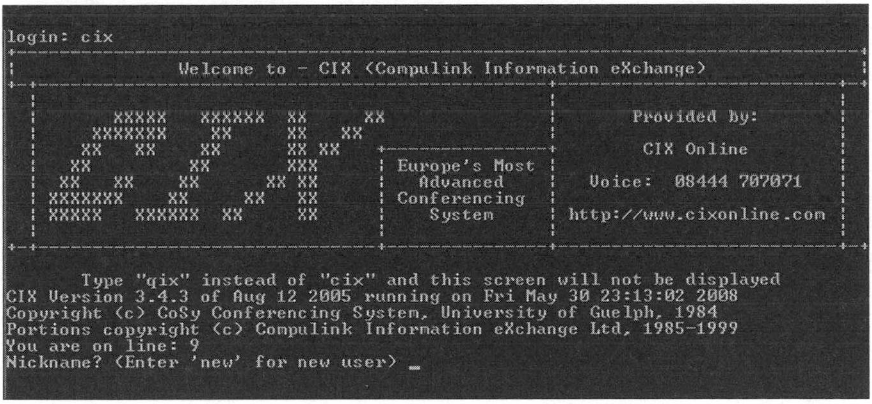

Figure A-10. CIX

1989

The first public Internet service provider, The World, is opened by Software Tool & Die Company. Quantum Computing puts Applelink–Personal Edition online; a few months later, friction between Apple and Quantum pulls the plug on the service. Quantum puts a revamped Apple service online, using the same GUI. Quantum opens PC-Link, a partnership with Tandy for IBM-compatible computers. CompuServe buys The Source and pulls its plug. Internet relay email testing is done by CompuServe and MCI Mail. MCI Mail is connected to the Internet. A Japanese version of CompuServe, called

Nifty-SERVE, goes online. Word of the Tiananmen Square Massacre spreads through online services before any conventional news media report it. On October 17, an earthquake in San Francisco knocks out all telephone service and most online services. However, a satellite uplink owned by GEIS allows GEnie members to report on conditions through email, chat, and bulletin boards.

1990

Quantum opens Promenade, an all-IBM online service with its own GUI, devoted to IBM's new personal computer, the PS/1. Quantum reopens its Apple II service, calling it America Online. Prodigy is launched nationwide with a flat rate of $9.95 per month, and declares itself the "first consumer online service" (conveniently ignoring AOL, CompuServe, and the other consumer services). Hypertext Markup Language (HTML) is developed by Tim Berners-Lee at CERN in Switzerland. GEnie responds with its "Star*Services" flat-rate option, providing selected services during non–prime time hours at $4.95 per month. Tim Berners-Lee begins his hypertext project in Berne, Switzerland. He coins the phrase "World Wide Web." ARPANET is decommissioned, its old 56.6Kbps lines taken out of service, leaving NSFNET the backbone of the Internet. Electronic Frontier Foundation (EFF) founded.

1991

NSFNET upgrades to T-3 (45Mbps) lines, and all networks and users are connected to this high-speed backbone. CSNET is decommissioned. NSFNET creates NREN, a research network that studies high-speed Internet technology. AOL (Figure A-11) "co-mingles" PC-Link and AOL for Apple II and Macintosh. AOL releases America Online for DOS, called PCAO and running under GeoWorks. CompuServe offers to buy AOL for $50 million; the offer is turned down. Quantum Computer Services legally changes its name to America Online, Inc. James Kimsey retires and Steve Case is named CEO of AOL. AOL experiments with local services. Sierra On-Line puts the ImagiNation Network (later the Sierra Network) online. It is the first online service devoted to multiplayer, real-time online gaming. US West and France's Minitel combine to offer a Minitel-type service. Internet tools gopher and WAIS are introduced. The first email message from space is transmitted from the Space Shuttle *Atlantis*, using a Macintosh Portable computer running AppleLink software.

Figure A-11. AOL

1992

After Congress removes prohibition of the commercial use of the Internet, DELPHI is the very first online service to provide Internet access. It offers Internet mail, newsgroups, telnet, FTP, and gopher. AOL goes public and provides Usenet newsgroup access. Several daily newspapers in cities around the country have been or are experimenting with dialup online services, usually free. The Internet Society is chartered. NSFNET is upgraded to T-3 (44.736Mbps). CERN releases the World Wide Web.

1993

The Mosaic graphical browser for Windows is released (Figure A-12). America Online for Windows is released, attracting tens of thousands of new customers immediately. AOL begins developing eWorld for Apple (Figure A-13); less than a year later, Apple cancels the service. Prodigy institutes per-minute charges for its most popular services and, in doing so, sparks an online revolt. Prodigy for Windows is released. The first consumer online service in Spain, Servicom, goes online. AOL responds with a flat-rate pricing plan. Magazines and newspapers flock to establish online presences. The number of subscribers to online services in the United States passes 3 million. NSF creates InterNIC (Network Information Center), responsible for domain name and IP address allocations. Through various divisions InterNIC handles Internet registration and information services through 1998.

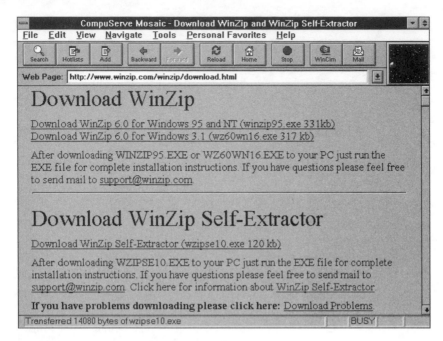

Figure A-12. CompuServe's version of the Mosaic web browser

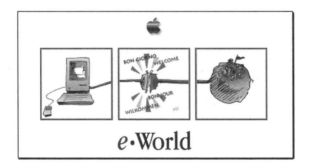

Figure A-13. eWorld

1994

New networks link to the Internet, along with hundreds of thousands of hosts. NSFNET installs 145Mbps lines, known as ATM (Asynchronous Transmission Mode). Q-Link and PC-Link are shut down. AOL offers an Internet Services area. In a public online chat, Steve Case says that it is "highly unlikely" that the service would ever go to flat-rate pricing. GEnie membership reaches 350,000. Prodigy offers web access and web-page hosting. Netscape 1 is released. A Prodigy press release claims credit for bringing the Internet to life, starting just 11 years earlier. AOL reaches 1 million members, and announces development of a web browser. Time Warner announces the Full Service Network (FSN), planned to provide video, games, shopping, and interactive services via cable TV; it is doomed to failure. News Corp. buys DELPHI. CompuServe opens Internet access via telnet. CIX reaches a peak of 16,000 members active in hundreds of conferences. Rumors about a Microsoft online service are rampant (Figure A-14).

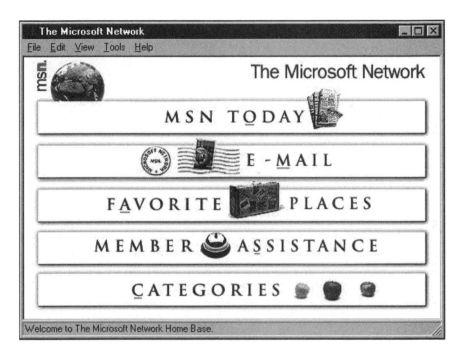

Figure A-14. Microsoft Network

Bibliography

Allan, Roy A., *A History of the Personal Computer: The People and the Technology*,
    ISBN: 978-0968910801

Bagnall, Brian, *On the Edge: The Spectacular Rise and Fall of Commodore*,
    ISBN: 978-0973864908

Biggs, John, *Black Hat: Misfits, Criminals, and Scammers in the Internet Age*,
    ISBN: 978-1590593790

Chapman, Merrill, *In Search of Stupidity: Over 20 Years of High-Tech Marketing Disasters*,
    ISBN: 978-1590597217

Freiberger, Paul, and Michael Swaine, *Fire in the Valley: The Making of the Personal
    Computer*, ISBN: 978-0071358951

Hafner, Katie, *Where Wizards Stay Up Late: The Origins of the Internet*,
    ISBN: 978-0684832678

Hafner, Katie, *The Well: A Story of Love, Death and Real Life in the Seminal Online
    Community*, ISBN: 978-0786708468

Klein, Alec, *Stealing Time: Steve Case, Jerry Levin, and the Collapse of AOL Time Warner*,
    ISBN: 978-0743247863

Kleinrock, Leonard, *Communication Nets: Stochastic Message Flow and Delay*,
    ISBN: 978-0486458809

Linzmayer, Owen, *Apple Confidential 2.0: The Definitive History of the World's Most
    Colorful Company*, ISBN: 978-1593270100

Livingstone, Jessica, *Founders at Work: Stories of Startups' Early Days*,
    ISBN: 978-1590597149

Naughton, John, *A Brief History of the Future: From Radio Days to Internet Years in a
    Lifetime*, ISBN: 978-1585671847

Norman, Jeremy M., *From Gutenberg to the Internet: A Sourcebook on the History of
    Information Technology*, ISBN: 978-0930405878

Okin, J. R., *The Internet Revolution: The Not-for-Dummies Guide to the History,
    Technology, and Use of the Internet*, ISBN: 978-0976385769

Ornstein, Severo M., *Computing in the Middle Ages: A View from the Trenches, 1955–1983*,
    ISBN: 978-1403315175

Standage, Tom, *The Victorian Internet: The Remarkable Story of the Telegraph and the Nineteenth Century's On-line Pioneers*, ISBN: 978-0802716040

Welsh, David and Teresa, *Priming the Pump: How TRS-80 Enthusiasts Helped Spark the PC Revolution*, ISBN: 978-0979346804

Veit, Stan, *Stan Veit's History of the Personal Computer*, ISBN: 978-1566640305

Founders

Service	Founder	Year Began
AT&T Mail	AT&T	1983
ALOHAnet	University of Hawaii/ARPA	1970
American People/Link (PLink)	American Home Networks	1983
America Online for Apple	America Online	1990
America Online for DOS (PCAO)	Quantum Link/America Online	1991
America Online for Windows	America Online	1993
Antiope	France Telecom	1975
AppleLink	Apple (hosted by GEIS)	1986
AppleLink–Personal Edition	Quantum Computer, with Apple	1989
ARPANET	Advanced Research Projects Agency	1969
ASCII-Net	ASCII Publishing (Japan)	1985
Bildschirmtext (BTX)	Deutsch Telekom	1978
BIX	BYTE Magazine	1985
Boston Citilink	Applied Videotex Systems	1984
Bunker Ramo	Simon Ramo	1969
CAPTAIN	Japanese Ministry of Post & Telecommunications	1979
CBBS	Ward Christensen and Randy Seuss	1978
CEEFAX	BBC	1972
CERFnet	Susan Estrada	1988
CIX	CIX Online	1987

Service	Founder	Year Began
CNR	Citicorp, Nynex, RCA	1986
CompuServe	Compu-Serv, Inc.	1978
Covidea	AT&T, Chemical Bank, Bank of America, Time, Inc.	1985
CREN	Corporation for Research and Education/merger of CSNET and BITNET	1996
CSNET	National Science Foundation (NSF)	1981
Cyclades/France	Institut de Recherche d'Informatique et d'Automatique (IRIA)	1972
DasNET	DA Systems, Inc.	1987
Data Courier	Louisville Courier-Journal	1984
Datapac	Trans-Canada Telephone System	1976
DELPHI	General Videotex Corporation	1981
Dialcom and Dialmail	Robert F. Ryan	1970
Dialog	Lockheed Corporation	1971
Dow Jones News/Retrieval	Dow Jones, Bunker Ramo	1971
Eaasy Sabre (as SABRE)	American Airlines	1960
EasyLink	Western Union	1982
E-COM	United States Postal Service	1982
Electra	Taft Broadcasting	1984
Eunet	European UNIX Network	1982
European Informatics Network (EIN)	(Multinational project)	1976
eWorld	Quantum Computing with Apple	1983
FidoNET	Tom Jennings	1983
Gameline	Control Video Corporation	1982
Gateway	Times-Mirror Publishing, AT&T	1982
GEnie	General Electric Information Services	1984
GEIS time-sharing network	General Electric Information Services	1965
Georgia OnLine	Louden, et al.	1984
Ibertex	Spanish Postal Office	1977

Service	Founder	Year Began
ImagiNation (Sierra Network)	Sierra On-Line	1991
INDAX	Cox Cable Company	1982
Info-Look	Nynex	1984
Internet Relay Chat (IRC)	Jarkko Oikarinen	1988
InterNIC	NSF	1993
Japanese teletext experiment	NHK (Japan Broadcasting Company)	1979
JANET (Joint Academic Network)	UK academic and research network	1971
JUNET	Japan University NETwork (Tokyo University, Tokyo Institute of Technology and Keio University)	1984
Keycom/Keyfax	Centel, Honeywell, Newscorp	1984
Lexis	Mead Data Central	1973
MCI Mail	MCI Telecommunications	1983
MEDLARS	National Library of Medicine	1970
MILNET	Defense Communications Agency	1984
Minitel	France Telecom	1980
MSN (Microsoft Network)	Microsoft	1995
MUPID	Herman Maurer (Graz University of Technology)	1981
NABU Network	NABU Manufacturing	1984
NAPLPS Videotex Protocol	Canada Telidon and AT&T	1977
NewsNet	NewsNet	1982
New York Times Information Bank	New York Times	1969
Nexis	Mead Data Central	1979
Norwegian Televerket	Telenor	1994
NSFNET	National Science Foundation (NSF)	1984
NSF teletext experiment	Mitre Corporation	1971
OAG	Official Airline Guide	1983
Oracle	Independent Television (ITV/United Kingdom)	1974
Packet Radio Network (PRNET)	ARPA	1979

Service	Founder	Year Began
Playnet	Howard S. Goldberg, David Panzl	1984
QUBE	Warner-Amex Cable	1977
PC-Link	Quantum Computer, with Tandy	1989
Prestel	BBC	1979
Prestel (Hong Kong)	Hong Kong Telecom	1982
Prestel (Netherlands)	Telenor	1978
PROFS	IBM	1981
Promenade	Quantum Computer, with IBM	1990
Prodigy	Sears, IBM	1988
PSS (X.25 network)	British Telecom	1980
Quantum Link (Q-Link)	Quantum Computer	1985
RCP (Reseau a Commutation par Paquets)	French PTT	1974
RELCOM (Russian Internet)	Computer Center of the Kurchatov Atomic Energy Institute	1990
The Source	Telecomputing Corporation of America	1978
Symbolics.com	Symbolics, Inc.	1985
T-Online	Deutsch Telekom	1983
Teledata	BBC	1971
Telenet and Telemail	Telenet	1975
Teletel	France Telecom	1980
Televerket	Telia AV (Swedish Televerket)	1979
Telset Finland	Helsinki Telset Oy	1982
Test-TV teletext	Sveriges Radio, and Televerket	1979
Transpac (X.25 network)	French PTT	1978
Trintex	Sears, IBM, CBS	1982
Tymnet	Tymeshare	1974
USA Today Sports	USA Today/LINC Networks	1985
UUCP	Bell Labs	1976
UUNET	Usenix	1987
Venture One	CBS, AT&T	1982

Service	Founder	Year Began
Videotel/Italy	Videotel	1982
Viewdata	British Post Office	1974
Viewtron	Knight-Ridder Newspapers, AT&T	1983
The WELL	Stewart Brand, Larry Brilliant	1985
The World	(First commercial Internet access provider)	1990
World Wide Web	Cern	1991

Index

A

Abstracted Business Information (ABI/INFORM), 177
Academic American Encyclopedia, 72
ACCESS, 53
additions to book, 177–178
ADL (Anti-Defamation League), 147
ADP (Automatic Data Processing, Inc.), 10
Advanced Research Projects Agency (ARPA), 2, 76–77, 179
Advanced Research Projects Agency Network (ARPANET), 63, 77, 162, 164, 182, 189
AHCL (Analog Hybrid Computer Lab), 15
Aladdin, 124
Allen, Paul, 133
ALOHAnet, 76
AlterNet, 163
America Online. See AOL
American Newspaper Publishers Association (ANPA), 65, 69
American People/Link (Plink), 103–105

American Society of Composers, Authors, and Publishers (ASCAP), 68
American Standard Code for Information Interchange (ASCII) code, 180
Analog Hybrid Computer Lab (AHCL), 15
Anderson, Jack, 36–37
ANPA (American Newspaper Publishers Association), 65, 69
Anti-Defamation League (ADL), 147
Antiope teletext system, 184
AOL (America Online), 120–121, 192
  commingling, 129–131
  for DOS (PCAO), 192
  and Gameline and Control Video Corporation, 89–90
  independence, 127–128
  marketing, 134–137
  overview, 127
  for PCs, DOS and Windows, 131–133
  planning ahead, 133–134
  and Playnet, 90–93
  Promenade, 128–129
  and The Source, 89
  Steve Case at, 95–101

AOL Germany, 159
Apple Computer, 100, 161
AppleLink, 100, 116, 117–119
ARPA (Advanced Research Projects Agency), 2, 76–77, 179
ARPANET (Advanced Research Projects Agency Network), 63, 77, 162, 164, 182, 189
ASCAP (American Society of Composers, Authors, and Publishers), 68
ASCII (American Standard Code for Information Interchange) code, 180
Asimov, Isaac, 3, 38
Asynchronous Transmission Mode (ATM), 194
AT&T Mail, 80
ATM (Asynchronous Transmission Mode), 194
Automatic Data Processing, Inc. (ADP), 10

B

Baran, Paul, 179
batch computing, 7
Batten, Jim, 65
BBN (Bolt, Beranek, and Newman Corporation), 5, 12
BBS (bulletin board system), 185
BCE (Boston Computer Exchange), 81
Because It's Time Network (BITNET), 76, 163
BellSouth, 99
Berners-Lee, Tim, 192
Bertelsmann Group, 159
Bibliographic Retrieval Services (BRS), 10, 64
Bildschirmtext, 185

BITNET (Because It's Time Network), 76, 163
BIX (Byte Information eXchange), 106, 154, 171, 172
BIXNAV (Byte Information eXchange NAVigator), 125, 171
Blasko, Larry, 69
Bolt, Beranek, and Newman Corporation (BBN), 5, 12
Boston Computer Exchange (BCE), 81
Brand, Stewart, 107
Brandt, Jan, 134
Brilliant, Larry, 107
BRS (Bibliographic Retrieval Services), 10, 64
Bruns, Dan, 80, 154, 172
bulletin board system (BBS), 185
Bunker Ramo, 9
Bush, Vannevar, 179
Business°Talk, 118
Byte Information eXchange (BIX), 106, 154, 171, 172
Byte Information eXchange NAVigator (BIXNAV), 125, 171

C

Cable & Wireless, 28
cache.dat file, 150
Cadillac Modern Encyclopedia, 80
CAPTAIN (Character and Pattern Telephone Access Information Network), 160, 185
Card, Orson Scott, 82
Case, Steve, 95, 111, 116, 132, 192
Cathode Ray Tube (CRT), 8
Caufield, Frank, 97
CB Simulator, 54, 104
CBBS (Computerized Bulletin Board System), 47

CBS Venture One, 75
CCSC (Credit Card Service Corporation), 36
CDC (Control Data Corporation), 126
Ceefax, 40, 182
censorship, Prodigy, 147–149
Cerf, Vint, 13, 76
CES (Consumer Electronics Show), 95
Character and Pattern Telephone Access Information Network (CAPTAIN), 160, 185
chat rooms, 54–56, 155–156
Chesley, Harry, 105
Christensen, Ward, 47
CIM (CompuServe Information Manager), 166
CIX (Compulink Information eXchange), 106, 159, 190
Club Caribe, 110
Collaborative Novel, 80
command characters, 104
command mode, 51
command-driven system, 50
Commercial time-sharing computers, 8
commingling, 129–131
Commodore, 91, 100, 116
competition, 122
Comp-U-Card, 17
CompuCom, 33, 184
Compulink Information eXchange (CIX), 106, 159, 190
CompuServe, 15–24, 57, 59
CompuServe Information Manager (CIM), 166
Computer Science Net (CSNET), 76, 162
Computerized Bulletin Board System (CBBS), 47

Conference on DELPHI, 81
conferencing system, 56
Consumer Electronics Show (CES), 95
consumer movement, 70–71
consumer services, 79–93. *See also* AOL
    DELPHI, 80–82
    dot-com bust, 84–85
    GEnie, 85–89
    overview, 79–80
    regional online services, 82–83
Control Data Corporation (CDC), 126
Control Video Corporation (CVC), 89
Cooperative Defense Committee, 149
Corporation for Research and Educational Networking (CREN), 190
corrections, 177–178
Costykian, Greg, 144
CoSy conferencing system, 106
Credit Card Service Corporation (CCSC), 36
CREN (Corporation for Research and Educational Networking), 190
Crosstalk, 123
CRT (Cathode Ray Tube), 8
CSNET (Computer Science Net), 76, 162
CVC (Control Video Corporation), 89

D

DARPA (Defense Advanced Research Projects Agency), 182
DARPANET (Defense Advanced Research Agency Network), 2, 11

DASnet, 112
Data Courier, 177
database services, 186
Datapost, 41
Davies, Donald, 5
DBC (Digital Broadcast
    Corporation), 30, 37, 41
DCA (Defense Communications
    Agency), 48
DDN (Defense Data Network),
    76–77
DEC (Digital Equipment
    Corporation) PDP-10
    computers, 13
DECnet (Digital Equipment
    Corporation's network), 76
default text, 49
Defense Advanced Research Agency
    Network (DARPANET), 2, 11
Defense Advanced Research Projects
    Agency (DARPA), 182
Defense Communications Agency
    (DCA), 48
Defense Data Network (DDN),
    76–77
DELPHI, 77, 80–82, 125, 154, 165,
    171, 172, 193
DeskMate, 3, 119, 129
Dialcom, 13, 33
Dialog, 10, 64, 125, 168
Digital Broadcast Corporation
    (DBC), 30, 37, 41
Digital Equipment Corporation
    (DEC) PDP-10 computers, 13
Digital Equipment Corporation's
    network (DECnet), 76
direct mail campaigns, 135
distributed processing, 19
DJNS (Dow Jones News/Retrieval
    Service), 64, 182
DNS (Domain Name System), 188

dot-com bust, 84–85
Dow Jones News/Retrieval Service
    (DJNS), 64, 182
Dow Jones–Bunker Ramo News
    Retrieval Service, 10
Dyson, Esther, 155

E

EasyLink, 71, 177
EasyNet, 71, 177
EasyPlex, 177
echomail, 158
E-COM (Electronic Computer
    Originated Mail), 177, 187
EDI (electronic data interchange),
    175
Education Resources Information
    Center (ERIC), 9, 63
Edwards, Elwood, 121
EFF (Electronic Frontier
    Foundation), 192
Eisenhower, Dwight D., 2
Electra, 83
Electronic Computer Originated
    Mail (E-COM), 177, 187
electronic data interchange (EDI),
    175
Electronic Frontier Foundation
    (EFF), 192
Electronic Mall, 111
emoticons, 105
encyclopedias, 72–73
Ender's Game, 82
ERIC (Education Resources
    Information Center), 9, 63
European Unix Network (EUnet),
    187
eWorld, 161

F

Fax Net, 30
Federal Communications
     Commission (FCC), 11
Fedida, Sam, 185
FidoNET, 158, 163, 188
file sharing, 53
files download area, Prodigy, 152
forums, 186
     CompuServe, 57–59
     file libraries, 57
Freenet, 177
front ends, 122–125
FSN (Full Service Network), 195
FTP program, 156, 166
Fuhrman, Debbie, 93
Full Service Network (FSN), 195

G

Galactic Network, 3
Gameline and Control Video
     Corporation, 89–90
Gameline Master Modules, 89, 98
games, online, 51–52
Gard Sr., Harry, 15
gateways, 63–64
GCOS (General Comprehensive
     Operating System), 86
GEIS (General Electric Information
     Services), 85, 86, 116, 153, 174
General Comprehensive Operating
     System (GCOS), 86
General Electric Information
     Services (GEIS), 85, 86, 116,
     153, 174
General Videotex Corp. (GVC), 80
GEnie, 85–89, 142, 153, 159, 174
Georgia OnLine, 84
GeoWorks Corporation, 131
GIF graphics format, 191

Gillen, Albert, 75
Global Network Navigator (GNN),
     166
GNN (Global Network Navigator),
     166
GO commands, 51
Goldberg, Howard S., 91
Golden United Life Insurance, 15
Goltz, John, 16
Google Adsense ads, 146
Graham, Katharine, 65, 69
Graham, Marshall, 36
graphical user interface (GUI), 115
Greene, Judge Harold H., 99
GTE Telenet, 42
GUI (graphical user interface), 115
GVC (General Videotex Corp.), 80

H

hardware/network play, 22
Heart, Frank, 5
Herzfield, Robert, 180
HMI (Host Micro Interface), 123
Home Music Store, 67
Honeywell, 83
Host Micro Interface (HMI), 123
HTML (Hypertext Markup
     Language), 192

I

IAB (Internet Activities Board), 188
Ibertex, 184
IBM Forum, 57
IDT Corp., 174
ImagiNation Network, 192
IMP (Internet message processor), 5,
     182
income. *See* money
INDAX interactive cable, 187
Info-Look, 177

Infoplex, 22
Information Processing Techniques
    Office (IPTO), 4
information superhighway, 11–14
Intergalactic Network, 180
international Internet expansion,
    158–160
Internet, 1–6, 157–175
    and Apple, 161
    history of, 1–6
    international expansion, 158–160
    newcomers to, 169–170
    online services, 165–175
    opening up, 161–164
    overview, 157–158
Internet Activities Board (IAB), 188
Internet Mall, The, 167
Internet message processor (IMP), 5,
    182
Internet Protocol (IP), 76
Internet Relay Chat (IRC), 177
Internet service providers (ISPs),
    107, 169
Internet Worm, 191
InterNIC (Network Information
    Center), 193
inter-system email delivery, 112
IP (Internet Protocol), 76
IPTO (Information Processing
    Techniques Office), 4
IRC (Internet Relay Chat), 177
ISPs (Internet service providers),
    107, 169

J

Japan Broadcasting Corporation, 184
Jennings, Tom, 188
JIX service, 159
Journalism Forum, 57
JUNET, 189

K

Kahn, Robert, 5, 13, 76
Keener, Al, 84
Kemeny, John, 86
Keycom, 83
KI (Knowledge Index), 71, 177
Kimsey, James, 97, 121, 132
Knowledge Index (KI), 71, 177
Kozin, David, 124
Kussmaul Encyclopedia, 81
Kussmaul, Wesley, 72 80

L

Langsam, Edward, 140
Lead Line, 105
Leonard Kleinrock, 3
Lexis/Nexis, 72, 168
Licklider, J.C.R., 3, 179
Livewire, 87
Lockheed, 9
Los Angeles Gateway service, 83
Louden, Bill, 20, 24, 52, 84, 124, 142,
    153, 172, 190
Lucasfilm Games, 110

M

MadMaze, 144
Marill, Thomas, 4
marketing, AOL, 134–137
Marrill, Thomas, 181
McCarthy, John, 7
McGinnish, Richard L., 105
MCI Mail, 79
Mead Data Central, 70, 72
MEDLARS (Medical Literature
    Analysis and Retrieval System),
    9, 10
memex, 179
menu text, 49

Merit Network, 162
Metcalf, Robert, 184
microcomputer bulletin boards, 45–48
microcomputers, 17
MicroNET, 23, 32, 184–185
Microsoft Network (MSN), 177
Mike Wingfield, 5
MILNET, 77, 189
Minitel, 39, 159
MIX (Multi-user Information eXchange), 106, 178
money, 8–14
    information superhighway, 11–14
    online content, 8–11
Mosaic web browser, 163
MS-DOS system, 150
MSN (Microsoft Network), 177
MUDs, 165
Multi-user Information eXchange (MIX), 106, 178
MUPID, 187
Murdoch, Rupert, 172

N

NABU Network, 115, 178
NAPLPS (North American Presentation Level Protocol Syntax), 74, 142, 156
National Information Infrastructure Act of 1993, 165, 167
National Information Utilities (NIU), 68
National Library of Medicine (NLM), 9
National Public Radio (NPR), 68
National Science Foundation (NSF), 162, 164
National Science Foundation Network (NSFNet), 80, 161, 162, 164, 167, 189–190

NCP (Network Control Protocol), 13, 76
netmail, 158
Network Control Protocol (NCP), 13, 76
Network Information Center (InterNIC), 193
Network Measurement Center, 5
News Corporation, 172
newsletters, 69–70
NewsNet, 70
newspapers, 69–70
Nexis, 70
Niehoff, Patricia, 126
Nifty-SERVE, 192
Nikkei-MIX, 159
NIU (National Information Utilities), 68
NLM (National Library of Medicine), 9
North American Presentation Level Protocol Syntax (NAPLPS), 74, 142, 156
NPR (National Public Radio), 68
NREN, 192
NSA (Nuclear Science Abstracts) Database, 9
NSF (National Science Foundation), 162, 164
NSFNet (National Science Foundation Network), 80, 161, 162, 164, 167, 189–190
Nuclear Science Abstracts (NSA) Database, 9

O

OAG (Official Airline Guide), 64, 178
OCLC (Online Computer Library Center), 31
OCR (Optical Character Recognition), 72

OEM (original equipment manufacturer) products, 135
Official Airline Guide (OAG), 64, 178
omissions, 177–178
online advertising, Prodigy, 144–146
Online Bibliographic Retrieval of Information Time-Shared (ORBIT), 10
Online Computer Library Center (OCLC), 31
online content, 8–11
online gaming, 52
online mall, 167
online services, 165–175
Optical Character Recognition (OCR), 72
Oracle (Optional Reception of Announcements by Coded Line Electronics), 183
ORBIT (Online Retrieval of Bibliographic Information Time-Shared), 10
original equipment manufacturer (OEM) products, 135

P

packet switching, 181
packet-switched network (PSN), 12, 16, 104, 106
Panzl, David, 91
Papes, Theodore C., 152
PARTIcipate, 33, 56, 126
Patricof, Alan, 111
Paul Baran, 5
PC Pursuit, 48
PCAO (America Online for DOS), 192
PC-Link, 119–120
PhoneNet, 162
pirate software, 52

Playnet, 90–93, 100, 115, 191
Plink (American People/Link), 103–105
POP (points of presence) configuration, Prodigy, 146–147
Portal, 178
Postel, Jon, 76
Prentice Hall, 34
Prestel, 40, 61
pricing, Prodigy, 153–155
Procomm Plus, 123
Prodigy, 125, 131, 139–156, 168
    censorship, 147–149
    chat rooms, 155–156
    files download area, 152
    history of, 139–141
    improvements, 142–144
    online advertising, 144–146
    overview, 139
    POP configuration, 146–147
    pricing, 153–155
    spyware, 150
    Videotex, 141–142
Prodigy Classic, 175
Promenade, 128–129, 192
PS/1 computer, 128
PSINET, 164
PSN (packet-switched network), 12, 16, 104, 106

Q

Q-Link (Quantum Link), 108–112, 136, 190
Quali-Comm, 178
Quantum, 116
Quantum Link (Q-Link), 108–112, 136, 190
QUBE, 32, 74, 140, 184
Quinn, John C., 66

R

Rabergrau, Philippe, 125
Rader, Louis, 86
Radio Shack, 19
Ranshaw, Russ, 20, 22
Reader's Digest Association, 62
Redux, 116–117
regional online services, 82–83
relay systems, 46
Rensselaer Business Incubator, 91
Rensselaer Polytechnic Institute
    (RPI), 91
request for proposal (RFP), 181
RFP (request for proposal), 181
Roberts, Larry, 4, 11, 181
RPI (Rensselaer Polytechnic
    Institute), 91
Ryan, Bob, 33
Ryder, Bernard, 28

S

SAGE (Semi-Automatic Ground
    Environment) radar system, 1
same-day hard-copy letter delivery,
    79
Sandground, Mark, 29
SATNET, 76
Sceptre terminal, 83
Schrage, Michael, 29
Scientific and Technical Aerospace
    Reports (STAR) database, 9
Scientific Development Systems
    (SDS), 5
Sculley, John, 121
SDC (System Development
    Corporation), 4
SDS (Scientific Development
    Systems), 5
Securities & Exchange Commission,
    99

Semi-Automatic Ground
    Environment (SAGE) radar
    system, 1
"SEND" program, 23
Seriff, Mark, 35, 90
services play, 22
Servicom, 193
Seuss, Randy, 47
Sierra Network, 192
Sierra On-Line Network, 178
SIGs (special-interest groups), 186
Sinback, Warner, 86
slash commands, 104
Smith, Clive, 100
Snapaks, 58, 61
SOFTEX (software exchange), 53
Source Telecomputing Corporation
    (STC), 41
Source, The, 25–89, 185
    customer loyalty, 43–44
    end of, 126
    growing pains at, 41–42
    growth, 43–44
SPAN, 76
special-interest groups, 56–57
special-interest groups (SIGs), 186
SportsWare, 107
SprintMail, 178
Sputnik, 179
spyware, Prodigy, 150
squelch, 55
stage.dat file, 150
Stampazine, 36
STAR (Scientific and Technical
    Aerospace Reports) database, 9
Star°Services plan, 153
STC (Source Telecomputing
    Corporation), 41
Stickles, George, 93
Sturtz, Larry, 84
Sutherland, Ivan, 180

System Development Corporation (SDC), 4
system operator, 57

T

Tandy, 119, 129
Taub, Jack, 31, 35, 37, 39, 41, 62, 68
Taylor, Dave, 167
Taylor, Robert, 4, 180
TCA (Telecomputing Corporation of America), 32
TCP (Transmission Control Protocol), 76
TCP/IP (Transmission Control Protocol/Internet Protocol), 13, 183
TDX Systems, Inc., 28
Telecomputing Corporation of America (TCA), 32
Teledata, 182
Telemail, 13, 178
Telemax, 28
Telenet, 12, 159
Telepost, 28
teletext, 40, 159
Teletypes, 8
TeletypeWriter eXchange (TWX) network, 11
Televerket Videotex system, 185
Telidon Canadian Videotex system, 184
Test-TV, 185
timeline, 179–195
Tomlinson, Ray, 182
Transmission Control Protocol (TCP), 76
Transmission Control Protocol/Internet Protocol (TCP/IP), 13, 183
transoceanic networkers, 159
Trevor, Alexander, 16, 50, 124

Trintex, 113, 141
TRS-80 Videotex, 61
TWX (TeletypeWriter eXchange) network, 11
Tyme, 178
Tymnet, 13, 159

U

United Press International (UPI), 35
U.S. Office of Education (USOE), 9
USA Today Sports Center, 107
Usenet, 44–45, 156, 166, 168
user publishing, 53
USOE (U.S. Office of Education), 9
UUNET, 164

V

van Vogt, A.E., 3
V-Chat, 105
VCO (Voice COnferencing), 105
Venture One, 139
Videotex, 32, 39–41, 50, 73, 140, 141–142, 159
Viewdata, 75, 183
Viewtron, 74, 140, 186
Voice COnferencing (VCO), 105
von Meister, William F., 25–38, 41, 62, 67, 89, 959

W

WAN (wide area network), 4, 181
Warnock, Thomas, 68
Weil, Audrey, 131
WELL (Whole Earth 'Lectronic Link), 107–108, 168
Western Union, 27
Whole Earth 'Lectronic Link (WELL), 107–108, 168
wide area network (WAN), 4, 181

Wilkins, Jeff, 15, 25, 70
Wilson, Kemmons, 69
Windows, 131–133
WIX (Windows Information
    eXchange), 178
World, The, 191
World Wide Web, 38

Z

Ziff-Davis, 152
ZiffNet, 178

You Need the Companion eBook

Your purchase of this book entitles you to buy the companion PDF-version eBook for only $10. Take the weightless companion with you anywhere.

We believe this Apress title will prove so indispensable that you'll want to carry it with you everywhere, which is why we are offering the companion eBook (in PDF format) for $10 to customers who purchase this book now. Convenient and fully searchable, the PDF version of any content-rich, page-heavy Apress book makes a valuable addition to your programming library. You can easily find and copy code—or perform examples by quickly toggling between instructions and the application. Even simultaneously tackling a donut, diet soda, and complex code becomes simplified with hands-free eBooks!

Once you purchase your book, getting the $10 companion eBook is simple:

❶ Visit **www.apress.com/promo/tendollars/**.

❷ Complete a basic registration form to receive a randomly generated question about this title.

❸ Answer the question correctly in 60 seconds, and you will receive a promotional code to redeem for the $10.00 eBook.

ERROR 404

Page not found